AUSTRALIAN GOTHIC

Borgo Press Books by JAMES DOIG

Australian Gothic: An Anthology of Australian Supernatural Fiction (editor)
Ghost Stories and Mysteries, by Ernest Favenc (edited by James Doig)

AUSTRALIAN GOTHIC

AN ANTHOLOGY
OF AUSTRALIAN
SUPERNATURAL FICTION

JAMES DOIG, EDITOR

THE BORGO PRESS

MMXIII

Classics of Fantastic Literature
Number Nine

AUSTRALIAN GOTHIC

FIRST BORGO PRESS EDITION

Published by Wildside Press LLC

www.wildsidebooks.com

DEDICATION

To Douglas A. Anderson,
for his kind assistance and
support over the years

CONTENTS

INTRODUCTION

The chief aim of this anthology is to illustrate the richness and variety of Australian supernatural fiction in the second half of the nineteenth and the early twentieth centuries. In Britain and the United States this period is regarded as the "Golden Age" of supernatural fiction—a period that produced Joseph Sheridan Le Fanu's 'Carmilla' (1872), Robert Louis Stevenson's 'The Strange Case of Dr. Jekyll and Mr. Hyde' (1886), Bram Stoker's *Dracula* (1897), Henry James's *The Turn of the Screw* (1898), M. R. James's *Ghost Stories of an Antiquary* (1904), and many other great tales that are regarded as masterpieces of the genre. But no Australian stories appear in any of the many anthologies that claim to represent the best supernatural tales of the period. Hugh Lamb wrote in his anthology, *Victorian Nightmares* (1977), "Australia is a very rare source of Victorian tales of terror, both in location and author nationality".

The fact is that Australian supernatural fiction has been poorly served by anthologists, researchers and academics. The *Encyclopaedia of Australian Science Fiction and Fantasy* (1998), published by Melbourne University Press, mentions only one of the writers represented here (Guy Boothby), in a general entry on "Early Science Fiction and Fantasy", and the *Oxford Literary History of Australia* (1998) lumps supernatural fiction together with melodrama and gives it short shrift. The entry on Australia in John Clute's *Encyclopaedia of Fantasy* (1997) omits supernatural fiction altogether. The only historical anthology of Australian supernatural fiction is Ken Gelder's excellent *Oxford Book of Australian Ghost Stories* (1994), but as the title suggests it focuses narrowly on ghosts. Almost all the stories in Gordon Stewart's *Australian Stories of Horror and Suspense From the Early Days* (1978) and Bill Wannan's *Australian Horror Stories* (1983) are non-supernatural "grim" stories of the type exemplified by Barbara Baynton's celebrated collection *Bush Studies*, published in 1902.

One reason for the neglect of Australian supernatural fiction is the sheer rarity of many of the collections and periodicals in which they appeared, most of which are unobtainable outside of the National and State Libraries. It was in these publications that popular fiction flourished in the days before radio and cinema. Periodicals like the *Bulletin* (1880-), *Australian Journal* (1865-1962), *Australasian* (1864-1946), and *Australian Town and Country Journal* (1870-1919) published popular British and American authors such as Le Fanu, Mary Elizabeth Braddon, H. Rider Haggard, and Harriet O'Brien Lewis alongside home-grown talent. These periodicals satisfied popular demand for adventure, romance and historical fiction as well as for sensational and supernatural fiction. Fitz-James O'Brien's famous supernatural tale about an invisible monster, 'What Was It?', appeared in the *Australian Journal* in 1866, while Arthur Machen's 'The White People', regarded by many as the greatest supernatural horror story ever written, was published in the *Australian Home Journal* in 1904.

In fact, the taste for gothic and supernatural fiction was just as evident in Australia as it was elsewhere, and Australian writers cashed in on the popularity of the genre. Many of these home-grown writers sought literary fame and fortune overseas, such as Guy Boothby and Rosa Praed. A few stayed in Australia and eked out rather precarious writing careers, for example Ernest Favenc and Mary Fortune (who as Waif Wander penned the weekly 'Detective Album' in the *Australian Journal* for over forty years). Both died penniless and forgotten; we don't even know the year of Mary Fortune's death. Other writers, such as

Hume Nisbet and J. E. P. Muddock, were émigrés who settled in Australia for a time and wrote about their experiences there. Australian publishers like George Robertson and The Bulletin Company regularly produced single author collections of short stories gathered from colonial periodicals. On the other hand, Australian authors who lived in Britain, such as Boothby and Praed, often appeared in more lucrative British periodicals like *Chambers*, *Belgravia*, and *Pall Mall*, and their short story collections were brought out by British publishers. Many of the stories in this collection are taken from these Australian and British collections.

Nevertheless, it took some time for the Australian public to develop a taste for sensational literature. In the early days of settlement, up to about the middle of the nineteenth century, Australia did not produce the mass of gothic stories and "penny dreadfuls" that were such a feature of popular literature in the United States and Europe. Part of the reason for this is because for many Australians there were enough real life horrors to cope with—aggressive natives (which often prompted massacres of aborigines), the unforgiving land, and, of course, the horrors of convict life. In England sixpenny chapbooks and penny broadsides appeared with titles such as *The Horrors of Transportation*; *The Fell Tyrant, or the Suffering Convict*; *A Complete Exposure of the Convict System, Its Horrors, Hardships and Severities, including an Account of the Dreadful Sufferings of the Unhappy Captives*. It may be no coincidence that Australian supernatural tales began to appear in greater numbers after transportation was abolished (in New South Wales this occurred in 1840, the rest of eastern Australia in 1852, and Western Australia in 1868).

Some of the authors represented in this anthology are well known. Marcus Clarke wrote arguably the greatest Australian colonial novel, *His Natural Life* (1874), while Rosa Praed, G. A. Walstab, Ernest Favenc and Louis Becke were critically acclaimed mainstream writers. J. E. P. Muddock and Guy Boothby were well-known mystery writers, Boothby for his Dr. Nikola series, and Muddock for his Dick Donovan stories. Mary

Fortune was one of Australia's earliest detective story writers; although she was extremely popular and published hundreds of stories, only one collection was published in her lifetime. Others like Dulcie Deamer and A. F. Basset Hull are more obscure and are credited with only one or two short story collections, while Frances Faucett would be completely unknown but for the fortuitous survival of a single story. Lionel Sparrow, who has two stories in this anthology, did not publish a book in his lifetime, and his tales of gothic horror can only be found in the pages of the *Australian Journal*.

While many of the stories gathered here are set in the colonies, I have also included stories that are set in other places. Louis Becke's 'Lupton's Guest', J. F. Dwyer's 'Cave of the Invisible', G. A. Walstab's 'The House By the River', and Guy Boothby's 'The Death Child' are set in Asia and the South Pacific. Rosa Praed's tale 'The Ghost-Monk' is set in France, while Dulcie Deamer's werewolf tale, 'Hallowe'en', and Marcus Clarke's 'Cannabis Indica' are set in an imagined Middle Ages. In casting a wide net I have included several different sub-genres in the field, which I hope will indicate something of the range and interests of Australian writers.

The stories set in Australia are particularly interesting for the way in which traditional English elements of the supernatural tale appear in new forms or are moulded afresh to a harsh, new environment—the haunted house is no longer a rambling manor, but an abandoned shanty or rundown homestead; the English wood, shadowy lair of ancient evils and creatures from folklore, becomes the oppressively hot, fly-infested bush; and the wind-swept moor is the empty, endless Australian outback with its blood-red sands and emaciated myall trees. European colonists struggled to cope in the harsh landscape and climate and were frequently claimed by it, most famously the explorers Burke and Wills in 1861, and Ludwig Leichhardt, whose expedition to traverse Australia from east to west disappeared without trace in 1848. The land itself seemed a malignant force that exacted a terrible revenge on those who challenged it or wandered thoughtlessly into it. Thus, in many of the stories here, people frequently fall victim to the bush; indeed, often it is children, symbols of innocence and European naiveté, who are claimed.

European artists, too, had difficulty coming to terms with the Australian landscape and native fauna: the strange, diffuse light of the bush, the blinding glare of the outback, the bizarre animals that seemed travesties of the natural world (when Bernard Shaw saw a platypus for the first time he looked for the tell-tale marks where duck and mole had been sewn together) were beyond the experience and skill of colonial artists and it was many years before they were accurately portrayed. Ernest Favenc effectively exploits this notion of Australia as a country of evolutionary and natural oddities in his 'Haunt of the Jinkarras'. Writers, no less than explorers, artists and settlers, were challenged by the environment, and this is reflected in many of the following stories. Australia, indeed, is a gothic landscape.

One final point: most of the research for this book was carried out at the National Library of Australia, an unparalleled resource for rare periodicals and collections. I have endeavoured to choose stories that are rare and have not been reprinted since their first publication. In this way the book is offered not only as an entertaining read—a "pleasing terror" as M. R. James put it—but also as a contribution to a neglected area of both supernatural fiction and Australian literary history.[1]

—James Doig
Palmerston, Australian Capital Territory

---

1. Note that I have retained original spelling and punctuation in these stories.

THE SPIRITS
OF THE TOWER

by Mary Fortune

Between 1865 and 1908 Mary Fortune (1833-1910?),
under her pseudonym Waif Wander, wrote more than
500 crime stories in her column of detective stories,
the 'Detective's Album', in the *Australian Journal*.
Born in Belfast, Ireland, she followed her father to the
Victorian goldfields in 1855. Her life was punctuated
by several crises, including the birth of an illegitimate
son, the death of her first child, and two failed mar-
riages.

After her death she fell into obscurity until the Australian writer/researcher Lucy Sussex rediscovered her
and established her contribution to Australian crime
fiction. Mary Fortune also wrote an excessive gothic
serial novel, *Clyzia the Dwarf*, and a number of supernatural and horror stories. 'The Spirits of the Tower',
a ghost story from the 'Detective's Album', was published in the *Australian Journal* in March 1883.

It is fully twenty years ago, that I was stationed at a miserable up-country camp on the borders of a river to which I need
not give a name, but the name of the few houses about two
miles off was Calandra, and it had once been a digging that had
stretched promisingly toward the spot where the police station

had been built, and then died out as suddenly as it had arisen, leaving us poor troopers in a wild spot all by ourselves and with scarcely a habitation within sight.

I never was in a duller station than that of Calandra. Of all the wretched sights a man can picture I think a deserted diggings is one of the most depressing, and I had nothing to do but go to the door to see one in all its misery of decay. Deep, treacherous shafts, with their mouths wreathed and half-hidden by wild green growth, through which the glimmer of unwholesome water could be seen when the sun shone into the depths, and great holes where paddocking had been done and left the heaped-up stuff to be filtered slowly back at each fall of rain during many months, were there in that gully by hundreds, with the rotting windlass props and slant, and decaying posts of some long-ago tent creaking when the wind blows like the wailing cries of some dead digger who had lost his soul for gold.

"If I am not removed I'll resign," I had said to myself over and over as days and weeks went by, and there was nothing but feigned duty to be done; and I said it again on the very evening that the first page of the story I am going to tell was opened in my hand.

It was an unusually wretched evening, even for Calandra. There was thunder in the air, and heavy, gloomy clouds in the sky. A damp wind was floating up from the dark river, and the long branches of the yellow box-trees were swaying to and fro in it with a sad monotony. Along the river, low down where the sedges were thick and rustling lonely, a curlew was crying out his awful "Murder!" while along the bush track, so faintly lined to and from the miserable township, not a living speck could be discerned.

"There are places in which any sane man would become mad, and Calandra is one of them," I muttered to myself. "No wonder that black pile remains empty and almost ownerless, for who would live, if he could choose his residence, with such a dreary desolate hillock as that tower must command?"

I was looking at the only wall within view from the door of

the station; a three-storied tower that formed part of a building of some pretensions called by the unusual title of "The Moat". The property belonging to it had been originally a pre-emptive right affair, but the diggers had rushed it in search of the precious metal, and there only remained belonging to and surrounding it about a hundred acres of purchased land. The house was on a rise near the river and hemmed almost in by timber; a gloomy stone building it was, with its nailed up windows and dark walls streaked with the green slimy damp of broken spouting, and there was nothing to be wondered at in the few neighbours avoiding it, as there was nothing pleasant to see or steal, entirely outside the report of its being (as all empty houses most certainly are) haunted.

"Ugh!" I said with a shudder, "I hate to look at that place!" and I looked no more just then, for a black moving spot became visible on the distant track, and very soon also the sound of horse's feet preceded my recognition of the rider, who was no other than my friend Tom Mason.

"This is a doleful sort of a country," he said as he dismounted; "and I don't wonder that your face is as long a fiddle."

"Don't you?" I growled. "I hope they've sent you to relieve me, for I'm sick of the blessed place."

"No relief for you, me boy; I'm only going on to Carryl's with despatches."

"A-hem the despatches! Talk of wasting the country's money! I'd like to know what else it is to keep a police station in a place like this."

"Resign," Mason said philosophically, as he unstrapped his rug and prepared to make his horse comfortable for the night. "Resign, by all manner of means, me boy."

"I'm going to when I'm ready. What news have you?"

"None. Oh, I forgot I have. You're going to have a new neighbour to-morrow."

"A new neighbour? In the name of goodness how can that be? There isn't a place to live in within ten miles."

"There is a gentleman coming to live in some place called

the Moat. He's driving a trap and baited at York's, but one of the horses wanted shoeing, or something, so he decided on stopping all night."

"Well, I wish him joy of the place—you can see it over there—and if of his own free choice he comes to live there he quite deserves being eaten up by rats, or frightened out of what small remains of sense he may be possessed of by the spirits that haunt the Moat."

"Is it haunted? By George, but that's jolly, Mark! I'll call and ask him for a night's lodging as I come back, for I have an awful craving to see a ghost."

"Stuff! What kind of chap is this Moat man?"

He gave me a card.

"There it is. 'Mr. T. Cyrus', not a bad name, eh? and when he sticks 'The Moat' after it, it will be quite too awfully aristocratic."

"What sort of a man is he?"

"Why, he's a dark-haired, white-faced fellow, with a haunted look about him, and I'm sure the ghosts of the Moat will cotton to him as a spiritual mate at once when they see him."

That was all the description I could get from my then volatile friend, but when Mr. Cyrus alighted at the station on the following day I found that it to a certain extent applied to his appearance. He was dark-haired and dark-whiskered, and his pallid face made his great eyes look darker than even they were. He was gentlemanly though and quietly spoken, while his well-chosen words and low musical voice were indicative of a man of culture and intelligence.

"A trooper I had the pleasure of travelling some miles with yesterday advised me to call at the station," he said. "Is he here?"

"Mason has gone about an hour, but he mentioned you, Mr. Cyrus, and I have been looking out for you."

"That is kind. Your name is Sinclair, I think"

"Yes."

"Is that the Moat?" and he pointed toward the dark tower that floated as it were, on the gloomy tops of the dense wood.

"Yes, that is the Moat. I am afraid you will find it a dull residence."

"Yes, I expect that. Have you any idea what sort of condition it is in?"

"The very worst, I should say. I was over there but once, and it gave me the idea of a decayed and desolate dwelling indeed."

"But it is furnished?" he said, in apparent astonishment.

"Furnished? I should never have guessed that, but if it is the furniture must of necessity have suffered from neglect. At all events, you must not dream of putting up there without some previous firemaking."

"There is no place else," he said.

"There is the police station. I shall be happy to give you room for a little."

"But I should be taking advantage of your kindness by accepting your offer," he said hesitatingly.

"If you know the life of loneliness I lead in this miserable hole, you would know how thankfully I see a break in upon it in a visitor's face. Pray say no more, but let us put your horses in the stable, and after you have had something to eat and drink, I will ride over to examine the Moat with you."

It was so arranged, and as we lunched together I had an opportunity of more closely examining the appearance of my new acquaintance, as, when his hat was removed, I found him a much handsomer and a much younger man than he had appeared before. I don't think he was over thirty, yet there were white hairs among his dark locks. He was a naturally silent man, I should say; or some great sorrow which had to be confined to his own breast had made reticence habitual to him.

"I am more than surprised at what you tell me about this property of mine," he observed after a longer period of silence than usual; "for I had reason to suppose that there was a caretaker living on it, in the house in fact."

"I have been here some months and never heard of any one being in charge of the Moat," I said. "I could almost count the residents within a mile of it on my fingers. What was the man's name you were led to expect to find taking care of it?"

"Richard Neilson."

"There is a man of that name living in the township—a strange, sullen customer he is; but I never heard that he had anything to do with the Moat."

"He has been drawing the pay for taking care of it, at all events," Mr. Cyrus said; "and I think we had better see him before going over. The township is not far away?"

"Just beyond the bend of the road."

"Then we will go and try to see this Neilson, if you will be so good as to accompany me. Are you alone here?"

"Oh, no; I have a mate to help me do nothing. He is gone on some little business of his own but will be back this evening."

"I am glad of that, for I can hope to see a good deal of you without leaving the police station destitute of a policeman."

We started for Calandra quite early, for it was not an hour past noon, both mounted and riding easily as the day was young. The very first hut on entering the little collection of dwellings was that of the man we were in search of, and, as it happened, he was at his door when we came within sight of it, doing something to a strong fishing-rod, to which a suitable line was attached.

As I had told Mr. Cyrus, this man was of strange sullen manner, and I never took to him. He spent a good deal of his time on the river, I had always heard, and he was a grey-haired man of fully sixty years. When we drew rein before him he looked at us inquiringly, but he did not speak or cease his work.

"This gentleman has some business with you I think, Neilson," I said, introducing my companion as it were.

"Ay? I can't guess what that may be."

"I will tell you," the gentleman begun. "I have come to reside at the Moat House, and I have come to you for the key."

"Ye are come to live in the Moat House, and ye want the key? Ye'll have an order to that effect?"

"I have," and a paper was quietly passed to the man, who laid down his rod and took it with an expression of some far deeper feeling than surprise in his dark face.

"You know the signature and the writing?"

"Ay, I ken baith. And so ye've bought the Moat place?"

"I have bought it, yes."

"Weel, much good may it do ye, for I never thought that any man could be found to live of his own free will in siccan an awfu' house, and I think ye'll maybe be glad to get oot o't again afore very long."

"What do you mean, man?" I asked, for Neilson's manner was, to say the least of it, disagreeable, and his visage had an unpleasant scowl on it as he handed the order for the key back to Mr. Cyrus.

"Ye know well enough what I mean, constable, a' the country knows that the place is haunted visibly."

"Visibly?" asked Mr. Cyrus inquiringly. "Have you yourself *seen* any spiritual manifestation?"

"Ay, have I, seen that which has made me cold to the very heart"—and he shuddered as he spoke—"seen the faces of dead men and heard their groans and their cries."

"You knew, and were in the service of the late Mr. Malbraith, the owner of the property, I understand?" said Mr. Cyrus as he keenly watched Neilson's bowed face.

"Ay, I knew him and worked for him for many a year,"

"Is it his spirit that haunts the Moat?"

Neilson lifted his eyes and looked full into his questioner's face as he drew a rusty key from his pocket and tossed it toward Cyrus.

"There is the key, take it, and find out for yourself who and what it is that haunts the Moat. I wouldn't own it or live in it to be made Emperor of Australia."

"Yet I was just going to ask you if you would enter my service, as you are used to the property."

"Your service—in what capacity?"

"That to be decided on. Of course I shall want a man to look after things generally, but I can talk to you again about that if you should think any arrangement possible between you and me."

Neilson was silent for a little as he steadily scanned the speaker's countenance and then he spoke in a strangely suspicious tone—

"Have I ever seen you before?"

"No; it is impossible. I have but now arrived from a far land in which most of my life was spent, and I am at least sure that I have never looked in your face until to-day. Why do you ask?"

"Because I seem to ken your features, and there's a something in your eyes that reminds me o'—I kenna what."

He passed his hand over his face as he spoke, and then, as if on a sudden thought, he offered to go with us to the Moat.

"I might be able to give ye some useful information, as I ken the place so long, and if ye like I'll go with you to see it."

Cyrus willingly agreeing to this, we rode on our way to the old place, Neilson taking a short cut through the bush that would lead him there in time to open the gate for us.

"You know that man, Mr. Cyrus!" I observed to that gentleman as we left.

"I assure you I have never seen his face before," he said, with an approach to a smile, as his eyes met mine. "I have heard of him though, and some day I may be able to tell you how and when."

"Ay, and *what*," I returned, "for there is something not over good to know."

"You guess that?" he asked, quietly, and then no more was said until we neared the rusty iron gate that was just creakingly opening to the hand of Neilson, who awaited our entrance.

We rode in, and I noticed that my companion's eyes were never removed from the building from the moment it came within view at a bend of the gloomy avenue, grass-grown and shadowed by great tangled branches of the old trees that grew beside it. The tower I have previously alluded to stood nearest the river, and a stout stone wing of one story joined it to landward, as it were. The dark stone of the building, on which summers and winters of years had traced many stains and discolourations, with its boarded-up windows and weed-grown threshold, formed as gloomy a picture as any man need to avoid, and I could scarcely wonder at Neilson's disinclination to live in the weird-looking house.

"If ye will open the door," Neilson said, as we dismounted, "I will get some tool at the back, and ding aft some o' these boards frae the windows; it winna be hard to do for they're rotten."

And so in a quarter of an hour many scattered boards were lying on the grass, and once more light and air penetrated to the interior of the decayed mansion.

I was surprised to find that the house was, after a way, furnished, but on every article of old-fashioned use and garniture the dust of time and decay lay thickly. There was a large dining-room to the south, and several smaller apartments, as well as sitting-rooms, in the principal part of the house; but it was to the tower that the attention of Cyrus was most closely directed.

This tower was two stories higher than the other portion of the dwelling, and its whole contents above the roof of the wing consisted of two rooms, one on each story. The upper or top room was arranged as a bedroom, and from its windows a wide and not unpleasant view of river and hill and forest was commanded, whilst the apartment under it was fitted up as a study, in which cobwebs wreathed the books on the shelves, and the dust lay thickly on the writing-table and large couch that stood in one corner of the room. On this couch I noticed Cyrus turn his eyes strangely ere he turned to Neilson, who stood at the door, and spoke—

"It was in this room that the last owner of this house died," he said, and Neilson's face was expressive of more than just astonishment as he heard the observation.

"How do ye know that?"

"The agent told me."

"Ay, it was in this room and on that very couch that he died."

"You were here at the time?"

"Ay, I was here at the time."

"How long ago was that?" I asked myself.

"Nearly five years."

"And his brother—Mr. George Malbraith—where did he die?" the strange gentleman asked.

"The brother? Why, he dinna die at all that I ken. Mr. George, the late master's elder brother just walked out one day and never was seen or heard o' after. Mr. Matthew inherited the property under will from Mr. George."

"He may not be dead at all then," I said, "and if he should turn up your purchase would be valueless."

"Oh, he's dead, sure enough; he'll never come back again to trouble the living or the dead," and as he spoke the man drew back and looked behind him, as if he heard something on the stairway, while Cyrus regarded every look and movement of the gloomy caretaker with the deepest interest.

"Neilson," he said suddenly, "surely you need not be afraid of ghosts in the daylight? Couldn't you and I come to terms about work here in the daytime, and you might go home to sleep? You will lose something by this place being sold, and it might not be inconvenient to you to earn something in another way."

"It's not the money," the man replied, with a quick look out to the stairway again. "Mr. Malbraith put my name down in his will, and I've enough to live on, but I have a hankering after the auld place, so I've no objection to give ye a helping hand till ye get a better on the terms ye propose."

"All right then. Go to work and make up good fires in every part of the house, and open every window and every door. I shall go back and bring up my trap, and sleep here this very night."

"Here? Not in *this* room?"

"Yes, in this very room. I have a fancy for it."

"I warn ye again doing it. I warn ye not to live in this room."

"Why?"

"Why? Listen even now! I can hear the feet o' dead men and the cauld air wafting roun' their white faces! But ye must hear and see for yourself ere ye'll believe, but dinna ask me to come up here by day or by night," and with white cheeks and trembling limbs the speaker hurried downstairs, and out into the air, where we could see him from the window, with his hat raised and his mouth agape, as of a man suffering from a deadly oppression.

"The man is crazy!" I said, with disgust, as we followed him downstairs.

"No, I think he is sincerely afraid."

"Of ghosts? Faugh!"

We were riding back toward the police station as I emitted these sneering words, and Cyrus turned on me such a queer look that I met it with one of wonder.

"Don't you believe in ghosts, then?" he asked, seriously.

"Surely it is unnecessary to ask any person of common sense such a question; of course I do not believe in any such chimeras."

"Do you accredit me with any portion of common sense?"

"Well, as far as I can see, I presume—"

"That I am at least not quite mad? Well I can assure you that I firmly believe in spiritual appearances, for I have been three times visited by one. But as I am about to make a request of you, we will leave the further discussion on this point. Will you spend the night with me at the haunted house?"

"Certainly, if my mate returns, nothing would give me more pleasure; for, not believing in spirits revisiting the earth, I am of course not afraid of them."

That settled, the conversation turned on matters connected with Mr. Cyrus's domestic arrangements, and I was surprised to find that after all he proposed to make no long stay at the Moat House, and his remark to me on driving in his trap from the station was—"I suspect you will know all about it to-night; mind and be over before dark this evening!"

One would require to have lived the lonely uneventful life I had been doomed to at Calandra to understand what an impression the unusual break in upon it had upon me during the latter hours of the day. Until my mate returned I was in a fever lest I should be disappointed, and when all was right in that quarter every hour I had to wait seemed interminable. I don't know what I hoped or expected to see or hear, or could I account for the attraction that drew me to the moat, but I walked toward the house when evening fell in an abnormally pleasant start of imagination, and found Mr. Cyrus awaiting on the threshold.

In the dull light of evening the place looked even more dismal and gloomy than it had done in the day, but all the windows were still open, while smoke was issuing from every chimney in the house. Only in the tower the flue against which the weather-stained flagstaff leaned exhibited no tokens of life, for Neilson would not go up the awful stairs, nor indeed had Mr. Cyrus urged it on him to do so.

"I am glad to see you," was the greeting from my host; "and I have waited for so many long and anxious months for this night, that I am sure it will bring me some dread revelation. I pray you do not look at me so suspiciously, for I am as sane as you are yourself, and you will acknowledge it when you hear what I have to tell you!"

I must now follow Richard Neilson's movements so as to relate some matters connected with this story which were afterwards detailed in evidence by a man named Connel Craig, who has not yet made an appearance in these pages.

Connel Craig was the owner of a few acres on the banks of the river on the opposite side to the Moat House, and about a mile above it. He was an apparently industrious widower with one grown up girl, who kept his household matters right, and so eked out his living by fishing, the produce of his line being of ready disposal within about ten miles of his hut.

On the evening of the day when the new proprietor had taken possession of the Moat, Connel was sitting in his old boat, making ready for a fishing excursion, when the familiar sound of oars caused him to raise his head. Another boat was coming in view from under a shaded bend of the river, and Connel at once recognised the rower as Richard Neilson.

"It *is* him, by Jupiter!" he muttered aloud, "and the devil's to pay when he ventures to pass *that* spot after sundown.

"Yes, something is wrong, I see it in his hangdog face," and the speaker bent his deep-set sharp eyes on the approaching boat.

Neilson truly rowed as a man ill at ease; every now and then he cast backward glances over his shoulder, and pulled so hard as if from pursuit that when he laid his skiff by the side of Connel's the sweat was pouring from his face and dropping from his brawny arms.

"What the—is the matter?" asked Connel, as Neilson drew a great breath and began to wipe the damp from his face. "Are the bobbies after you?"

"Curse you, shut up, you and your bobbies!"

"Oh, not my bobbies if you please, Mister. I thank the Lord I have nothing to do with the police or laws, unless, indeed, it might be for keeping my mouth too close about other people's business."

"Keep it closer yet,—you! You're paid for holding your tongue, ain't you?"

"No. I'm not. I haven't seen the colour of your money this month yet, Richard Neilson, and all the money you have wouldn't pay me for your jaw, so I'll take none of it. Who the mischief are you that you're to come here and bounce a decent man that wouldn't put his finger to murder if—"

"By—I'll brain you if you don't shut up!"

The man Neilson had stood up and seized one of the sculls. As he stood with it raised in a fierce threatening posture, and the whiteness of an awful rage in his distorted face, he was a fearful sight; but Connel Craig was not afraid of him. Before the oar was poised a revolver was presented at Neilson, and the fierce order rang out on the river—

"Down with that oar, or I'll put a bullet through your treacherous brain!"

The oar was dropped as suddenly as it had been lifted, and Neilson fell to his seat with a groan.

"I am mad," he said—"clean mad."

"You never spoke a truer word, mate; but, mad or not mad, you shan't murder me unawares. Ever since I knew of *that* job

I've carried this day and night. But what is up? What put up your danger? And, above all things, what gave you courage to tempt the water when the shadows of night cross it?"

"Danger!" was the stern reply; "danger to me, and loss to you."

"Loss to me? That's comin' home, Neilson, so you'd better tell me the why and the wherefore."

"The Moat House is sold."

"Sold is it? Well, I don't see how that can affect either you or me."

"You will know soon. The owner is in the house, and is going to live there. If I had had any warning, if that cursed town court had sent me proper notice, all would have been well; but the first I heard of it was the order for the key this day."

"I suppose you've lost your billet, eh? Is that the trouble?"

"Fifty times worse, for I have lost all I sinned for—every piece of gold is in the house."

"What of that? Nothing can be easier than to get it out."

"That's where you are mistaken; I can't without your help in some way or other. I planted the gold in Malbraith's room, and you know well that I daren't go into that room except in daylight even to save my life."

"You can go in by day then, surely?"

I thought so. I meant to have done it to-day, as I will tell you presently, but when I went up to the room it was locked. That confounded policeman is in it too, for he has knocked up an acquaintance with the new owner, and it is time for me to clear out, Connel"—the man spoke this ultimatum with a great sigh and a deep gloom on his dark bowed face "—not that I think he or any man has the least suspicion, but how do I know the hour that all may be revealed by themselves?"

"By the spirits you mean?"

"Yes, by the spirits of the dead."

"Nonsense, I don't believe in such trash! I wonder at you."

"I do, for I have *seen* them—ugh!" and he trembled as with cold, though a warm air was rippling the water at his boat's keel.

"But what has this all to do with me or my gains?" Connel Craig asked, with a keen look into his companion's face. "It is nothing to me what you have done with your ill-gotten money; my part of the business is to take my share of it for keeping your secret; if I don't get my share I don't keep the secret, that is all."

"And you would betray me after all the payments I have made you?"

"Betray you? I would have betrayed you when your accomplice was alive to share your punishment, if you had not forked out double, so as to have him under your own thumb; and you may believe I won't think twice about it when you begin to talk about my losing over the bargain."

"I thought that you would help me," Neilson said, "as it is to your own benefit I thought you would try to get the money out for me."

"Me! Me make a robber of myself to save you? No, thank you, I have kept myself free of the law as yet, and I mean to do the same while I hold out. And now I want to talk no more about this matter, but I won't be hard on you, for I'll give you a week to pay up in full. If you don't, you know what will be the consequence."

"Yes, I know," replied the man Neilson; and his deep-set eyes blazed with rage as he answered, "I know you for the first time Connel Craig, and I see that it is with you my money or my life, eh?"

"Any way you like to put it, mate; you know well what I mean."

"All right, it is as well that you have spoken out at last;" and Neilson resumed the sculls and pushed his boat into the river.

"There goes my murderer, if he can manage it," muttered Craig, as he looked after the boat; "but he's too big a coward to try it single-handed; he'll bolt for it I guess, and so let him for all I care."

And meanwhile Neilson rowed on his way down the river, along whose banks the shadows of tree and verdure were darkening more and more with each passing moment; but for once the man felt not his accustomed terror as he passed a spot from whence he could lift his eyes and see the old Moat tower looming dim in its surrounding of heavy forest land. He was in too fierce a rage to shudder as he passed one awful spot on the bank, or to fancy, as he had many a time done before, that a terrible white face gleamed at him among the surging sweep of his own oar. Fearful oaths were on his lips, and threats that would have made a hearer's blood run cold were flung on the breeze that swept his hot face without cooling it any more than if it had been the plates of a furnace within which the fires of a great force were trying to expend themselves.

If one believes at any time in the ubiquitous power of the Evil One, surely it must be when occasions such as those to which my story has reached lay to the hands of evil-doers the most suitable tools to assist them in the working of an evil deed. The heart of Richard Neilson was boiling with impotent revenge, and his grip on the oars was as on his enemy's throat, when a soft but peculiar whistle from the left bank of the river held his hands as he let the boat drift and looked eagerly shoreward. He saw no one, but some one saw his pause, and the whistle was repeated when the suspended oars dipped again into the water and the boat was propelled toward the sound.

As he laid his boat alongside the reedy shore, and drew in his oars, an exclamation that was almost a shout escaped from his lips, and Neilson bounded ashore. A man was standing on the grass in the shelter of some undergrowth—a man stout of form and coarse of face, with worn and dusty attire and tangled hair and beard.

"By—, it is you!" Neilson had said. "The devil helps his own. If of all the world I could have had my wish this moment, I should have wished to see your face."

"Hold your mad yells!" the man replied, as he stepped into the boat and sat down. "If you had a rope around your neck you would not make such a row. Get in and get home."

"In trouble again?" asked Neilson, as he obeyed and seized the oars.

"Ay, and will be as long as there is money to be made by a blow. I was at your hut, but guessed you were up the river when I missed the boat. How are things working with *you*, Dick?"

"Badly,—badly just now, and if ever a man wanted a helping hand I do, and I know you're game to give it to me, Dan Whelan."

"Ay am I, 'in for a penny in for a pound' is my motto, mate; so spit out your trouble, Dick, for there can't be listeners on the river. Pull out more into the stream and then go ahead."

The speaker struck a match as he spoke and lit his pipe, in readiness to listen to Neilson's story, which was told as the water rippled by them in silvery sparkles, where the nearly full moon crept through the trees to its bosom, and while the sweet breeze from the Bugong Hills softly touched the cheeks of the plotters in a vain attempt to whisper of a sweetness and a purity they could not comprehend. As further events will reveal the result of their plans, I need not enter into them more fully, but leave them in the hut of Neilson at Calandra until a later hour.

"We may as well go upstairs," Cyrus said to me after we had lingered long in front of the haunted house, and when the moon was beginning to throw her pale light freely over the forest tops. "It is getting late, and I have a story to tell you."

So I followed him in and up the stairs, after he had carefully seen to the fastenings of the door. There was no light save what struggled through the uncurtained windows on the staircase, and I confess that I did not feel at ease, even though I was no believer in ghosts, and was glad when Cyrus had struck a match and lighted the candles ready placed on the writing-table in the room he had selected to occupy.

"You would never think of living altogether alone in this place?" I said, as he placed a decanter and some refreshments on the table. "Putting spirits entirely out of the question, the loneliness and gloom of this house would set a man crazy."

"I never meant to be here long," he answered; "indeed I hope my business will not take many days. You see my preparations are but slight," and he pointed to his bedding as it lay on the old-fashioned couch I have mentioned before; "but although my belief in spirits is entire, I am not afraid, for I know that those who revisit this house will not harm me."

"No, I am sure they won't!" I replied, as though I should say "for there are no such things;" but my new friend looked so solemn as he drew the dusty curtain far back from the window and let the moonlight through the dim panes, that I helped myself to a glass from the decanter, and sat down to hear the story he had promised me.

Cyrus took out his watch and laid it on the table. The hands marked half-past ten as he detached the albert from his vest.

"I am impressed with the belief," he said seriously, "that whatever of a supernatural seeming occurs here this night will take place between half-past eleven and twelve o'clock, so that I have more time to relate my tale to you than its length will require. Shall I begin?"

"If you will be so obliging. I confess that my curiosity is great."

"I want to tell you a little of the history of the brothers who both lived and both died in this house. You are already aware that the family name of these gentlemen was Malbraith; the youngest of them, George Malbraith, was a single man; the eldest was a widower, with one son, but a disowned one in consequence of an unhappy marriage to which I need not revert. Mr. Mathew Malbraith was a man of property, and on the disunion and separation between him and his son taking place he took up a closer intimacy with his brother, who was very many years younger than himself, and a poor man. The result of this intimacy was their emigration together to this country and the purchase of this property. There was, however, no house on it then, and Mathew Malbraith designed and had the Moat built, calling it after his English home, and designing to pass the remainder of his days in it, as indeed he eventually did.

"For ten years before his death Mathew Malbraith heard no word of his banished son, yet his brother had betrayed the absent youth so far as to hide all knowledge of the letters he received from him from the unhappy father, who, in his loneliness, repented him sadly of his son's loss, and would have made him amends in all ways could he only have found out the whereabouts of his ill-used lad. When I tell you that the name of the dead man's son was Cyrus Malbraith, you will anticipate my story in a measure."

"Yes," I replied. "You are the son of Mr. Mathew Malbraith yourself?"

"I am; I am Cyrus Malbraith."

"Pray go on, for I am more and more interested now that I know that."

"You are, of course, but now comes the part of my narrative that will most astonish you. I had been for years in San Francisco, the father of a happy family, and in prosperous circumstances, when I, one night, awakened from a strange dream. I had dreamed that I had heard my father's voice crying aloud to me, 'Come! O Cyrus!' and in, as it sounded, the most awful bodily agony. I awoke with my heart beating with abnormal rapidity, and moisture breaking through every pore of my body, and it was some moments before I could compose myself in the belief that I had not really heard my own name uttered loudly.

"Well, I slept again, and was awakened by the same call, but the cry, 'Cyrus, O Cyrus!' was fainter. I sprang from my bed and drew on some clothes, determined to keep awake and reason myself out of the nightmare that seemed to have taken possession of me, so I sat down in an armchair by the bed.

"As I sat there, with my hand on my forehead, that felt hot and throbbing, I raised my eyes and saw between me and the door a man's form lying, as it seemed, upon the floor, with a bruised and bloody face turned toward me with its appealing eyes fixed on mine. The face was my father's, and I got up to stagger toward the form, but it was gone, and I fell forward on my face to the spot where it had appeared. I was found there insensible, and lay for many weeks after in the grasp of a violent illness, to the approach of which, I was constrained to ascribe the fancied appearance and voice of my parent."

"Doubtless you were already delirious when you dreamt of

the call," I said.

"I do not think so; nor, I think, will you when you are aware that it was on that very night and at that very hour my poor father was murdered in this house, but it was not for long after that I knew that, or that it was my Uncle George's hand that struck the death-blow. That news reached me in this letter that was delivered to me in due course by the foreign mail, and the contents of which brought me to Australia—read it."

He placed the letter before me, and I read—

From The Moat House,

29th October, 18—.

Nephew Cyrus,—I cannot die without confession of my great sin to you before I go hence and am no more. I write this from my death-bed in this house, that my hands desecrated with the blood of my brother, Cain that I am, and was accursed and deprived of hope. Here I lie in grievous and sore pain, and with none to close mine eyes save him who aided me in my crime, and from whom I have to hide the knowledge of this my confession, lest he should with his own hands avenge your father's death by adding to the stains already upon them that of the poor blood that courses so feebly in the veins of these fingers which I now for the last time hold this pen. In the tower room above this where my bed is we despoiled foully my brother and your unhappy father of his life, and here I expiate in pain of body and despair of soul a deed done on the 29th day of October 18—, at between half-past eleven and twelve o'clock at night. My life has been one long misery since that hour, which has never been repeated upon the dial that our victim's form has not haunted my bed. I do not ask your forgiveness, for I have forfeited that of the God who made me.—

Your unhappy uncle,

GEORGE MALBRAITH

I raised my eyes as I finished the perusal of this letter, and saw that the gaze of Cyrus Malbraith was fixed on the dial plate of his watch, and that the hands were approaching the hour I was now awaiting with the strangest feelings.

"What do you think now?" he asked. "The very hour of the month there confessed to was that in which I heard my father's call and saw his face."

"I do not know what to think. My God! What is that?"

We both arose to our feet as a heavy fall seemed to take place on the floor above us, and a dreadful sound of scuffling and stamping of feet, as though a deadly struggle for life were going on in that long closed room. We neither spoke or moved until cries and stifled shrieks for mercy gave place to one loud call, and "Cyrus, O Cyrus!" was heard as plainly as though uttered by human lips.

"I am here father; I am coming!" shouted the poor son, as he darted toward the door and opened it just as the very silence of death itself succeeded the previous noise above.

"You forget, you forget!" I cried, as I also ran to the door with the intention of closing it; "you cannot help the dead." But he waved me off and whispered, "Hush! It is not over," as the door above opened and heavy steps seemed to bear some heavy burden, tramp, tramp down the stairs and past the open door where we stood.

I don't know what came over me, but I suppose it was the courage of desperation. The brilliant light from the pair of candles on the table poured out into the landing as I dashed outside and planted myself in the middle of it. My revolver was in my hand, and its muzzle was pointed up the stairs, down which I yet heard the approaching tramp.

"In the name of Heaven, stand back; it is close upon you!" said the horrified watcher; but I saw nothing and only heard the heavy footsteps as they sounded nearer and nearer.

"Where is it? I see nothing!" I said, as a strange rustle seemed to pervade the air around me and my outstretched hand encountered the cold features of a dead body. Yet there was nothing. My hand was stretched into a space fully illuminated by the candles, yet I felt the dead features and the damp hair and heard a faint groan that might have been the last from a dying man's lips, and then there was a silence unbroken save by my own hard and terrified breathing.

I drew back into the apartment and closed and locked the door behind me. Cyrus had already gone, and was leaning weakly against the window through which the moonlight streamed. He indeed seemed incapable of speech, but all at once he beckoned me to his side.

"Look, is this the end?" he whispered.

I went to his side and looked out. Beneath the tower lay the grass-grown garden with its overgrown shrubberies casting dark, heavy shadows across the white patches of moonlight, and straight down toward the river was an opening in the trees, through which the broad gleam of water was visible as it sparkled in the moonbeams or hid in the shelter of sedge and willow. As I followed the eyes of Cyrus, mine rested on the apparent figure of a man staggering, as it seemed, under a heavy burden that hung limply over his shoulders.

This dead apparition crossed the grass and moved down the vista toward the river, disappearing suddenly by the bank just as the edge of a great cloud touched the moon and covered her up with a pall of sable. It was as though between us and the awful scene a curtain of darkness had been suddenly dropped to shut a deed of blood from the sight of man forever. Cyrus turned and, dropping into his chair, hid his face with his hands.

I did not know what to think or how to persuade myself that I had been the victim of some cheat, for how could my sense of sight as well as my sense of touch be at fault? Had I not felt the touch of cold features, with which my hands yet trembled, in a spot occupied by nothing as my eyes assured me? Had I not heard noises and voices where there was no one? What was I to think or believe?

"I should like to visit that room above us," I said abruptly, and Cyrus got up and took a light in his hand.

"There is nothing to prevent you, there is the key," and he handed me a key as he spoke. Seizing the other candle I preceded him, going up the stairs, however, with a tremor I should not like to have avowed.

The door was on the side of the small landing, in exactly the same position as that of the room beneath it, and I satisfied myself that it was fastened before I unlocked it.

"Stop a moment before you open," said my new friend, as he laid a hand on my arm, "I want to tell you the condition in which I left it a few hours ago when I thoroughly examined it. The room was in perfect order save for the dust of years that lay even upon the dark bed-cover, so that a touch left the impress of fingers upon it and the fingers brought away impurity."

"You think it will be changed now?" I asked.

"How can I help thinking so? No struggle such as we heard could take place without leaving traces."

"The struggle was but of sound; I saw nothing on the stairs, though I felt it."

"But I saw it; I saw the dead face of my father that you felt, and I saw but too well the features of the man who bore the corpse on his shoulder—it was my uncle's and it was awful in its terror of the burden so close to it."

I opened the door and we entered, to find that my companion's suspicion was correct, the room bearing every trace of a mortal struggle in which blood had been spilled. In fact, the tale could almost be gathered from the indications left in the haunted chamber. The bed-clothes were disordered and partly dragged to the floor, as if with the grasp of the victim who had been torn from his slumber to die. A small night-stand was overturned, a chair fallen on its back, and the bits of carpet that had lain decently on the floor were shuffled about and, in one spot, exposed the bare boards, on which red spots and stains were visible as though but a week old. The very atmosphere felt heavy as if with death, and a shudder went through me as though from a chill wind.

"In the name of him who can alone understand these mysteries, let us get out of this!" I exclaimed; and, far more rapidly than I had ascended, I went down again to the comparatively safe shelter of the lower apartment, the door of which I carefully locked, as if that could be any security against the spirits of the tower.

"Are you not a bit nervous?" I asked of my host, as I hastily replenished my glass and emptied it.

"Not in the least. I believe that I have been especially summoned from a far land to avenge my father's death, and that the things we have seen and heard and felt have been as especially sent to guide me in securing that vengeance."

"How so? There was nothing to show more than you already know."

"Oh yes, there was a great deal. I know the particulars now. I know that my father was dragged from his bed and foully murdered, and that his own brother carried the corpse down those stairs and down the avenue toward the river. I shall search in that spot for the remains of a murdered man."

"You may have a satisfaction in interring the bones," I said; "but no more, since your uncle is dead."

"You forget there was an accomplice," he said impressively.

"Ah, yes, I had forgotten that; but I see now, you think the name of that accomplice is—"

"Richard Neilson. Yes, I do."

"But you can prove nothing against him?"

"Not yet; but I feel that I shall be able to do so. I was not brought all these long watery miles on a futile errand."

Now I am going to rejoin the suspected Neilson and the unscrupulous man he had called Dan Whelan. It was between eleven and twelve of the same night that Neilson's boat containing them both was pushed from the shore at the back of Calandra and rowed into the stream. It was Neilson who handled the sculls, and in the stern sat Whelan, grim and uncompromising-looking, while his companion was white as chalk and weak as a young child.

"You will have to row, Dan, I can't do it!" he said, as the shadows along the shore deepened into the overhanging bush; "my grip will not hold on the sculls."

"You are the—coward!" the other muttered, as he rose and changed seats with Neilson, "and you have nearly half a gallon of spirits in you too. If I had as weak a liver as you I'm—if I would ever dip my fingers in anything thicker than muddy water."

"I can't help it, but God forbid that I should ever again feel the blood of a murdered man on my hands. More to the right, Dan—keep close to the bend to keep out of Connel Craig's sight, his hut is just opposite."

"Once more I say what is the use of bothering with this dead man? I could cut that Craig's weaxand before half a grave could be dug. Say the word, Dick, and I'll go ashore and do it."

"No! no! I say, never again, never again, no more blood, never again!" and the miserable, trembling wretch half rose in his terror to stay the hand that would have directed the boat toward the opposite bank of the stream.

"Faugh!" he cried with disgust, as he shook off the limp hand of Neilson. "If ever a man deserved to die for his cowardice you do, and if I didn't owe you more than one good turn I'd jolly quick leave you to do your own resurrection work. Waken up, man, and point out the place to me. How the deuce do you expect me to row there when I don't know a foot of the way?"

"Steer for that fallen tree and run your boat up against it. The place is not fifty yards from that."

Following these instructions the boat was soon fastened in the shadow of the log, and picks and shovels, with a dark lantern, a coil of rope, and a huge bottle, were taken from it to the land. It was in a wild spot of tangled scrub and fallen timber, and with great sprawling branches straggling out over it for many acres of uncultivated forest, through which Richard Neilson led the way with a desperate courage supplied him anew by a fresh attack at the spirits ere he left the boat.

In this tangle the shadows were deeper, and the spots which the moonlight reached through the straggling branches were few and far between, but they lay bright and full upon a green hillock as soft and rounded as though it had been raised on some sunny green lawn.

"This is the place," whispered Neilson, "for I know it by that cut I put in the log; but who has dragged the branches from it, or planted the grass to grow so green?"

"The ghosts you talk about of course," said Dan with a sneer. "Put down the rope and fall to work with your mouth shut, for the sooner this job is over the better it will be for us both."

"How deep is it?" he asked again, when the mould had been flying from their shovels for some time. "Ah! You needn't answer, I can see we are near from your white face. Get up, man, and take your shaking carcass out of that. I can't bear the sight of you."

Only too glad to obey the mandate, Neilson crawled out of the grave, while Whelan carefully scraped the soil from a rough coffin that had now become partly visible, and on which the strokes of the shovel sounded awfully in the murderer's ears. Once Dan came up to the surface, and took a long pull at the big bottle before he went down again, carrying the coil of rope with him.

"Now the course is clear," he cried, as he returned to his companion's side. "Pull away at your rope, and we'll have him up. Steady—steady. Hold fast! My end's caught. All right. There we are!" And the clay-soiled box that hid its awful secret lay on the grass, while drops of agony fell heavily from the murderer's face over his victim's breast.

It was then, as it lay by the rifled grave which Whelan was rapidly filling up, that the curtain-like cloud that obscured our view from the tower window fell over the moon and blotted out its light. It was by the pale glimmer of stars that the two men bore their dread burden through the wood, and laid it in the bottom of the boat, and when they had shoved out once more into the stream it was Whelan who held the sculls, while Neilson had fallen weakly and speechlessly into the stern.

He did not seem to see anything but the awful object that lay at his feet, or to hear anything but the death groans of the man whose blood he had spilled treacherously. In vain his companion addressed words of inquiry. He did not speak, for the cold grip on his heart seemed to him the grasp of a dead man's hand.

All at once he shuddered and looked up. Right before him on the slope above the river gleamed the starlike light in the tower window of the Moat House, and the rays from it appeared to point directly to him as he sat in the boat, with his rigid knees drawn up to avoid contact with the terrible coffin. Suddenly, and with a gasping breath, he started to his feet, and, dragging the nearest oar from Whelan's grasp, waved it above his head frantically, as if about to strike his companion.

"You did it on purpose," he shouted wildly, "you did it that I might see him again on the very spot where the water was red with his blood as he sank! My God, he is there, with his awful face and his glassy eyes staring at me!" and with an awful cry of agonised despair, Neilson dropped the oar and fell backwards into the water.

A horrible imprecation grated from between Whelan's teeth as he tried to steady the boat that was nearly overturned by the sudden disappearance of Neilson. On the spot where the miserable man had disappeared unsteady ripples spread circlingly and big bubbles arose and burst upon the surface, but the form whose struggles as he died must have moved the waters into unholy shapes never re-appeared on its surface again, though Dan's eyes were strained in every direction to see and succour him. But all at once a sense of his own insecurity overwhelmed him, as he heard distinctly the sound of horse's feet on the road that skirted the river.

"A trooper's horse, by Jove!" he muttered, "and here I am to account for two dead men. Curses on my luck! I'll have to swim for it, or I'll get into this job of Neilson's myself!"

As he spoke he had slipped over the side of the boat, leaving it and its dread burden to drift helplessly where it listed, while he himself made his escape to Neilson's now-deserted hut to secure a change of clothing and such money as he could find to help him in his further flight—for he was far on his way from Calandra when daylight broke over the Moat House.

Fair and sweet broke the morning around the Moat House, with the dewdrops glittering on the verdurous river banks, and the sparkling water rippling along the sedges by the cool, refreshing breeze of early day. Connel Craig rowing leisurely down the river and thinking of his interview of yesterday with Richard Neilson, felt uneasy as he looked toward the tower and saw its window open, and a faded curtain flapping outside it in the soft wind.

"That Dick will come to no good end, and I am a fool to trust him," he was thinking; "yet I can't bear to get him into such heavy trouble after hiding it so long."

Thus as he was looking up toward the tower and the curtain flapping in the open window, and then, as he was getting too far in shore, he plied one oar and turned his head over his shoulder to see his course, what he did see was the awful boat of the previous night, as it drifted strangely to and fro, yet scarcely ever left for many yards the spot from which Richard Neilson had fallen.

The astonished man made a few strokes and then drew in his oars.

"It's Neilson's boat," he said aloud, though there was no living man to hear him. "What can have happened?" And then his eyes caught sight of the oar the man had dropped in his last horrible vision of his victim; it was lying against a bed of sedges, whose sad rustling might have been the whisper of ghostly voices mourning for the sins of men.

"What can have happened?" Craig repeated, as his boat sidled up to the other, and he rose to his feet and looked into the unmanned boat, where he saw the rough coffin with the damp clay yet clinging to its sides, and the horrified man fell back with a dread cry as he recognised it; for it was his own hands that had rudely put its boards together.

"The hand of Heaven is in it," he gasped, "for it has come back to the very spot from whence I dragged it myself!"

We were at breakfast at the Camp when Craig, whose face was white as ashes, came into the room. I had persuaded Mr. Cyrus Malbraith to return with me and share the meal, and I was relating to Mason the terrible events of the night, as he had returned sometime during the small hours, when Connel entered. No one could doubt that something out of the common had happened when they looked at his face, and I asked him what it was as I rose from the table.

"Yes, it is something terrible," he replied; "and although I have had something to do with it, I can't keep it on my mind any longer. You have heard of Mathew Malbraith, of the Moat? Well, his dead body is lying in Richard Neilson's boat in the river, within sight of the tower; you had better see to securing it, for I would not touch it again, and the boat seems adrift."

Cyrus started to his feet.

"Do you mean my father's body?" he cried as he laid his trembling hand on Craig's arm.

"If you are the son of Mr. Mathew Malbraith, former owner of the Moat, yes, I do mean it; and I will tell you all I know about it as soon as the police have got hold of that awful boat."

Having made all arrangements, we went down to the river where Craig's boat awaited us, and after a short spell at the oars we came in sight of the strangely moored craft as it swayed to and fro, lapping the water with its sucking bows as they rose and dipped among the sun-gleamed ripples.

"She is moored in some peculiar way sure enough," said Mason, who was bending over the bows as we neared the silent boat of the dead man, "for there is a rope overboard from the stern, and the end of the rope is *fastened under the coffin*."

"Steady, Connel, and we will haul it in."

As I said the words I lifted the wet rope and tried to draw it to me, but vainly, though it seemed attached to something that swayed strangely back and forth beneath the water; another pair of hands were added to the rope, and with a strong pull the hold gave way and up to the surface we dragged the dead body of Richard Neilson.

The staring eyes glared with an awful vacancy, and in the clutched hands were grasped the roots of reeds and water-weeds that had held him to the bottom until our united strength had broken them. The rope by means of which his body had moored the boat containing Malbrath's remains over the very spot to which they had been first consigned by the murderers had become entangled with Neilson's legs as he fell out of the boat, and remained so wound and wrapped around him that it was with difficulty we freed him from its folds.

All due investigation ordered by law having taken place, the bodies were buried, the one lying far distant from the other, as was but right; and now, when I have given you Craig's evidence almost in his own words, I shall have finished this story of the Moat House.

"I was out fishing late one night four years ago," he related, "and, as my luck would have it, happened to be in the shade of the trees opposite the Moat, with my lines out, when I saw two men coming down to the bank. I guessed they were up to no good, especially when I saw that one of them bore something like a human figure on his back, and that the other one was Richard Neilson. I was too far away to hear what was whispered, but the moon was bright and I saw them sink the body in the river and then go back to the house.

"I wondered what I would do. There was no police at Calandra then, and besides I guessed that the secret would be worth money to me. Once I thought of raising the body without a word and so disposing of it that I should at all times and seasons have the murderers under my thumb; but then, again, I reflected on the danger I might run of having myself done the deed I had only been in part a witness of, so I watched my chance to see Neilson alone, and I told him he was in my power.

"'I did not do it,' he declared; 'it was my master. Surely you wouldn't hang an innocent man so?'

"'I know nothing of your master,' was what I answered him. 'Yours is the only face I could swear to, and it is to you I shall look for what may shut my mouth; get it how you like, but money I will have, and you know that money you can get.'

"'I will do my best,' he said; 'but the secret must be between us two.'

"'All right, so long as I agree with you no one else shall ever know from me. But there is one thing I say, and that is that the poor man must be decently buried, and not lie down there to be food for fishes. His body must be raised and buried like a Christian.'

"He pleaded hard to let the awful thing lie, but I would not listen, and I would not help him touch it; but I made the coffin as I best could, and brought it down the river in my boat, and when he put the corpse in I helped him to take it up the river again and bury it in Marshland Scrub. I wish I had never had a hand in it, for I shall never pass that spot again without fancying I see Neilson's boat floating there silently, with one dead man anchoring it to the ground, and the other floating in his coffin over the place where his corpse first plunged."

LITTLE LIZ

by B. L. Farjeon

B. L. Farjeon (1838-1903) is best known these days as the father of the well-known children's author, Eleanor Farjeon, whose ghost story 'Faithful Penny Dove' has often been anthologised. Benjamin Leopold Farjeon came to Australia from London in 1854 and spent seven years on the Victorian goldfields. In 1861 he went to New Zealand and worked for a newspaper before publishing *Shadows on the Snow: A Christmas Story* (1866), which he dedicated to Charles Dickens. Dickens responded encouragingly to the book and Farjeon promptly returned to England to make his name as a writer.

He wrote over fifty books, many of them crime and mystery stories, some of them with Australian content. He also wrote many novels of the supernatural and occult, including *Devlin the Barber* (1888), *A Strange Enchantment* (1889), *The Last Tenant* (1893), *Something Occurred* (1893), *The Mesmerists* (1900), and *The Clairvoyante* (1905). 'Little Liz' is a harrowing tale from his elusive first book, *Shadows on the Snow*. This version is from a reprint published in 1867.

When the Victorian gold-fever was at its height, people were mad with excitement. Neither more nor less, I was as mad as the others, although I came to the colony from California, which was suffering from the same kind of fever, and which was pretty mad, too, in its way. But Victoria beat it hollow; for one reason, perhaps, because there was more of it. The strange sights I saw and the strange stories I could tell, if I knew how to do it, would fill a dozen books. In my time I have lived all sorts of lives and have worked with all sorts of mates, picked up in a rough-and-tumble kind of way, which was about the only way then that mates picked up each other. One day you did not know the man that the next day you were hob-a-nob with. I had some strange mates, as you may guess, but the strangest I ever worked with, and the one I liked more than all the others put together, was Bill Trickett. Bill was as thin as a lath and as tall as a maypole, and had come to the colony under a cloud. I don't mean by that that he had done anything wrong at home, and was sent out at the expense of the Government, like a heap of others I mated with; but he was obliged to run away from England for a reason I didn't know when I picked him up, but which I learnt afterwards. He had brought his wife out with him—a poor, weak, delicate creature, who died soon after he landed, leaving behind her a baby, a little girl, the only child they had. This child Bill left with some people in Melbourne, and came on to the gold-diggings to try his luck. I was working at that time in Dead-dog Gully, near Forest Creek, which was just then discovered, and Bill and me came together as mates. A better one, to do his share of the work and a little bit over, I should be unreasonable to wish for. I never had anything to complain of. On the contrary. He never shirked his work, seeming to like it more than anything else in the world. And once, when I was laid up with colonial fever—some of you have had a touch of it, I daresay, and know how it pulls a man down—he nursed me with the tenderness of a woman, and worked the claim without a murmur. Those are things one doesn't easily forget. Soon after I got well our claim was worked out, and we had to look else-where for another; for every inch of Dead Dog was taken up. I remember well the night we parted. We were sitting in our tent, Bill and me, with our gold before us and our revolvers at full cock on the table. We had to look out pretty sharp in those days, mates. Many's the man who has been robbed and disposed of, without any one being the wiser; many's the man that has been murdered, and thrown down deserted shafts. Queer things were done on the diggings during the first fit of the fever, that human tongue will never speak of. Murder will out, they say; that isn't quite true. I've seen some sights that make me shiver to think of, the secret of which will only be known on the Day of Judgment.

Well, we were sitting there, with our gold before us. Our claim had been a rich one, and we had three hundred ounces to divide, after all our sprees—and we had a few, I can tell you.

"Tom," said Bill, as he sat looking at the gold, "if I had had as much money as that when I was in the old country, I should never have come out to the gold-fields, and my dear wife would not have died."

"That's more than you can say for a certainty," I answered.

"Not a bit of it," he said; "my wife would have been alive, and we should have been living happily together. I'll tell you how it was. I was a contractor in a small way at home, and had lots of up-hill work, for I commenced with nothing. While I was courting Lizzie, an old hunks of a money-lender wanted to marry my girl. She had a nice time of it, poor lass! With her father on one side trying to persuade her to marry the old hunks, and me on the other, begging her to be faithful to me. But I had no need to do that. There was only one way out of the difficulty; we ran away, and got married without their knowing. We were as happy as the days were long, and should have remained so, but for the old money-lending thief. To spite me for taking the girl from him, he bought up all my debts—about three hundred pounds worth—and almost drove me mad. And one morning I caught the villain in the act of insulting my Liz. I didn't show him any mercy; I beat him till he was sore, and then I kicked him out of the house. The next day the bailiffs were on the look-out to arrest me for debt, and I had to run for my liberty. He sold me up, root and branch, and turned my wife into the streets, and we came together to Liverpool, where Lizzie was confined. I tried hard to get work, but couldn't; starvation or the workhouse was before us. All my chances at home were gone, and there was nothing for it but emigration. I shipped before the mast, and a friend assisted me to pay Lizzie's passage in the steerage. A fortnight after we were out at sea, she told me that the doctor who attended her in her confinement had said that a long sea voyage would probably be the death of her. His words came true; she died within the year. So, you see, if I had had my share of that gold at home, I could have paid that damned old scoundrel, and my wife would not have died. I want to get a heap of gold, and go home and ruin him. I should die contented then."

He rose, and walked up and down the tent, cursing the man who, he believed, had killed his wife.

"I tell you what, Tom," he said, after a bit, "I shall tramp to Melbourne to see my little daughter, and then I shall go prospecting. There are places, I'll stake my life, where the gold can be got in lumps, and I mean to find them out. I dreamt the other night that I came upon it in the rock, and that I had to cut it out with a chisel."

I didn't like the idea of losing my mate, and I did my best to persuade him not to go; but I might as well have talked to a lamp-post. So we divided the gold, shook hands, and the next morning he started on the tramp to Melbourne.

I didn't see or hear anything of him for a good many months after this; and somehow or other, when I lost him I lost my luck. Every shaft I bottomed turned out a duffer. I could hardly earn tucker. I worked in Jackass Gully, Donkey-woman's Gully, Pegleg, Starvation Point, Choke'm Gully, Dead-horse Gully, and at last made my way to Murdering Flat—nice, sociable names!—pretty well down on my luck. I had been in Murdering Flat three weeks, and was sitting alone in my tent one night, reckoning up things. In those three weeks I hadn't made half-an-ounce of gold, and there wasn't two pennyweights in my match-box—so that I didn't feel over amiable. That day, I had been particularly unlucky, having made about three grains of gold, which I flung away in a rage. I was just thinking whether I mightn't just as well go to the grog-shanty, and have a drink—it was past nine o'clock at night—when who should walk straight into my tent but my old mate, Bill. I scarcely knew him at first; for he had let his hair grow all over his face, and he was almost covered with it, up to his eyes and down to his breast.

"Bill!" I cried, jumping up.

"Yes, it's me, Tom," he said. "Are you alone?"

"Yes, Bill."

"Stop here, then, till I come back, and don't let anybody in but me."

He went out, and returned in about ten minutes with a beautiful little girl in his arms.

"Hush!" he said, stepping softly. "Speak low. She's asleep."

She wasn't above six years old but she was so pretty, and looked so like a little angel—such as I never expected to see under my roof—that I fell in love with her at once. Of course I was a bit surprised when he brought her in, and he couldn't help observing it as he laid her carefully upon my stretcher.

"This is my little girl, Tom," he said, answering my look. "If I ever go to heaven, I shall have her to thank for it. She is my good angel."

"Where are you come from?" I asked, after we had covered the pretty fairy with a blanket. He looked cautiously round, as though he feared some one was in hiding, and then, sitting opposite me at the table, rested his chin on his hands, and said, in a whisper,

"I've found it, Tom!"

There was such an awful glare in his eyes that I felt quite scared as I asked him what it was he had found.

"I've found the place where the gold comes from," he said, in the same sort of hoarse whisper. "I am *on* it, Tom! I knew I should find it at last. Look here."

First going to the door, to see that no one could get in without warning, he pulled from his breast-pocket a nugget of pure gold that must have weighed near upon seventy ounces, and five or six others, from fifteen to twenty ounces each. Lord! how my heart beat as I handled them, and how I wished I could drop across some of the same kidney! I don't know how it is with you, mates; but although I don't believe I value the gold much when I've got it, there's no pleasure in life so great to me as coming suddenly upon a rich patch. I think the sight of bright shining gold at the bottom of a dark shaft is one of the prettiest in the world.

"Is that good enough for you?" he asked, as he put the nuggets back into his pocket.

I laughed.

"Any more where they came from, Bill?"

"More than you could carry."

I stared at him, believing he had gone mad. "It's true. How are you doing?"

"I can't make tucker, Bill. My luck's dead out."

"It's dead in now," said he; "I've come to put fifty ounces a day in your pocket. What do you say? Will you go mates with me again?"

That was a nice question, wasn't it, to put to a hard-up digger, without an ounce of gold in his match-box?

"Will I, old fellow?" I cried. "Will I not! When shall we start?"

"Stop a minute, Tom," he said gravely. "I've something to say to you first. I want you for a mate again, and shall be glad to have you; but we've got to strike a bargain. You see my little girl there?"

I nodded.

"She is the blood of my heart! I am like a plant, Tom, which would wither if deprived of God Almighty's blessed dew. She is my dew. If anything was to happen to her I should wither, and rot, and die. I want you for my mate, because I believe you to be honest and true. And I am going to show you a place where the gold grows—a place which, of my own free will, I would not show to another man in the world. I have hunted it and tracked it, never heeding the danger I have run. But do you know, Tom, that since I have had my little pet with me"—and he laid his hand, O, so gently upon her cheek!—"all my recklessness and courage seem to have gone clean out of me. For it is her life I am living now, not my own! And I think what will become of her if I die before my time—if I should slip down a shaft, or it should tumble in upon me, or I should fall ill of a fever, or anything of that sort should happen to me that would deprive her of a protector. These thoughts haunt me day and night, and presentiments come over me sometimes that fill me with fears I can't express. Now, Tom, listen to me. The place I am going to take you to will make you rich. If we can keep it to ourselves for a few months—(though there is another in the secret, but he won't peach, for his own sake)—we shall get at least five thousand ounces—perhaps double as much: there's no telling whether we sha'n't drop across a mountain of gold. Now, lay your hand upon your heart, and swear by all you hold dearest that if anything should happen to me, you will take care of my little darling, and be a second father to her when I am gone!"

I bent over the dear little one's face—I can feel her sweet breath again upon my cheek—and kissed her. She stirred in her sleep, and smiled. Then I said,

"That kiss is a sacrament, Bill. By all that's holy, I will be a second father to your little girl, should she need me. So help me, God!"

He took my hand, and the big tears rolled down his beard. It was full five minutes before he was calm enough to speak.

"Now I'll tell you all about it. You remember my leaving you to go to Melbourne, after we had worked out our claim in Dead-dog Gully. Well, when I got there, I found that my little girl was not being well treated. The people she was living with had taken to drink, and had neglected her. And my heart so grew to her—I can see my Lizzie's face in hers—that I made up my mind never to leave her again. So, when I was ready to start, I brought her away with me, and we've travelled together, since that time, I don't know how many hundreds of miles."

"How in the world did you manage it?" I asked, in wonder.

"The little thing couldn't walk!"

"And if she could," he answered, "do you think I would have let her blister her pretty feet? My darling! Manage it, Tom! Sometimes I carried her, and I got her odd lifts, now and then, upon the drays and wagons going our way. There was never a drayman or a wagoner that refused to give my little girl a ride, and that wasn't sorry to part with her—good luck to them! Why, some of them came miles out of their way for her sake, and would never take anything for it but a kiss from her pretty lips! And do you know, Tom," he said, "she saved me from the bushrangers once. We were in the Black Forest, and they were on me before I knew where I was. We had just finished tea, and I was stooping over the log-fire to get a light for my pipe, so that the little girl was hidden from them at first. I turned, with my heart in my mouth—not for myself, Tom; for her—and looked at them. There were four of them, splendidly mounted, dressed in red serge shirts and bright silk sashes. "Stand!" they cried, levelling their revolvers at me; "stand, for your life!" Well, my girl jumps up, and runs to my side, and takes hold of my hand. They were dumbfounded. "Well, I'm damned!" said one, under his breath; and then in a louder tone, "is that yours, mate?" "Yes," I answered, looking into their faces for pity. Upon that, they put up their pistols, and one of the men got off his horse, and came close to us. "Don't be frightened, little one," he said. "I'm not frightened," lisped my pet, playing with the fringe of his red silk sash. "I'm not going to harm her, mate," he said to me; and he knelt before my darling, and put her pretty hands on his eyes, and kissed them again and again. "If every man had an angel like this by his side," he said softly, "it would be the better for him." Then he took off his sash, and tied it round my girl's waist; and I had to lift her up to the other men to kiss them. That being done, they wished me good-night, and rode off. That was a lucky escape, wasn't it? However, after a time I found I couldn't get along as quickly as I wanted, and besides, when I was on the track of the gold I've discovered, I had to travel through country where I didn't meet with drays or wagons. So I bought a wheelbarrow."

"A wheelbarrow?" I cried, more and more surprised.

"Yes, Tom," he said, with a comical look; "a wheelbarrow; and I put my little darling in it, and wheel her wherever I want to go. Well, to get along with my story, I came one day to the place where I'm working now, and where I want you to join me. Directly I saw it, I knew the gold was there, and I put up my tent. Before the week was out, I had a hundred ounces. I went to a cattle-station about twelve miles off, and bought a stock of provisions. Then I set to work in earnest. The whole place is a great gold-bed; wherever you dig, it peeps up at you with its bright eyes. There's plenty of quartz on the hills, and you can't search five minutes without finding it. At the top there's more quartz than gold; deep down, I'll lay my life there's more gold than quartz. I worked by myself in this gully for four weeks, making about a hundred ounces a week, when one day, as I was panning out the gold in the creek hard by, I saw a man looking at me. He had wandered by accident to the place, and had discovered me working. My mind was made up in a minute. I took him for my mate, so that the secret might be kept, and we worked together till the day before yesterday."

"What has become of him, then?" I asked.

"O, he's there still, getting gold, but not so much as he might if he was one of the right sort. For I know of a gully that's worth a dozen of the one we've been working in, and I don't intend that he shall put a pick in it. No, Tom, that's for you and me. I haven't parted from him without good reason. My little darling never liked him from the first, and would never let him kiss her. Then there's Rhadamanthus—"

"Rhadamanthus!"

"Don't be scared, Tom. It's only a dog, that was given to me by a drunken scholar—or rather, given to Lizzie in the bush—on the condition that we were always to call him Rhadamanthus—which we do, though at first it was a jaw-breaker. Then, as I say, there's Rhadamanthus. He won't let this mate of mine that was, come near him; snaps at him; snarls like the very devil if he tries to pat him on the head. That's a kind of instinct I believe in. And Lizzie's is a kind of instinct that I'd stake salvation on. But I put up with the fellow till a week ago. He wanted Lizzie to kiss him, and she wouldn't. He tried to force her, and I came upon them when she was struggling in his arms, screaming out to me for help. I helped her—and helped him, to the soundest thrashing he ever made acquaintance with. I broke with him then and there, and came away in search of you, pretty certain I should be able to find you. You're pretty well known, Tom."

"And Rhada—"

"Manthus. Out with it, Tom! It'll come as easy as butter soon."

"Where is he?"

"Outside in the bush, a couple of hundred yards away, keeping watch over the wheelbarrow. I want to start right away; we'll have to be careful that we're not followed."

"I'm ready this minute, Bill," I said. "I'll just take my blankets and tools. I'll leave the tent up; it'll keep off suspicion."

I wasn't long getting ready, and Bill, lifting his little girl from the bed, held her, still asleep, tenderly to his breast, and led the way into the bush, where Rhadamanthus and the wheelbarrow were waiting for us.

Rhadamanthus, the raggedest dog that ever breathed, with the most disgraceful tail that ever wagged, fixed his eyes upon me in a kind of way that said, "Now, what sort of a chap are you?" We laid pretty little Liz in the wheelbarrow, making her snug, and covering her up warm. Her face, as she lay asleep in the wheelbarrow, had a curious effect upon me. Made me choke a bit, as I'm doing now. When she was snugly tucked in, I kissed her, and a sweet and new feeling crept into my heart as once more she smiled at my kiss.

"It's a trick of hers," said Bill; she always smiles in her sleep when any one kisses her that she likes. God bless you, Tom!"

"All right, mate," said I.

"Rhadamanthus sidled up to me, and licked my hand.

We travelled the whole of that night, taking it in turns to

wheel little Liz, who slept soundly all the time. Rhadamanthus trudged along by our side, watching his child-mistress with true affection in his eyes. It was a beautiful star-lit night, and everything about us was quiet and peaceful. The scenes through which we passed were full of strange beauty to me, who had hitherto looked upon them with a careless eye. Now and again in the distance we saw a camp-fire burning, with the diggers lying around it; and occasionally we heard the tinkling of bells on the necks of horses who stumbled about with hobbles on their feet, while their drivers were sleeping between the shafts of the wagons, walled round with canvas, on beds of dry leaves. We kept out of the track of men as much as we could, and met with no obstacles on the road that we did not easily overcome. We had to lift the wheelbarrow over fallen logs sometimes, and once over a creek, and we did it gently, without disturbing our little one. That walk through the solemn and lovely woods was to me very much like a prayer. When we made our way through the tall straight trees of silverbark—when I looked up at the wonderful brightness of the heavens, which filled the woods with lovely light, among which the shadows played like living things—when upon a distant hill I saw a flock of sheep asleep, with the moon shining clear upon them—and when I gazed at the peaceful and beautiful face of the child asleep in the barrow—I could scarcely believe that it was not all a dream. The remembrance of that night's tramp has never left me, and its lessons remain. Too often, mates, do we walk through life, blind to the signs.

During the day we camped, and took it in turns to sleep, and on the third night we came to the end of our journey. We had had three or four hours' heavy up-hill work, but I didn't feel tired a bit. My body was as light as my heart.

"Over that range, Tom," said Bill, "and we're there."

It was the steepest of all the ranges, and took us a time getting to the top, and then, looking down, I saw a great natural basin, shut in by high hills. You would have thought there was no outlet from it, unless you climbed over the hills which surrounded it;

but when you got down, you discovered a number of artful little turns and windings, which led to gullies and smaller basins which you could not discern from the heights. We had to wake little Liz, as there was some danger wheeling the barrow down so steep an incline. She jumped out quite bright, and let me carry her some distance. If she had been my own child, I could not have felt more tender towards her. Presently Bill pointed out his tent, and said he should not wonder if his old mate were sleeping in it. Sure enough, when we were within six yards of the tent, he rushed out with a revolver in his hand, and fired at Rhadamanthus, who had sprung at him the moment he made his appearance.

"Lie down, Rhad!" cried Bill, pushing the dog away with his foot; "and you, Ted, drop that revolver, or I'll wring your neck for you!"

Almost on the words, Bill leaped at the fellow, wrested the revolver from his hand, and sent him spinning a dozen yards away. It was not done a moment too soon, for I believe he was about to fire on us. He was a desperate-looking fellow was Teddy the Tyler. A white-faced, white-livered, flat-footed bully. I heard some queer stories about him afterwards.

"You murdering villain, you!" said Bill, as Teddy the Tyler rose from the ground with an evil look, and tightened his belt. "Do you know you might have shot my little girl?"

Little Liz was clinging to her father, trembling in every limb.

"A good job if I had," muttered Teddy the Tyler.

Bill strode quickly up to him, and seizing him by the collar, forced him to the ground by dint of sheer muscular strength.

"If ever again you raise your hand," he said, between his clenched teeth, "against me, or my little girl, or my mate, or my dog—you so much as lift your finger against them, say good-bye to the world. I'll break your infernal back for you, as sure as the Lord's in heaven!"

"What do you bring loafers into the gully for?" growled Teddy.

"That's my business," answered Bill. "I discovered this place, and I've a right to bring a friend. This is my mate now. Call him a loafer again, and I'll knock your ugly teeth down your throat; keep a civil tongue in your head, and I'll not interfere with you. I make you a present of this gully, every inch of it." Teddy's face brightened. "I know where there's a richer one—ah, you may stare, but you'll not put your foot in it! To-morrow I shall take my tent away, and you can work here by yourself till you rot, if you like. I don't think you're fool enough to get the place rushed, for that would put an end to your little game. Pick up the revolver, Tom, and stick it in your belt. It's mine. And throw out of the tent everything that belongs to the thief."

I carried his blankets and clothes out to him, and threw them at his feet.

"There's something else in there belonging to me," he said. "My neckerchief."

I found it, and flung it to him. A bright-coloured neckerchief, which he slung about his neck, sailor fashion. The light of the moon shone upon it, and I noticed particularly the combination of bright colours in which it was woven.

As he gathered up his things he had a parting word to say, and he spit it out with foam about his lips, like the hound he was.

"I'll make this the worst night's work you have ever done! You shall cry blood for the way you've served me! By this, and this, I swear it!"

He wiped the foam from his mouth, and, flicking it to the ground with a snap of his fingers, walked slowly away.

We took no further notice of him, but putting the chain on Rhadamanthus, we went into the tent, and lay down till morning.

We were up with the lark, and out. As we passed along the gully, I noticed that Teddy the Tyler had put up a sort of mimi, and that he was asleep under it.

"Now then, Tom," said my mate, "I'll show you something that will open your eyes. That fool there knows nothing about it. I discovered the place three weeks ago, and held my tongue, having my doubts of him."

Coming to the end of the gully we walked over a pretty

considerable rise in the land, Bill leading the way, through more than one heavy clump of timber on the other side. We might have walked half a mile through thick clusters of trees, when Bill clapped his hand upon my eyes, and told me to close them. We might have walked a hundred yards further, when he took his hand away, saying we were there. It was a strange-looking spot, completely hidden by wood-growth; a piece of land that appeared to have been scooped out of the hills, in the exact shape of a saddle.

"Look around you," said Bill; "see the hills, every one of them, shelving down into this hollow. Look at the veins of quartz, auriferous every bit of it, all running down to one point. Here's a piece of the stone"—picking it up—"with gold in it, here's another with more gold in it. That's evidence. Now take your fossicking knife, and dig up some of the earth at the trunk of that tree with the large spreading roots. Dig into the roots. I thought as much. You can see the gold in it without spectacles. The stuff there'll yield an ounce to the tin dish. Why is the gold just at that spot? Because it has slid down the heights with the rains, and the roots of that tree have caught some of it in its descent, and held it fast in crevices. This hollow beneath us contains all the gold that has been washed for ages off these golden hills, and it is all ours—all ours, every ounce of it!" He was on the ground, showing me proof of his theory in small lumps of gold that he dug out here and there. "Tom, kneel down here by my side, and I'll tell you why I worship it." He held it in the palm of his hand, and gazed with glowing eyes upon it. "I see this educating her; I see this making her fit to hold her own with the best lady in the land; I see it bring smiles to her lips, roses to her cheeks; I see her doing good with it; I see her, the light of my days, removed from the hard trials that make life so sad to many; I see lifelong joy and happiness in it for my pretty Liz, my pretty, pretty Liz!"

He let the gold fall to the ground, and hid his face in his hands. I understood then how perfect love can be.

We returned to the old gully, and carried away our tent and

all that belonged to us. Before night we had our fireplace built, and our tent fixed in a spot where it would be secure from floods. The next day we set to work.

Bill was a true prophet. The hollow was heavy with gold. We did not find a regular gutter of it, though Bill said if we sank deep we should be sure to come upon one; but within a few feet of the surface, and sometimes almost on the surface, we lighted upon rich pockets of gold. Talk of jewellers' shops! This dirty hollow took the shine out of all of them. And as day after day went away, and our bags of gold got heavier and heavier, we laid plans for the future. We were to go home and buy a farm; Liz was to be educated and grow into a beautiful young woman and get married, and we were all to live together and take care of the children—how the little one laughed when we came to this part of the story! for we spoke freely before her;—it was all settled, and certain to come true. Those five weeks that we lived together were the happiest of my life. Liz was like a star in our tent, and made everything bright and beautiful. We all worshipped her— Bill, me, and Rhadamanthus—and lived in her, so to speak. The tricks she played, the stories she had to tell, the discoveries she made, gladdened the days, and drew our hearts closer and closer to her. One day she saw a rock exactly the shape of a goat's face and beard, and we had to go with her and christen it, "Goat's Rock"; another day she picked up a beautiful crystal, which she declared was a charm to keep everything bad away; another day she found a new kind of wild-flower, which she prattled over in the quaintest and prettiest fashion; another day she discovered that Rhadamanthus was a fairy who had changed himself into a dog to take care of her. The faithful, ragged beast! She announced the amazing discovery to him in the most impressive manner, kneeling before him, and putting his paws on her shoulders, the while he looked into her face, and blinked in confirmation. A baize partition separated the compartment in which she slept from ours, and one night, when I heard her, before going to bed, lisping her prayer that God would bless dear father and dear Tom and Rhad, my thoughts went back to the time when I, too, prayed before I went to sleep. On Sundays we would take a walk, and Bill, in the evening, would read a chapter from a Bible he had—which him, nor me, nor Rhad, would ever have thought of but for our dear little angel. Those Sundays, with Bill, and the little girl, and the ragged, faithful dog, are never out of my mind. I wish I had always spent my Sundays in the same way.

During this time we had only seen Teddy the Tyler once. About a fortnight after we started working he strolled upon us. A tin dish with nearly a pound of gold in it was lying on the ground, and he threw a woefully covetous look at it. He had his pick and shovel hanging over his shoulder, and walking past us he stuck his pick in the ground, and tucked up his shirt-sleeves.

Bill, following him, took the pick and shovel, and pitched them a dozen yards off.

"I told you you shouldn't come into this gully," he said.

"It's as much mine as yours," replied Teddy the Tyler. "I mean to fight for it, mate, at all events."

"That's fairly spoken," said Bill. "Fight you shall, and if you lick me, we'll give you this gully, and get another. Tom, come and see fair play."

To it they went. But Teddy might as well have stood up against a rock as against my mate. Bill was the strongest man I ever knew, and he gave Teddy such an awful thrashing that he threw up his arms in less than a quarter of an hour.

"Had enough, mate?" asked Bill.

Teddy shouldered his pick, and walked away without a word, throwing a devil's look behind him as he went.

"He'd murder the lot of us, Bill," I said, "if we gave him a chance."

"Daresay," said Bill; "we won't give it to him."

In eleven weeks we got eleven hundred ounces of gold, and then a thing happened that makes my blood turn cold to speak of. I started one night to get a stock of provisions. We used to start in the night so that we shouldn't be discovered, and when we made our appearance at the cattle station early in the morning for meat and flour, the people there didn't suspect we had been walking all the previous night. I was pretty well the whole day getting back, for I had to be cautious, to prevent being followed. Within half a mile of our gully I met Bill, with a ghost's face on him, and looking as if he had gone mad in my absence.

Running towards me, he said wildly,

"Tom, for God's sake answer me quickly! Have you seen Lizzie?"

"Not since last night," I said, with an uncomfortable feeling at Bill's wild manner.

"She's lost! She's lost!" he screamed.

"Lost!"

"I've been hunting for her all the day. O my pet, my darling! if I don't find you, may the world be burned, and all that's in it!"

I was almost as mad as he was, for you know I loved the little thing as if she were my own daughter.

"Keep cool, Bill," I said, as quietly as I could, though I felt my words trembling with the trembling of my lips; "if we want to do any good, we mustn't lose our wits."

"I know, I know!" he said, beating his hands together; "but what am I to do—what am I to do?"

"When did you miss her?"

"This morning. I got up at day-light, and left her sleeping in her crib. She was asleep, and I kissed her before I went out. I shall never kiss her again! I shall never kiss her again! O my pet, my pet!"

And he broke into a passionate fit of sobbing. It was awful to see. I waited till he was a bit calmer, and then I told him to go on.

"I came back to breakfast, and she was gone; and Rhad's off his chain, and gone too. I've been hunting for her all the day. O God! tell me where she is!"

"I am glad the dog was with her," I said. "How long is it since you were at the tent?"

"Not an hour ago. But all this talking won't bring her back. Let's go on searching for her. Perhaps she has climbed over the ranges, and is lost in the bush beyond."

"She could never do it, Bill; she hasn't strength enough, the dear little thing, to walk to the top of these hills. Now, Bill, I am cooler than you are, and I intend to keep cool. Although I'd give my legs and arms rather than any hurt should come to our pretty darling,"—I had to hold myself tight in here, to keep myself from breaking down—"I'm not going to let my feelings run away with me. If I am to help you, I must know everything. Let us go back to the tent, and start from there. Here's my hand, Bill; I'll search for our darling till I drop."

He grasped my hand, and we ran to our tent. The first thing I did was to examine the dog's chain. It had been unlocked in the usual way, and the key was lying on the table.

"That's plain proof," I said, "that Liz herself let him loose, and took him out with her. Had she all her things on?"

Yes; her hat and mantle were gone, and also a little basket she used to take with her, to fill with wild flowers."

"You see," I said, "she went out flower-gathering. Now which way did she go?"

Naturally, I considered, she would take the road she knew best—the one that led to the gully Bill first worked in. There was a creek on the road, pretty deep in parts, and the dreadful idea struck me that she might have fallen in. All this time Bill was behaving in the wildest manner. He took every little thing that belonged to her, and kissed them again and again. He called her by name, as if she could hear him; cried to his dead wife, as if she were standing before him; and altogether was about as useless as a man well could be. Then, taking a chamois-leather bag filled with gold, he threw it on the ground, screaming,

"To the Devil with all the gold! Devil gold! devil gold! why did I come here and lose my pet for you? O Lord! take all the gold, and give me back my child!"

"Come along, Bill," I said, without appearing to heed his ravings, for that, I knew, was the best way; "I am going to the creek to look for her."

"She hasn't fallen in!" he cried. "How do you know she has

fallen in? It's not true! My pet is not drowned! No, no!"

"I don't say she is drowned," I said. "God forbid that she is! Behave like a man, Bill, and keep your senses about you, or we may as well give her up altogether."

I was bound to speak in that way to him, and after a time I got him to be a little more reasonable. Then we started for the creek, calling out "Liz! Liz!" at the top of our voices, and whistling in the old familiar way to Rhadamanthus. No sound answered us, and the solemn stillness of the place, when we were not speaking, fell upon my heart like a funeral pall. We tracked the creek from one end to the other, and then I sat on the bank to consider.

"Bill," said I, "she can't be drowned, thank God! Rhad can swim, and if he couldn't have saved her, he would be somewhere about. Besides, her basket would float, and we should see some signs."

And then a thought flashed into my mind. "Bill, have you been to Teddy the Tyler?"

"Great Lord! Do you think—"

"I don't think anything. Let's go and see him."

We walked to Teddy's tent, calling and listening to imaginary answers as we walked. It was late in the evening by this time, and Teddy was sitting outside his tent smoking his pipe. He barely looked up as we approached; but I noticed that he hitched close to him with his foot an axe that was lying on the ground.

"Good-evening, mate," I said, by way of commencement, though I felt more inclined to spit in his face than be civil to him.

Bill shook with excitement, and there was a dangerous gleam in his eyes.

Teddy did not reply to my "Good-evening," but sat still, smoking. He had his eye on the axe, though; I didn't miss that.

"Are you deaf?" I asked.

"No," he snapped. "Are you?"

"Look here, mate," I said.

"And look you here, mate," he interrupted; " I don't want any of your "Good-evenings" or any of your company. What are you loafing in my gully for? I'll split your skull open if you stop here much longer."

"We've come here for a purpose," I said. "I am going to ask you a question or two—that you'll have to answer, my lad, if you wish ever to answer another."

"You can ask a thousand," said Teddy. "Fire away. You won't get me to answer one."

"We shall see. We are in search of little Liz. She hasn't been home all day. Have you seen her?"

Teddy gave us both a sharp, quick look, and did not answer. Bill never took his eyes from Teddy's face.

"Have you seen our Liz?" I repeated. "Has she been here today?"

Still no answer.

Without any warning, Bill made a spring at him; but Teddy was on his legs like lightning, brandishing the axe over his head. Bill avoided the blow, catching the handle on his arm, and, closing with Teddy, had him on the ground in no time, with his knee on his chest, and his hand at his throat.

"Hold off!" Teddy choked out. "Take this madman off, or he'll throttle me!"

"Answer that question," said Bill, with set teeth; "if you don't, I'll kill you!"

"She hasn't been here to-day," the fellow gasped.

"Have you seen her anywhere, you devil?"

"No," was the sullen reply.

"You may get up," said Bill, rising. "Let me find that you are lying, and I'll tear your heart out. Mark me, Teddy the Tyler! If I discover that you have seen my child to-day, and have been telling us lies, you shall do what you threatened I should do, and what I *am* doing, God help me! You shall cry blood. Come away, Tom; the sight of him turns me sick."

We had a weary night of it. We searched in every likely place; we lighted fires on every rise, so that they might catch the child's eye, if she was anywhere near; but when the morning came, we were as far off finding her as ever. What puzzled me most was the absence of Rhadamanthus. We could find no trace of him. If anything had happened to the child, I thought, the dog's instinct would surely have led him home to the tent. We trudged back, sore and disheartened. We had not eaten a morsel the whole night. Bill, I believe, hadn't put food to his lips since he first missed little Liz. He hadn't even smoked a pipe. I was thinking to myself, what shall we do next? when my mate, who had thrown himself on the ground, whispered to it in a voice so low that he seemed to be afraid of my hearing him,

"The old shafts—the deserted shafts—we haven't looked there for her!"

The idea that our little girl might be lying at the bottom of one of the deserted holes, dying perhaps, made me dizzy for a moment.

We turned out of the tent in silence, and recommenced our search, Bill trembling like a man with the palsy at every hole we stopped at. I went down myself, to save him the first shock of the awful discovery, if she were lying there. But I discovered nothing.

"Let's go to the old gully again," said Bill.

The sun was rising over the hills, bathing them in seas of gold and purple, and the laughing jackass was waking everything up with its gurgling laughter. Teddy the Tyler was not out of bed, and I went down the shaft he was then working. The noise disturbed him, and he came from his tent, half dressed, and, with a death-like scare on his face, asked us what we were up to now.

"It's only fair to tell him," said Bill. "We're looking for my child. She might have tumbled down a shaft, you see."

We searched every hole in the gully without result, and then we went away.

And now, mates, something happened that I have thought of over and over again with wonder. I was a better man then than I am now, for I had the impression of those peaceful and happy Sundays, with the readings out of the Bible, and the quiet walks with little Liz, full upon me. And I believed at that time that God Almighty had sent some little birds to assist us to the end of our search. We had got away from Teddy's gully, fully a mile from it, and were passing a cluster of gum-trees, upon one of which half a dozen laughing jackasses were perched. As we passed they set up a chorus of mocking laughter, which so grated upon me, that I threw my stick at them, and sent them flying away. Going to pick up my stick, which had fallen some distance off, I observed an abrupt turn in the ranges, leading to a chasm in the hills which neither of us had ever trodden before. But for these birds, we should not have discovered it. I called out to Bill, and he followed me into the declivity.

"Here's a shaft sunk," I said; some one has been prospecting."

The shaft was about twenty feet deep, and, holding on to a rope that I tied to the stump of a tree, I lowered myself down. Before I reached the bottom, I saw that our search was at an end. There lay our little Liz, with her face turned upwards, as though she was sleeping. I could not distinguish her features, and indeed I was so startled that I did not pause to think or look more closely.

"Liz!" I whispered.

No answer came, and I called to her again. All was silent. The rope to which I was clinging was not long enough to tie a slip-knot by which we could raise her. Another and a longer rope was in Bill's hands above. I climbed into the sunlight, and, taking the rope from Bill, prepared to make a sling of it.

Bill allowed me to take the rope, and looked at my fear-struck face with a terrible twitching of his features. He was trying to utter words, but for a moment or two he had lost the power. With a sound that was like a shriek and a sob he regained it.

"For the good God's sake, Tom, don't tell me she is down there!"

"She is there, Bill. No, no! What are you about?"

I flung my arms around him, to prevent him springing down the shaft.

"Bill, this is an awful moment, and Lizzie's life may hang upon our keeping steady. As you love your dear little one, don't give way yet awhile. She wants your help to raise her. Do you hear me? She wants your help."

"Ay," he replied vacantly.

"I am going to tie this rope round her. Will you stand steady here above, and raise her, while I support her below?"

He nodded, and made motions with his lips, as though he were speaking. But no sound came from them.

"For our precious darling's sake, Bill," I said, as I prepared to descend again, "be steady, lad."

I tied the rope round her slender body—ah, me! ah, me! the pretty little hands that did not respond to the touch of mine! the soft face that rested on my shoulders!—and slowly, slowly, we brought her to the surface, where I tenderly set her down.

She was dead! The angels had taken her from us.

As she lay with her eyes turned blindly to the sun that was smiling on the hills, and bathing them in light, I could scarcely believe that she was dead. In her innocent young face the roses were still blooming, and in her pretty little hands were grasped a few of the wild flowers she had been gathering. I stooped, and kissed her pure fresh lips. Then I turned away, for blinding tears were in my eyes, and a darkness fell upon me.

"O my darling! my darling!" I heard Bill say. "You are not dead—you cannot be dead! Look at me, speak to me, my pet! Throw your arms round my neck." And he pressed her to his breast, and kissed her many times.

"She is only sleeping. Feel her heart, Tom, it is beating. Feel, feel, I say!"

I placed my hand on her heart, to soothe him; alas, its pulse was stilled for ever!

"Bill," I said solemnly, for it was an awful thing was the sight of the dear angel lying dead upon the grass, "do not deceive yourself; she is dead. She has gone to a better world than this."

"Dead!" he cried, springing to his feet, and looking wildly upwards. "Then strike me dead, too!"

He threw himself beside her again; he clasped her in his arms, nursing and rocking her as he would have done if she had been sleeping; he called her by every endearing name; and suddenly became quite still.

"Tom," he said presently, in a strangely quiet and eager tone, "look at this mark on my child's neck. What is it? God! what is it?"

I looked. It was a discoloured mark, and I shuddered to think that it might have been caused by the grasp of a cruel hand. But I would not madden him utterly by a whisper of my suspicions.

"It is impossible to say what it is, Bill, without evidence."

"True," he replied, still more quietly; "without evidence. Where's Rhad?"

The absence of the dog had been puzzling me. That he would not have voluntarily deserted little Liz was as certain as fate.

"Stay here with my child," said Bill; "I am going to search for her dog. He loved my Liz, and was faithful to her. He would have laid down his life for her."

He disappeared in the bush, and within ten minutes I heard him call out that he had found Rhadamanthus. He stepped from the shadows of the trees, and placed Rhad at my feet. Poor Rhad! He was dead—shot through the heart.

"You see, Tom, he's been shot. Who did it? We want evidence. Whoever killed the dog killed my child."

I knelt and examined the dog's body. Three bullets had been fired into it, and there was something in the dog's mouth. Forcing the jaws open, I took it out, and recognised it immediately. It was a piece of the coloured silk handkerchief I had thrown out of the tent to Teddy the Tyler, the first night he came to the gully. The dog had evidently torn it away in a desperate struggle, for shreds of it were sticking between his teeth so firmly that I could not drag them away.

"There has been foul play here, Bill," I said.

"I know it, I know it. What is that between his teeth? Faithful Rhad! It is part of a handkerchief. O, I know without your telling me! But whose handkerchief?—do you hear me?—whose handkerchief? Speak the name. Out with it, man!"

"Teddy the Tyler's," I said.

I had no time to add another word, for Bill was off with the speed of the wind in the direction of Teddy's gully. I hurried after him, but he was too swift for me, and I lost him. When I reached the gully, neither Teddy nor Bill was in sight, and though I searched for an hour I could see nothing of them. Not knowing which way to turn to look for them, I hastened back to where our dear dead Liz was lying, and carried her in my arms to our tent. My first impulse was to put everything in order. I tidied up the place, and arranged our darling's bed, my scalding tears almost blinding me as I worked. Then I laid the body on it, and covered it up, all but the face, which was still bright with roses soon to fade. About her head I scattered some wild flowers growing near our tent; and on her breast I placed the Bible, our only book. This done, I went again in search of Bill, with no better success than before. I was full of fears, but was powerless to act. All I could do was to wait. My next impulse was to bring Rhad's body home. I did so, and placed it at the foot of the bed, on the ground. The hours went by, and Bill did not appear. Noon was past, and still no sign. The sun set, and still no sign. Half a dozen times at least I went to Teddy's gully, only to find it deserted. What was I to do? What could I do? I would have gone to the cattle-station, where we purchased our food, but that I was loth to leave our darling alone. It seemed like deserting her. No; I would wait till the morning. Night coming on, I lit a candle, and sat in the dim tent, keeping watch—for the living and the dead. It was an awful, awful time. Sounds without warned me that the weather was changing. Dark clouds were in the skies; the wind sighed and moaned. I knew the signs. A storm was coming. It came, sooner than I expected, bursting upon us with frightful fury. One of the most terrible storms in my remembrance. The rain poured down in floods—the thunder shook the hills—the lightning played about the peaceful face of little Liz, and cast a lurid glare upon the flowers and the Bible on her breast. I knelt by the side of the bed, and prayed, keeping my face buried in the bed-clothes, and holding the dead child's cold fingers in mine. I may have knelt thus for an hour, and the storm raged on without abatement. Then I raised my head. My heart leaped into my throat. At the door stood my mate Bill, haggard and white, with blood oozing from between the fingers which he pressed upon his heart. It was but a vision, and it lasted but a moment; but so terrible an impression did it leave upon me, that I ran into the open air for relief. And in that moment a voice fell on my ears:

"Liz! My pet! My darling!" The voice of a dying man. But the darkness was so thick that I could not see my hand before me.

"Bill!" I cried. "Where are you?"

I received an awful answer. A hand stretched itself from out the darkness, and, clutching me with a strength so fierce and resistless that I had no power to resist, forced me back into the tent. The candle was still burning, and by its light I saw my dear old mate standing before me, grasping with his other hand the lifeless body of Teddy the Tyler. Bill's hand upon my breast relaxed, and the body of the murderer slid from his grasp, and lay in a heap on the soddened ground.

"Liz!" whispered Bill. "My Liz! Life of my life! my pet!"

He saw her in her bed, and a ghastly smile of joy played about his lips. He staggered towards her, and fell down dead! Within twenty-four hours five hundred men were in the gullies. They helped me to bury Bill and little Liz in one grave, and to put a fence round it.

My story is done.

THE HOUSE BY THE RIVER

by G. A. Walstab

George Arthur Walstab (1834-1909) was born in London and migrated to Victoria in 1852. He served for two years in the Victorian Mounted Police and in 1857 he fought in India as a subaltern during the latter part of the Indian mutiny. After the mutiny he stayed in India for a few years working as a journalist and as a sub-editor on the Calcutta *Englishman*. He returned to Australia in 1865 and worked for a number of Victorian periodicals, editing the *Australian Journal* for a time. 'The House by the River', a classic ghost story that appeared in the *Australian Journal* in June 1883, draws on his experiences in India.

I give the tale exactly as it was written to me, without any comments whatever upon the extraordinary nature of the appearances mentioned in it. Some may laugh, some may sneer, and many may disbelieve. I can only say that the man who writes what he saw, or thought he saw—as different opinions may elect to accept the story—served as a cavalry officer through the Indian Mutiny, and that I never heard his courage or veracity called into question. Here is the mystery, for mystery even I can only call it:

My dear George,—At your request I give you as circumstantial an account as I can of the occurrences of two of the most extraordinary, or rather terrible, nights I ever passed in the course of a tolerably eventful life. Even to you, as an old friend, they may appear incredible, but I am sure that you will not doubt for one moment that I write what I firmly believe to have happened to me. It is easy enough for me to recall the circumstances; I wish, indeed, it were not so easy. But it is with great disinclination that I recall what I am almost ashamed to say I would far rather forget.

You are aware that, after the mutiny was over, I left the service, took to a literary life, and earned some repute as a writer of fiction. It is no fiction, however, that I am writing of now; I should be glad if it were, for even after the lapse of years the memory of those two nights comes back to me in my dreams too often to be pleasant.

You know also that, though a novelist, and therefore, it may be presumed, to some extent imaginative, I was never, in the good old days, a believer in the supernatural, but that, on the contrary, I was rather inclined to be sceptical on those subjects connected with the night side of nature, in which you and others took a deep interest.

You will remember even that, like Ingoldsby's Black Mousquetaire, I was nicknamed "Sans Foi" in the regiment by those who were in the habit of hearing me sneer at the mysteries some were inclined to believe in. I don't believe in many of them now. I doubt sometimes even my own remembrances. But I never sneer.

It was nearly three years after I left the service that I was attached to the staff of one of the papers in Calcutta. The wet season of the year I refer to had been a more than usually unhealthy one. King Cholera had been very exacting in his payment of tribute, and the small-pox, of which you in Melbourne have such a terror, had almost decimated the native quarter of the town, not halting even at the more healthy portion of the city.

You remember where I lived at the time, and you know also that, though close to Government House, it was not by any means the healthiest part of Calcutta. I was not, therefore, surprised when, in the midst of the sickness around us, the family doctor advised me to send away my wife and children, if only a short distance.

He was a believer in these changes, and as I remembered how young F—, of the—th N. I., had absolutely marched his detachment out of cholera range, I was the more inclined to agree with a man in whom I had in all respects the utmost confidence.

"Of course, old man," he said to me, "you must stick here; but the sooner the wife and bairns clear out the better."

I cleared them out accordingly, but not far. A friend of mine—poor Br—t; he is dead now—hearing that I wished to send my family out of town, told me that he had rented a house at Agrapurrah—about nine miles out of Barrackpore-road—but that his wife not liking it, he had moved into town again.

"It's a lonely place," he said, "on the river, but the house is large and roomy, and I believe healthy."

The doctor and I went out to look at it the next day, and his opinion was decidedly in favour of my accepting B—'s offer.

Not having to pay rent was, of course, an object to a man with scarcely captain's pay; but in the clear daylight the house and its situation were not unattractive.

It had been one of the Portuguese missions in the days when the memory of Sarajah Dowlah was yet fresh in men's minds. It stood close to the banks of the Hooghly, with a terrace and steps leading down to the river. The compound, or garden, was large. In the rear was a court-yard, on the other side of which was an unused building, formerly the nuns' dormitory, but now turned into a quarters for the native servants, and on one side was a chapel and a small cemetery. The first was closed, except on the occasional visits of the padre, and the latter was closed entirely.

All the rooms in the house had been furnished by my friend, but I determined to occupy only the upper story for sleeping purposes. The accommodation consisted of six rooms, three of which fronted to a long verandah looking out on the river. The largest of these I selected as a nursery for the children. On the one side were my wife's rooms, and on the other a dressing-room for myself, whenever I could manage to get out of town.

The communication with the dining-room and drawing-room below was by a long staircase, and attached to the bathrooms were the usual back staircases for the use of the sweepers.

Through a roofed-in passage you could pass to the dormitories, but this was only used by the servants.

I give you these details to show how difficult of explanation is what occurred afterwards. There are no Europeans within five miles, and the whole place was as retired as well could be.

Thinking, however, that my wife might be lonely in my absence, I arranged with a European professional nurse in Calcutta, the widow of a soldier who had been a corporal in my own troop, to stay with the family while they were at Agrapurrah. She was a practical, common-sense Scotch woman, had made two voyages home and back in charge of children, and was in all respects reliable.

In addition to this, I also sent my own bearer, or personal servant, who had been with me during the campaign, and who had evinced his more than Hindoo courage by, on one occasion, bringing me a drink of Mangofool under a decidedly unpleasant fire. Two ayas, were, of course, indispensable, so that, what with the Khansamah and the Khitmutgars, the house was full enough.

It was a wet day when I drove the party out, and the whole place wore by no means so cheerful an aspect as it had on the occasion of my first visit. Even my wife—by no means a nervous woman—was impressed by the gloominess of the surroundings, and spoke of the half-ruined dormitories and chapel in decidedly disparaging terms. The nurse, Mrs. H—, with the usual composure of a soldier's wife, said nothing. She had been in decidedly worse quarters often, and was proportionately philosophical. Certainly the idea of the supernatural was not present to any of us. I did notice that as Punchoo, the bearer, and the other servants took possession of their quarters, some of the people from a little village close by stood looking at them curiously, but the circumstance conveyed no meaning to me then, and I drove back to town highly satisfied with the whole arrangement.

That night, however, I could not sleep even in my own comfortable quarters, and when I did, I had wretched dreams. All through the next day, too, I was uneasy and low-spirited, and found buckling to my work a task of some difficulty.

I dined at my club in the hope of shaking off this feeling, which I attributed at first to the weather, which was simply beastly; but, even after the excitement of a game of billiards, the next night was as bad as the first, and as soon as day broke I ordered out my horse and rode to my "country seat".

It was about six in the morning when I reached the home. The ayas and the children were in the garden, and I was somewhat surprised at the embarrassed manner in which the nurse, who was with them, replied to my, "Well, Mrs. H—, how are you all?"

I said nothing, however, but went to my wife's dressing-room, where I found her in a decidedly bad temper. She was not nervous, but annoyed, and, on my asking the reason, she said that the English nurse has refused to remain in the place any more. She had asked her why, and after some hesitation she had said that the place was haunted.

"I won't tell you what I saw, ma'am," had been her answer; "but I saw something, and I won't stop any more. If the master's wise, ma'am, he won't let you or the dear children stop either."

"And it's very annoying, dear," continued my wife, "for the place agrees with the children."

"Haunted! Nonsense!" I replied. "The woman's gammoning you. She wants to get back, I expect, and is pretending this as an excuse, but I didn't think she would do it. I'll see her myself."

So I went down to the garden and interviewed her myself. At first she was very reticent, repeating only her determination to go; but on my looking into her eyes steadily and saying with some heat, that she ought to be ashamed of herself for trying to frighten her mistress, she replied very earnestly:

"I wouldn't frighten the mistress for the world, sir, and that's why I have told her nothing. But, as I am a Christian woman, I saw it, sir, and for God's sake, sir, take them all away before harm comes to them."

"Nonsense, Mrs. H—," I answered. "Saw it! What the deuce do you mean? You must have been dreaming."

"No, sir, it was no dreaming. I saw it distinctly. I am a soldier's widow, captain; my poor dead husband carried you out when you were shot, sir, and I wouldn't tell you a lie, sir, not to be made Queen of England. Don't ask any more questions, sir; take them away."

"Well, Mrs. H—," I replied, "I believe you think you saw *it*—whatever you mean by it—but I can't move them for such fancies as this, you know. If you won't stop, you must go, and I will send someone else out to-morrow. Of course you must stay to-night."

"God help me, sir, if I do;" and to my utter surprise, she burst into a fit of hysterical weeping. I soothed her as well as I could, but I could not quite get rid of the idea that she was pretending. I insisted upon a further explanation.

"Tell me all, Mrs. H—. I must know it before your mistress comes down. I won't have her alarmed by your whims."

"Indeed, sir, it's no whim, and I'll tell you all. If you let the mistress and children stop here then, it's your own fault. It happened at about one this morning, sir. I had been sitting with the mistress till past twelve—for she was very wakeful—but at last she fell asleep, and I went into the nursery. It was moonlight, though raining, and the light shone clear through the *jelmils*. The ayahs were asleep on the floor, but standing between the children's cots was a tall woman, dressed in a long grey robe. As God is my judge, captain, she was there. I could see no face, but she was weeping and moaning, sir, as if in pain. I tried to speak or move, but couldn't. As it says in the good book, the hair of my head stood on end. It was a spirit passed before me, and I can only pray that no harm comes to the little ones. I am a Christian woman, sir, and you know I wouldn't say anything that wasn't true to my husband's old officer."

"Come, come, Mrs. H——," I replied, considerably and disagreeably impressed by her manner, though still incredulous. "You must be dreaming, or, perhaps, some of the servants were playing you a trick."

"It was no trick, sir."

"Well, perhaps it wasn't. But you stop here to-night, and I'll come out before midnight and sleep here, and see what *it* has got to say to an old trooper. Was she pretty, Mrs. H——?"

"Oh, sir, I know you're brave enough, but don't joke. I didn't see her face."

"Well, don't say anything to your mistress, and I'll come out."

She agreed to remain after some hesitation, but when, after leaving me to rejoin the children, she took one of them in her arms and pressed it closely to her heart, as if to protect it, I was ashamed of doubting her.

Still, a ghost in the nineteenth century turning up to worry the children of an ex-dragoon was too much for my credulity.

I said nothing to my wife, except that Mrs. H—— had altered her mind about leaving, and that I was coming out again at night; but just before I mounted my horse before starting I called Punchoo, and questioned him closely as to whether he had seen anyone loitering about the compound the previous evening.

I will not trouble you with his answer. Native servants have a habit of giving answers not exactly straight. But he gave me to understand that, though he had seen no one, there was something about the place and the "gup"—"gossip"—of the village that he didn't like. I was now more convinced than ever that some native trickery was at work. It was a lonely place; robberies were by no means unknown in the outlying suburbs, and the low quarters of Cossipore were certainly not too distant for a budmash raid, if it was known that there was no Sahib in the house.

So I rode back to Calcutta with the firm determination to come back in the evening, and make it unpleasantly warm for anyone I could find unlawfully on the premises.

But, with all my determination, I could not shake off the depression of the previous day. I fought against it with a feeling something like shame, but it was of no avail. I was pursued by a haunting idea that something was going to happen, and though I dined merrily, with some old comrades in the Fort, I did not succeed in getting rid of it.

At last, about eleven o'clock, I ordered my buggy, and before starting placed on the seat my loaded revolver and my sabre, with which a few natives had already made an acquaintance. I was going to be my own shokeydar on this occasion, and ready to act accordingly.

It was not raining this night, and the moon was riding high and bright in, for a wonder, a clear sky. We passed nothing on the road except a solitary elephant, at whom my mare shied so violently as to spill the syce, who was clinging on behind, to the wild delight of the animal's driver. The little village near the house was as still as the grave, and Punchoo, who was waiting for me, informed me that no one had been near the place. My wife had some supper waiting for me in the dining-room, and after a hearty meal, a bottle of Baas, and a stiff glass of No. 1 Exshaw, we went to bed. Passing through the nursery, I noticed that Mrs. H— and the children were fast asleep, the ayahs being curled up on the ground, one at the foot of each cot.

I smoked a cigar for about half an hour after my wife had fallen asleep, and then placing my sabre and revolver on the table where the night light stood, I got into bed, dropped the mosquito curtains, and in a few moments was in a deep slumber.

How long I slept I didn't know, but I found out afterwards that it must have been one o'clock when I was awoke suddenly by a loud scream from my wife.

"Harry, look!" she cried, tightly clutching my arm as she sat up in the bed. "See the woman going through the door."

I looked as she spoke, and saw that the purdah, or door-curtain—ordinary doors are rarely seen in India—was shaking, as if some one had just passed through.

In far less time than it takes me to tell you, I jumped out of bed, seized my revolver, and rushed into the nursery.

The bright moonlight was streaming through the open Venetians, and the whole room was clearly visible. On the bed lay Mrs. H— in strong convulsions, the two ayahs were starting in wild terror to their feet, and the two children were screaming loudly. But there was no one else.

Calling to my wife to come to the children, I ran into my own dressing-room to get some water, intending, in my excitement—half anger, half fear—to treat Mrs. H— to a good sound douche of cold water.

But my purpose was changed when I returned to the nursery. My wife was leaning over the nurse, the ayahs were endeavouring to quiet the children, and near the foot of the beds, in the centre of a halo of bluish mist, stood *a tall woman in a grey robe.*

I am no coward, but for a moment my blood ran cold, and the water jug fell from my hand; while the figure turned and walked slowly toward my wife's room.

I was sure now that it was a trick, and, without pausing to think, I fired my revolver point blank at the figure's back, and dashed after it into the bedroom. The night-light was still burning, and the *room was empty.*

The shot awoke the servants, and the whole tribe, headed by Punchoo, crowded into the room.

I searched it thoroughly, and found nothing; I searched the bathroom, and there was nothing, while the back staircase door was locked. I searched the lower rooms, and found nothing, but on reaching the court-yard leading to the old dormitories Punchoo suddenly yelled out—

"See, Sahib; see the woman," and then stopped short, pallidly green with terror, and apparently unable to move.

I raised my eyes at once to the verandah of the dormitories, and there, pacing up and down, wringing its hands, and uttering from time to time a low moan, was the figure in grey I had seen in the nursery.

"Give me the lantern, you infernal idiot!" I shouted to Punchoo, who was shaking with fear, but still stuck to me, and, snatching it from his hand, I ran up the steps of the verandah. The figure had vanished.

Not one of the servants would answer my calls but Punchoo, and, with him carrying the lantern—I think he was more afraid of me than the figure—I thoroughly searched the cells and vaults of the dormitory and found nothing. I even knocked up an old native Christian in the village and made him hand over the keys of the chapel and cemetery, and searched them, too, with the same result.

I then returned to the house, leaving Punchoo with strict orders to keep watch in the court-yard till daylight. Whether he did so, or whether he retired to his mat and slept off his terror, I don't know, but he reported the next morning that he had seen nothing.

Mrs. H—, on emerging from her fit, only told her former story—which I could not now refuse to believe—but my wife admitted that she had only seen what she thought was the skirt of a woman's dress passing through the doorway, and nothing more. She had not seen the figure that I saw, and added, with more coolness than I had expected, that she was not a bit frightened after she saw me awake and armed.

Still I was not surprised at her objecting to remain alone in the home, as Mrs. H— would not, and that very day I removed the whole family back to town, highly disgusted with the result of my arrangements, but determined to say nothing to my friend B— until I had thoroughly investigated what I believed to be a trick of some of the villagers, who must have had some reasons of their own for wishing to keep the house empty. That I had seen a figure was certain, but I was still puzzled to find that my bullet—fired point blank at it—had lodged directly in the wainscot on the opposite side of the room, and yet not touched the object it was aimed at. This fact dispelled the idea that my pistol might have been tampered with while I was at supper, which had at first occurred to me. Still, I was determined to return some night and get to the bottom of the mystery. I did so. I will now tell you the result.

* * * * * * *

Convinced as I was that I had been the victim of a trick of some sort, I could not shake off the feeling of uneasiness I had before experienced, and it grew on me to such an extent that, at last, while dining one evening, about a week afterwards, with the—th Punjaubees, I told the whole story to Doctor K— of that regiment, a man whose professional attainments were known throughout India, a man of high literary ability, and a notorious sceptic.

As a matter of course he laughed at me.

"They called your fellows the 'Sheltan-ka-pultan' (the devil's regiment), my boy, and I suppose Sheltan came to look after one of his own."

But we talked the matter over in the ante-room after dinner, and eventually he and two subalterns—they are colonels now—agreed to drive down with me the next night, and 'draw the ghost', as the doctor put it.

"We'll have a rattling good supper, Harry," he said at parting, "and a bottle or so of simpkin (champagne), and then, in the words of Mark Twain, 'fetch round your ghost.'"

We drove down the next night accordingly, taking a well-filled hamper with me, and at midnight sat down to supper. I had placed a regular cordon of servants, under the direction of Punchoo, round the house, and the feeling of uneasiness had quite left me.

Supper over, we told stories and sang songs, until, just as the clock struck one, one of the subalterns said:

"Come on, Harry, the ghost won't turn up. She's afraid, poor thing. Give us the 'Marseillaise'".

Elated with champagne, I sprang to my feet, and the next minute the chorus of that most spirited of national songs rang through the lonely house. The last notes had just died away when, from the direction of the room my wife had occupied, came the sound of a low moan of the most despairing agony.

We all started to our feet, and turning round I saw standing in the doorway—but visible, as I heard afterwards, only to me—the same figure I had seen before, enveloped in the same bluish bright halo of mist.

Our revolvers and my sabre were lying on the sideboard. I seized the latter, and, with a loud cry to my companions to follow me, I sprang across the room and aimed a blow at the head of the figure, which brought the curtain rod, severed in two, to the ground. But the figure neither fell nor turned. On the contrary, it slowly lifted the hood that covered the head and showed me its face.

Never shall I, till my dying day, forget that face, or the lineaments that in my dreams have so frequently appeared to me since. A face worn and emaciated almost to the bone—a face covered with the livid greenish hue of corruption, but with eyes fixed on me, and an expression of unutterable woe, agony and despair.

My blood ran cold as ice, a low groan of horror burst from my lips, and then, as the sabre fell from my hand with a clash to the floor, I felt myself clutched by the throat.

I cannot tell what followed, but I heard afterwards that I drew back my hand as if to strike, and then fell heavily to the ground. I was insensible for two hours, and when they had taken me back to my home, I lay raving in delirium for some days. My own medical man and K— attended me through the illness that followed, and when I recovered they unwillingly discussed the matter with me at my own most earnest request.

I was the only one of the party who had seen anything, though all had heard the moan that followed my song, and seen the room filled with a bluish bright mist, which they attributed to a fog from the river, while the moan might have been uttered by one of the servants asleep on the verandah.

I disputed neither assumption. Neither did I dispute with the doctors when they advanced the theory that I must have been suffering from some mental or optical hallucination, brought on by overwork and literary excitement, encouraged by what I confirmed was a near approach to fast living. I was only too anxious to adopt the theory, and to be medically treated accordingly.

But what they could not account for, and what Dr. K— was especially puzzled at, was that for days after the event there remained on my neck the marks of *four female finger nails.*

"Perhaps some of you did it in opening my necktie," I suggested.

"No," said Dr. K—, hesitatingly; "they are women's nails, I'm sure."

"Perhaps," I added, "I did it myself in a sort of hysterical paroxysm."

And then, as they exchanged glances, and I looked down at my hands, I remembered that I had the bad habit of biting my nails, and could not therefore have done it myself.

It was no human fingers that had seized me, and, in the words of Job, "a spirit had passed."

I know well now that what I had seen was no human visitant or trick. I know, too, that none of those who were with me would ever afterwards allude to the subject in my presence. I know that my friend B— subsequently confessed to me that neither he nor his wife had lived in the home after a supposed dream of hers, and I know also that, on the vaults being searched by him again, an irregularity in the masonry attracted his attention, and that enclosed in a niche was found a female skeleton and the mouldering remnants of a robe, the victim, probably, of some monasterial discipline.

I know, moreover, that no one has lived in the house since, and that it is now ruinous and deserted.

I expect no one to share my belief as to what I saw, but I know as well that the two children, over whom that "perturbed spirit" moaned and wailed, are now in the land where such secrets are revealed, and I feel sure that once in my life there was lifted for me the veil between the Seen and the Unseen, for what reason is known only to the Great Spirit who holds the curtain-rings in His all-powerful hand.

I repeat, and with all humility, that I am no coward. I have served my Queen through a period when men rode daily with their lives in their hands into the valley of the shadow. I was one of a regiment which earned for itself a high reputation for dashing bravery, and I can say conscientiously that I never shrank from any peril in the path of my duty. But did the attainment of the Viceroyalty of India depend upon my passing another night in that house, I would not do it; and were the winning of that still higher honour, the Victoria Cross, made conditional on my doing so, I should decline the contest. I have told you the story now, and I wish I had never had it to tell.

Yours,

Harry

Such is one of the few authenticated ghost stories ever told to me. The man who told it was a good soldier as ever buckled on a sabre or mounted a charger, and I have no doubt of his veracity.

THE GHOST FROM THE SEA

by J. E. P. Muddock

James Edward Preston Muddock (1843-1934) was born in the New Forest near Southampton. Soon after he finished school he went to Melbourne where his uncle worked as a journalist and printer. He worked for a time in the goldfields before travelling extensively in Asia. He returned to Melbourne in 1868, but left soon afterwards for London. He was a prolific writer and wrote many books, many of them under his Dick Donovan pseudonym. *Tales of Terror* (1899) was published under the Donovan pseudonym, while *Stories Weird and Wonderful* (1889), from which this story is taken, was published under his real name. He never returned to Australia, but his last published book as Dick Donovan was *Out There: A Romance of Australia* (1922).

Towards the latter half of the fifties, Melbourne, in Australia, was startled by an extraordinary and terrible crime. It was at the very height of what was known as the "gold fever". A year or two before, news had spread like wildfire that gold had been discovered in enormous quantities in various parts of the country. That news literally seemed to turn people mad, and young and old, the halt, the lame, and even the blind, rushed away for the fabled regions of El Dorado. Whole families, who had been content to jog on quietly year after year, earning fair wages, and getting all the necessaries of life, were seized with the fever, and, selling up their belongings rump and stump, invested in billies, tomahawks, spades, pickaxes, washing-pans, and other etceteras, and shouldering their swags set off for the mysterious regions, where it was rumoured gold was lying on the surface of the ground in big nuggets. Fortunate, indeed, were those who had any belongings to sell in order to provide themselves with the plant required for roughing it in the bush; for many had nothing at all, save what they stood upright in, but, imagining that they were going to gather in the precious metal in sackfulls, they started off with the rest, only to perish, it may be, miserably of starvation, disappointment, and broken hearts. This period in the history of our Australian colonies is a startling record of human credulity, human folly, wickedness, despair and death. The fever was confined to no particular class of people. Clergymen, bankers, landowners, shipowners, merchants, shopkeepers, sailors, labourers, classical scholars and ignoramuses alike fell under the fascination. The worst passions of our nature manifested themselves; hatred, envy, jealousy, greed, uncharitableness. The parsons were no better than the paupers; the classical scholars than the ignoramuses. The thin veneering of so-called civilization was rubbed off, and the savage appeared in all his fierceness at the cry of "Gold! Gold!"

It is at such periods as these that the moralist finds his pabulum, and those good but weak-minded people who think that human nature has improved with the advance of time have only to get on the house-tops and utter the cry of "Gold!" again, to prove that we are not a whit better than our ancestors were three thousand years ago. This may not be very flattering to us, but alas! it is true. In those days of Australian gold rushes the bush was a veritable terra incognita. Explorers had attempted to penetrate into the mystic interior, but many never came back again, and to this day it is not known where their bones moulder. Those who did return were gaunt, famine-stricken, hollow-eyed, for they had looked upon death, and the stories they told were calculated to appal everyone but the most daring and reckless. But the report of the gold finds so turned the heads of people that, forgetting all about the dangers and privations they would have to endure, they started off into those unknown regions, and thousands literally perished by the way. The experiences of some of these unfortunate people are in themselves amongst the most pathetic and moving of human stories.

Melbourne at the time of this narrative was not the Melbourne of today. It was then simply a collection of canvas and wooden huts and houses, with a few buildings of a more substantial character. One of the most imposing houses in the place was that known as "Jackson's Boarding-house." It was built partly of wood and partly of stone, and was kept by a man and his wife named Jackson. Very little, if anything, was known of the Jacksons' history, beyond that they had come to the colony a few years previously. Jackson was a nautical man, and had purchased a schooner with which he traded up and down the coast, though with indifferent success.

At last his schooner was wrecked, and Jackson and his wife, who had always sailed with him, built a wooden shanty, in what was then known as Canvas Town—now Melbourne— where they sold liquors and provisions. They seemed to have done fairly well, for very soon they erected what was then quite an imposing building, and they called it "Jackson's Boarding-house."

Jackson was remarkable for an extraordinarily powerful physique. He stood about six feet high, and his muscular development was so great that it was said he could lift a cask of split peas, weighing nearly three hundredweight, from the ground, and raise it at arm's length above his head. He was an ill-favoured man, however, for he had a low brow, small cunning sort of eyes, and was exceedingly passionate in his temper. But it was notable that he seemed to be strongly attached to his wife, and they were never known to disagree.

Mrs. Jackson was a striking contrast to her husband, for she was a slightly built little woman, with a pink and white face, sickly blue eyes, and a mass of tow-like hair that was almost the colour of flax, whereas her husband was as dark as a raven.

Soon after these people had opened their boarding-house, there came to lodge with them a Mr. and Mrs. Harvey, who had recently arrived from England. They had, like many others, come out to try and improve their fortunes. A warm intimacy seemed to spring up between the two couples, and they lived apparently in the greatest harmony. It was understood that Mr. Harvey was a mechanic by trade. He was a strong, healthy man, very handy and useful, and did odd jobs for the community. His wife was a pretty, agreeable woman, and soon became a great favourite, for she played the piano and sang well, and was always ready to afford amusement or render assistance to anyone needing it, where it lay in her power. Her husband acquired the character of a rather indolent, good-natured sort of fellow, whose aim seemed to be to suddenly accumulate wealth without doing much labour for it.

At length the gold fever set in, and amongst those who started off in the first rush for the regions of fabulous wealth was Harvey, his wife remaining behind at Jackson's boarding-house. Some eight months later Harvey returned, and soon the report spread that he had brought thousands of pounds' worth of nuggets and gold dust. He remained in the town for four weeks, during which he and his wife denied themselves nothing, and it was evident that the report about his wealth was in the main true. Then, having furnished himself with an extensive outfit in the shape of tent, cooking-stove, digging and washing utensils, he started up the country again, Mrs. Harvey still remaining at the boarding-house. She purchased a horse and buggy, provided herself with fine clothes and jewellery, and common gossip had it that this little, blue-eyed flaxen-haired woman was the richest person in Melbourne. Two months later, her husband still being absent at the diggings, the community was startled one morning by a report that Mrs. Harvey had been murdered. The report proved to be only too true, and the story told by a female servant in the boarding-house was this. She went to the lady's room to see why she had not appeared, it being an hour and a half after her usual time of rising. She found the door locked, and, repeated knocking having failed to elicit a response, she informed her master, and expressed fears that something was wrong. Jackson at once went upstairs with some of the lodgers, and, failing to get an answer, he at once broke open the door, and then a terrible sight revealed itself.

Lying across the bed was the body of Mrs. Harvey. She was dressed only in her night-dress, which was disarranged and torn as if she had struggled desperately, as in fact she had, for further evidence of this was forthcoming. She was on her back, her head hanging over the farthest side of the bed. Twisted tightly round her neck until it had cut into the flesh was a crimson cord sash or belt, such as in those days was common—these sashes, or, more correctly speaking scarves, being worn by men round their waists to keep their trousers up, instead of braces. The horribly distorted features showed that the poor woman had been strangled, and subsequent medical examination brought to light that her head had been forced back with such tremendous force that the neck was absolutely broken. Discolorations about the mouth indicated that a heavy hand had been pressed there to keep her from screaming. There were also deep indents and bruises on the wrists, which proved that she had struggled and been firmly grasped there by the murderer. Other parts of the body were also terribly bruised, as if in the struggle she had been banged repeatedly against the massive wooden bedstead.

Murder had been done, that was certain. That the murderer was a man was equally certain, for no female could have exerted such tremendous force as had evidently been used. It was no less certain that robbery had been the motive, for a very large travelling trunk or box had been forced open, in spite of an unusually strong lock, and two iron bands round it which were secured with padlocks. All the poor creature's clothes had been turned out of the box, and were scattered about the floor, as well as her jewellery, nothing in that way being taken. Now what did that prove? It proved this: the murderer, with the cunning of a devil, knew that in such a place to possess himself of her jewellery, valuable as it was, would almost certainly lead to his detection. No, it was neither her jewellery nor her clothes he wanted, but the nuggets and gold dust her husband had brought from the diggings. No one could swear to gold dust or nuggets, and both were plentiful, for diggers, especially sailors, were constantly arriving from the diggings with hoards of gold, which they sold for ready cash far below their value: for at this early period there was no regular exchange or agency for the purchase of the precious metal.

The next question was: How did the murderer get into the room? Not by the door, for a dozen witnesses vowed that it was locked on the inside, the key still in the lock, when Jackson broke open the door. The only other entrance, then, was by the window, twenty-five feet from the ground. There was no indication that a ladder had been used, and so the theory was that the murderer had secreted himself under the bed, and when his fiendish work was completed he had gone out by the window, climbed up by means of an iron gutter pipe to the roof, and had then descended into the house through a skylight.

Now came the most important question of all: Who was the murderer? At the time of the crime there were nearly forty people staying in the boarding-house, mostly men, a good many of them being sailors. The police arrangements of the town were very primitive, and by no means equal to coping with such a mysterious tragedy, and unfortunately not an atom of evidence could be got that would have justified the arrest of any individual. The result was the mystery was destined to remain a mystery forever; and the times were too exciting and too changing for such a crime even as that to long occupy the public mind, and so, almost with the burying of the flaxen-haired woman who had been so cruelly done to death, the tragedy was forgotten for a time. Three months later, however, its memory was revived by the arrival of Mr. Harvey. He had written two or three times to his wife, had received no answer, had got alarmed, and had come to see what was the matter. The news almost drove him off his mind, for he had been passionately attached to his wife. He stated that he had left her with about ten thousand pounds' worth of gold; and he now offered to give anyone five thousand pounds' worth of gold who would bring the murderer to justice. The offer, however, proved of no avail; not the faintest clue could be obtained. Jackson had taken charge of the murdered woman's effects, and these he handed to the husband, who certified his belief that they were all correct except the gold, which was in nuggets and dust, one nugget alone being valued at between two and three thousand pounds. And so the poor husband departed, an utterly changed and broken man.

Another person in the community had also changed considerably. This was Jackson the boarding-house keeper. He generally bore the character of being a steady, industrious man, but he suddenly developed a craving for drink, and as a consequence neglected his business, which, of course, declined, the result being an opposition house was started, and Jackson's once flourishing boarding establishment lost all its custom. Jackson drank harder than ever then, and even his wife gave way to the vice. At length, a year after the murder, Jackson sold off his effects, and he and his wife took their passage for England, in a ship called the *Gloriana*.

This ends the first part of the record, but the sequel—startling and inexplicable—has yet to be told.

The *Gloriana* was a large, full-rigged, clipper ship, one of a line trading between the mother country and the colonies. She was commanded by a hard-headed Scotchman, Captain Norman Douglas, who was well known in the trade, and, in fact, was one of the most popular skippers on that route. He bore the reputation of being a singularly conscientious and truthful man, and utterly without sentiment or superstition. There are no doubt plenty of people still living who were acquainted with him, who would unhesitatingly endorse this statement.

The *Gloriana* had a fair complement of passengers, first and second class. Amongst the first class were Jackson and his wife. It is necessary, in order to make what follows more clearly intelligible, to describe one portion of the ship. She was fitted with what was known in the old days as a "monkey poop", with an alloway or passage running on each side. This passage was reached from the main deck by three or four wooden steps. Right aft a short flight of steps led to the poop, on which was a hurricane house, with a companion way going down to the cuddy, or, as it is now called, the saloon. In the break of the poop, flush with the main deck, so that his window and door faced the bows of the vessel, was the captain's state-room, and alongside of his door was the entrance to the cuddy from the main deck. The Jacksons' cabin was the first in the cuddy on the left side on entering, and next to the captain's, though it must be remembered that the captain had to come out of the cuddy to get into his room. That is, his door opened from the main deck, whereas the Jackson's opened from the cuddy, and consequently at right angles with the captain's.

The vessel made a splendid passage through Bass's Straits, the weather being magnificent, but it was noted with some astonishment that the Jacksons rarely appeared on deck, but remained in their cabin, and it was whispered about that Mr. Jackson was almost constantly muddled more or less with drink. He and his wife kept to themselves, and seemed to carefully avoid their fellow passengers. One night, when the ship was well out in the South Pacific, and bowling along under double-reefed top-sails, Captain Douglas was sleeping soundly in the middle watch, when his door was suddenly opened, and Jackson precipitated himself into his room, dressed only in his night shirt. He was ghastly pale, was trembling like an aspen leaf, and seemed to be suffering from the effects of a terrible fright.

Naturally thinking that something was the matter, the captain sprang from his bed, and was surprised to find Jackson on his knees, his lips blanched, his face streaming with a cold perspiration.

"What is the meaning of this?" the captain demanded.

"For God's sake save me!" Jackson moaned in terror. "Save

you from what and whom?" asked the captain, thinking that his passenger was suffering from delirium tremens.

"From her," groaned the man. "She all but lured me into the sea, but I broke the spell in time, and rushed in here."

This extraordinary remark naturally tended to confirm the captain's idea about the delirium, and so he soothed his passenger as well as he could, and then led him back to his cabin, where he noted that Mrs. Jackson was soundly asleep in her bunk. He helped Jackson into his bunk, tucked him well up with the clothes, and left him; and as he came out of the cuddy on to the deck to reach his own room again, he started back until he all but fell, for it seemed to him that a flash of brilliant light had almost blinded him, while something soft touched his face. He thought that this might be a sea-bird, but what was the light?

It was the second mate's watch, and that officer was walking the poop, while the portion of the crew on duty were lying or sitting about in the waist of the vessel.

"Mr. Harrington," sang out the captain to the second mate, "what was that light?"

"What light, sir?" asked the officer in astonishment.

"Why, didn't you see a brilliant flash of light?"

"No, sir," answered the officer, thinking the captain must have been indulging in a little too much grog.

"Ahoy, there, you fellows," roared the skipper to the watch on deck. "Where did that light come from?"

"What light, sir?" asked several voices.

"Good heavens! did you not see a flash of bright light?" exclaimed the captain angrily, for he thought he was being made a fool of.

"No, sir, we saw no light," answered the crew unanimously.

Captain Douglas was mystified. What did this mean? Was it a delusion? Had he been made a fool of by his senses, or what?

He went into his cabin again with his mind strangely disturbed. The ship was sailing splendidly, a heavy sea running after her, a gale was blowing, the sky was clear, the stars shining brightly, and neither in sea nor sky was there anything to account for that flash of light, or that *something* that had touched him. His officer and his men could not have been in collusion, and therefore Captain Douglas came to the conclusion that he had been made a fool of by his own senses, though, taken in connection with Jackson's strange remarks, Captain Douglas was affected as he had never been affected before.

Next day the crew told one another that "the old man" had been "soaking himself."

Captain Douglas was unusually thoughtful. He invited Jackson into his cabin and asked him what had been the matter with him during the night. Jackson appeared to be very ill, with a scared, cowed expression in his face. "I don't know," he replied a little sullenly, "I think I must have been dreaming."

"Well, I hope you won't dream again like that," remarked the captain, and then he told his own experience. As he heard this Jackson seemed to grow terrified again, and he groaned between chattering teeth:

"Heaven pity me then, it's a reality!"

"What is?" asked the astonished captain.

Jackson covered his face with his hands as he answered:

"Three times since we left Melbourne I have seen the vision of a woman, and she tries to lure me into the sea." He shuddered like one who was seized with palsy.

A few hours before this Captain Douglas would have roared with incredulous laughter had he been told such a thing. Now he was solemnly silent, for his own experience—the touch and the flash of light—permitted of no explanation that he could furnish. And so this tough old sailor, who had sailed the salt seas from his youth, and braved the perils of the deep in all parts of the world, was seized with a nameless fear that he could not allay.

The good ship continued to bowl along before favouring gales until she drew into the stormy ocean that roars around Cape Horn. During this time Jackson was seldom seen except for an hour or two in the early part of the day, when he and his wife would promenade the poop. He seemed to have changed very much. Everyone on board said that he looked ten years older since leaving Melbourne. His hair had blanched, his face was pallid and wrinkled, his eyes were restless as if from fear.

The vessel fell in with terrific weather off the Horn. Monstrous icebergs and field ice made navigation perilous, while the hurricane's wrath lashed the ice-strewn ocean into mountainous waves. The ship could only pursue her course under storm sails, and only then by ceaseless vigilance being exercised on the part of all the crew. For nearly a week the captain was on deck, snatching an hour or two's sleep as best he could during the twenty-four.

One night, when the *Gloriana* had nearly doubled the Horn the weather seemed to grow worse, so that it became necessary to heave the ship to under a close-reefed main topsail. The sky was inky in its blackness. Not a star shone out from the ebony vault; but over the sea were vast flashing fields of phosphorescent foam as the giant waves broke with an awful roar; while looming in the blackness were ponderous icebergs in whose hollows the sea thundered. Now and again unusually terrific squalls came howling up from the south, bringing showers of jagged ice and hailstones as big as marbles. It was a night of horror and danger such as those who have never sailed in that stormy southern ocean can form but a faint conception of.

Vigilant and anxious, and clad in heavy sea-boots and oilskins, Captain Douglas stood on the poop with the chief mate; the second mate and several of the crew being on the forecastle straining their eyes on the look-out for the ice, while both in the main and foretop a man was lashed also on the lookout. Suddenly as the captain and chief officer stood together at the break of the poop sheltering themselves under the lee of a tarpaulin lashed in the rigging, the captain staggered, and seizing the officer's arm exclaimed hoarsely:

"My God! what is that?"

And well might he so exclaim, for to his horrified gaze there appeared on the main deck a mass of trembling light that in an instant seemed to change into a woman's figure, a woman with long, streaming fair hair, while round her white neck a scarf was twisted. The captain and his mate were transfixed with horror, for they both saw it. But they were to see even a more fearsome sight yet. The apparition rose, waving her arms the while, and floating out over the howling waste of black, writhing waters; and as she rose there suddenly darted from the cabin doorway the half-naked Jackson, his hair streaming in the wind. The apparition still waved her arm, still floated out away from the ship, and then, before the terror-stricken men who witnessed the awful sight could move to stop him, the wretched man uttered a scream of despair and fear that froze the blood of those who heard it, and with one bound he leapt into the boiling waters, and at that instant the apparition disappeared like a flash of lightning.

It was some moments before either of the two men had sufficiently recovered to speak. Then they asked each other if their senses had fooled them. But the captain, remembering his former experience, rushed to Jackson's cabin. Mrs. Jackson alone was in it, and she was sleeping. It was no delusion then. Jackson had jumped overboard, lured by that ghost from the sea. It was impossible to make the slightest attempt to save him; he had gone down into the black and boiling waters never to rise again.

Mrs. Jackson was not informed of her husband's suicide until the following day, and when she heard of it she fell down in a swoon; and, on recovering, it was found that she had lost her reason, so that it was necessary to watch and guard her for the rest of the voyage. On arrival in England it was deemed prudent to place her in an asylum, where she died six months later. No word ever escaped her lips that would have tended to eluci-date the awful mystery. She seemed to be tortured with some indescribable anguish, and from morning till night she paced to and fro, wringing her hands and moaning piteously. But to those who witnessed that appalling scene off Cape Horn when Jackson went to his doom, the mystery required no explanation, for it explained itself. And that explanation was that it was he who had murdered poor Mrs. Harvey, and the phantom of his victim had lured him to a terrible death.

SPIRIT-LED

by Ernest Favenc

Ernest Favenc (1845-1908) is a name that should be better known to aficionados of supernatural fiction. He was born in Surrey, England, and came to Australia in 1864. He worked on stations in North Queensland before leading a number of exploration expeditions in Northern Australia. Later he joined the staff of the Sydney *Evening News* and drew from his experiences in his literary work, which included fiction and non-fiction.

He published three collections of short stories, *The Last of Six: Tales of the Austral Tropics* (1893); *Tales of the Austral Tropics* (1894), which includes the stories in the earlier collection with the addition of two others; and *My Only Murder and Other Tales* (1899). All three contain stories of horror and the supernatural, and there are other unreprinted tales in contemporary periodicals, especially the *Australian Town and Country Journal* and *Phil May's Annual*. I've chosen three tales that I hope will give a flavour of this writer's fine sense of the macabre.

CHAPTER I

It was the hottest day the Gulf had seen for years. Burning, scorching and blistering heat, beating down directly from the vertical sun, in the open, radiating from the iron roof which provided what was mistakenly called shade. In the whole township there was not a corner to be found where a man could escape the suffocating sense of being in the stoke-hole of a steamer.

The surroundings were not of a nature to be grateful to eyes wearied with the monotony of plain and forest. The few stunted trees that had been spared appeared to be sadly regretting that they had not shared the fate of their comrades, and the barren ironstone ridge on which the township was built gave back all the sun's heat it had previously absorbed with interest.

Two men who had just come in from the country swore that where they crossed the Flinders the alligators came out and begged for a cold drink from their water-bags; and the most confirmed sceptic admitted the existence of a material hell. Naturally there was little or no business doing and, just as naturally, everybody whose inclination pointed that way went "on the spree."

Amongst those who had not adopted this mode of killing old father Time were two men in the verandah of the Royal Hotel. (When Australia becomes republican it is to be presumed that a 'Royal' will cease to be the distinguishing feature of every township.)

The two men in question were seated on canvas chairs in the verandah, both lightly attired in shirt and trousers only, busily engaged in mopping the perspiration from their streaming faces, and swearing at the flies.

"Deuced sight hotter lounging about here than travelling," said Davis, the elder of the two; "I vote we make a start."

"I'm agreeable," replied his companion; "the horses must be starving out in the paddock. We shall have a job to get Delaine away, though; he's bent on seeing his cheque through."

"That won't take long at the rate he's going. He's got every loafer in the town hanging about after him."

"Hullo! what's that?" said the other, as the shrill whistle of a steam launch was heard. "Oh! of course, the steamer arrived at the mouth of the river last night; that's the launch coming up.

Shall we go down and see who is on board?"

The two men got up and joined the stragglers who were wending their way across the bare flat to the bank of the river. The passengers were few in number, but they included some strangers to the place; one of whom, a young-looking man with white hair and beard, immediately attracted Davis' attention.

"See that chap, Bennett?" he said.

"Yes, Dick, who is he?"

"Some years ago he was with me roving for a trip; when we started he was as young-looking as you, and his hair as dark. It's a true bill about a man's hair going white in one night. His did."

"What from? Fright?"

"Yes. We buried him alive by mistake."

"The deuce you did!"

"He had a cataleptic fit when he was on watch one night. The other man—we were double-banking the watch at the time—found him as stiff as a poker, and we all thought he was dead, there was no sign of life in him. It was hot weather—as bad as this—and we couldn't keep him, so we dug a grave, and started to bury him at sundown. He came to when we were filling in the grave; yelled blue murder, and frightened the life out of us. His hair that night turned as you see it now, although he vows that it was not the fright of being buried alive that did it."

"What then?"

"Something that happened when he was in the fit, or trance. He has never told anybody anything more than that he was quite conscious all the time, and had a very strange experience."

"Ever ask him anything?"

"No; he didn't like talking about it. Wonder what he's doing up here?"

By this time the river bank was deserted; Davis and Bennett strolled up after the others and when they arrived at the Royal, they found the hero of the yarn there before them.

"Hullo, Maxwell," said Davis, "what's brought you up this way?"

Maxwell started slightly when he saw his quondam sexton;

but he met him frankly enough although at first he disregarded the question that had been asked.

In the course of the conversation that followed Maxwell stated that he was on his way out to the Nicholson River, but with what object did not transpire.

"Bennett and I were just talking of making a start to-morrow, or the next day. Our cattle are spelling on some country just this side of the Nicholson. We can't travel until the wet season comes and goes. You had better come with us."

"I shall be very glad," replied the other, and the thing was settled.

Bennett had been looking curiously at this man who had had such a narrow escape of immortality, but beyond the strange whiteness of his hair, which contrasted oddly with the swarthy hue of his sunburnt face, and a nervous look in his eyes, he did not show any trace of his strange experience. On the contrary, he promised, on nearer acquaintance, to be a pleasant travelling companion.

The summer day drew to a close, the red sun sank in the heated haze that hovered immediately above the horizon, and a calm, sultry night, still and oppressive, succeeded the fierce blaze of the day-time. The active and industrious mosquito commenced his rounds and men tossed and moaned and perspired under nets made of coarse cheese-cloth.

The next morning broke hot and sullen as before. Davis had risen early to send a man out to the paddock after the horses, and was in the bar talking to the pyjama-attired landlord.

"You'll have to knock off his grog or there'll be trouble," he said; "he was up all last night wandering about with his belt and revolver on, muttering to himself, and when a fellow does that he's got 'em pretty bad."

"I'll do what I can, but if he doesn't get drink here he will somewhere else," replied the other reluctantly.

"Then I'll see the P.M. and get him to prohibit his being served. It's the only way to get him straight."

At this moment the subject of their remarks entered the

bar—a young fellow about five or six and twenty. He was fully dressed, it being evident that he had not gone to bed all night. The whites of his eyes were not blood-shot, but blood-red throughout, and the pupils so dilated that they imparted a look of unnatural horror to his face.

"Hullo, Davis," he shouted; "glad to see a white man at last. That old nigger with the white hair has been after me all night. The old buck who was potted in the head. He comes around every night now with his flour-bag cobra all over blood. Can't get a wink of sleep for him. Have a drink?"

His speech was quite distinct, he was past the stage when strong waters thicken the voice; his walk was steady, and but for the wild eyes, he might have passed for a man who was simply tired out with a night's riding or watching.

The landlord glanced enquiringly at Davis, as if to put the responsibility of serving the liquor on him.

"Too early, Delaine, and too hot already; besides, I'm going to start to-day and mustn't get tight before breakfast," said the latter soothingly.

"O be hanged! Here, give us something," and the young fellow turned towards the bar, and as he did so caught sight of Maxwell who had just come to the door and was looking in.

The effect of the dark face and snow-white hair on his excited brain was awful to witness. His eyes, blazing before, seemed now simply coals of fire. Davis and the landlord turned to see what the madman was looking at, and that moment was nearly fatal to the newcomer. Muttering: "By—he's taken to following me by daylight as well, has he? But I'll soon stop him;" he drew his revolver and, but that Davis turned his head again and was just in time to knock his hand up, Maxwell would have been past praying for. The landlord ran round the bar, and with some trouble the three men got the pistol from the maniac, who raved, bit, and fought, like a wild beast. The doctor, who slept in the house, was called, and, not particularly sober himself, injected some morphia into the patient's arm, which soon sent him into a stupor.

"By Jove, Davis, you saved my life," said Maxwell; "that blessed lunatic would have potted me sure enough only for you. Whom did he take me for?"

"He's in the horrors, his name is Delaine, and he's out on a station on the tableland. They had some trouble with the blacks up there lately, and, I suppose, it was the first dispersing-match he had ever seen. There was one white-haired old man got a bullet through his head, and he says he felt as though his own father had been shot when he saw it done. He's a clergyman's son; of course he drinks like a fish and is superstitious as well."

"I trust they'll lock him up until I get out of the town; but I'll remember your share of this. Wait until we get away and I will tell you what brought me up here, but don't ask me any questions now. Is your friend Bennett to be trusted?"

"In what way? Wine, women or gold? I don't know about the first two, but the last I can answer for."

"It's a secret. Possibly connected with the last."

"I hope so, I want some bad enough. I think I know where to put you on to a couple of good horses, and then we'll make a start."

CHAPTER II

The stove-like township is three days journey away; four men, Davis, Bennett, Maxwell, and a blackfellow are camped for the night by the side of a small lagoon covered with the broad leaves of the purple water-lily. In the distance the cheery sound of the horse-bells can be heard, and round the fire the travellers are grouped listening to Maxwell who is telling the tale he has never yet told.

"When I fell down on watch that night and became to all appearance a corpse, I never, for one instant, lost either consciousness or memory. My soul, spirit, or whatever you like to call it, parted company with my body, but I retained all former powers of observation. I gazed at myself lying there motionless, waited until my fellow-watcher came around and awakened the sleeping camp with the tidings of my death, then, without any impulse of my own, I left the spot and found myself in a shadowy realm where all was vague and confused. Strange, indistinct shapes flitted constantly before me; I heard voices and sounds like sobbing and weeping.

"Now, before I go on any further, let me tell you that I have never been subject to these fits. I never studied any occult arts, nor troubled myself about what I called 'such rubbish.' Why this experience should have happened to me I cannot tell. I found I was travelling along pretty swiftly, carried on by some unknown motive power, or, rather, drifting on with a current of misty forms in which all seemed confusion.

"Suddenly, to my surprise, I found myself on the earth once more, in a place quite unknown to me.

"I was in Australia—that much I recognised at a glance—but where abouts?

"I was standing on the bank of a river—a northern river, evidently, for I could see the foliage of the drooping ti-trees and Leichhardt trees further down its course. The surrounding country was open, but barren; immediately in front of me was a rugged range through which the river found its way by means of an apparently impenetrable gorge. The black rocks rose abruptly on either side of a deep pool of water, and all progress was barred except by swimming. The ranges on either hand were precipitous, cleft by deep ravines; all the growth to be seen was spinifex, save a few stunted bloodwood trees.

"What struck me most forcibly was that in the centre of the waterhole, at the entrance of the gorge, as it were, there arose two rocks, like pillars, some twelve or fifteen feet in height above the surface of the water.

"Below the gorge the river-bed was sandy, and the usual timber grew on either bank. At first I thought I was alone, but, on looking around, I found that a man was standing a short distance away from me. Apparently he was a European, but so tanned and burnt by the sun as to be almost copper-coloured. He was partially clothed in skins, and held some hunting weapons in his hand. He was gazing absently into the gorge when I first noticed him, but presently turned, and, without evincing any surprise or curiosity, beckoned to me. Immediately, in obedience to some unknown impulse, I found myself threading the gloomy gorge with him, although, apparently, we exercised no motion. It was more as though we stood still and the rocks glided past us and the water beneath us. We soon reached a small open space or pocket; here there was a rude hut, and here we halted.

"My strange companion looked around and without speaking, drew my attention to a huge boulder close to the hut and on which letters and figures were carved. I made out the principal inscription. 'Hendrick Heermans, hier vangecommen, 1670.' There were also an anchor, a ship and a heart, all neatly cut. I turned from these records to the man. He beckoned me again, and I followed him across the small open space and up a ravine. The man pointed to a reef cropping out and crossing the gully. I looked at it and saw that the cap had been broken and that gold was showing freely in the stone. The man waved his hand up the gully as though intimating that there were more reefs there.

"Suddenly, sweeping up the gorge came a gust of ice-cold wind, and with it a dash of mist or spray. Looming out of this I saw for a moment a young girl's face looking earnestly at me. Her lips moved. 'Go back. Go back!' she seemed to whisper.

"When I heard this I felt an irresistible longing to return to my discarded body and in an instant gorge, mountains and all my surroundings disappeared, and I found myself in the twilight space battling despairingly on, for I felt that I had lost my way and should never find it again.

"How was I to reach my forsaken body through such a vague, misty and indeterminate land? Impalpable forms threw themselves in my path. Strange cries and wailings led me astray, and all the while there was a smell like death in my nostrils, and I knew that I must return or die.

"O, the unutterable anguish of that time! Ages seem to pass during which I was fighting with shadows, until at last I saw a sinking sun, an open grave, and men whose faces I knew, commencing to shovel earth on a senseless body.

"Mine!

"I had felt no pain when my soul left, but the re-entrance of it into its tenement was such infinite agony, that it forced from me terrible cries that caused my rescue from suffocation."

Maxwell paused, and the other two were silent.

"You will wonder," he resumed, "what all this has to do with my present journey. I will tell you. You remember Milford, a surveyor up here, at one time he was running the boundary-line between Queensland and South Australia for the Queensland Government. A year ago I met him, and we were talking about the country up this way. In running the line he had to follow the Nicholson up a good way, until finally he was completely blocked. He described to me the place where he had to turn back. It was the waterhole in the gorge with the two rock-like pillars rising out of the water."

Again there was silence for a while, then Davis said musingly.

"It's impossible to pronounce any opinion at present; the coincidence of Milford's report is certainly startling. But why should this sign have been vouchsafed to you? Apparently this being you saw was the ghost of some old Dutch sailor wrecked or marooned here in the days of the early discovery of Australia. Had you any ancestors among those gentry?"

"Not that I am aware of," returned Maxwell, "but if we find the place we shall certainly make some interesting discovery, apart from any gold."

"And the girl's face?" enquired Bennett.

Maxwell did not answer for a minute or two.

"I may as well tell you all," he said then; "I was in Melbourne, after I saw Milford, and I met a girl with that same face, in the street. Strange, too, we could not help looking at each other as though we knew we had met before. That meeting decided me on taking the trip up here. Now, that is really all. Are you ready for the adventure?"

"I should think so," said Davis; "we have fresh horses at the camp, and nothing to do with ourselves for three months or more. Please God, on Christmas Day we'll be on Tom Tiddler's ground picking up gold in chunks."

"One question more," put in Bennett. "Have you ever had any return of these trances or cataleptic fits?"

"Never since, not the slightest sign of one."

CHAPTER III

There was no doubt about the strange proof or coincidence, whichever it should turn out to be. The three men stood on the bank of the Nicholson River gazing at the gorge and the waterhole, from the bosom of which rose the two upright pillars of rock. Two weeks had elapsed since they were camped at the lagoon.

"It is the same place," muttered Maxwell, and, as the overwhelming horror of his fight through shadowland came back to him, he leant on his horse's shoulder and bowed his head down on the mane.

Bennett made a sign to Davis and both men were silent for a while, then Davis spoke—

"Well, old man, as we are not possessed of the supernatural power you had when you were last here, we'll have to get over that range somehow."

Maxwell lifted his head. "We shall have to tackle the range, but I expect we shall have a job to get the horses over. How about leaving them here in hobbles and going up on foot?"

"Not to be thought of," replied Davis; "why, the niggers' tracks just back there in the bed of the river, are as thick as sheep-tracks. The horses would be speared before we got five miles away. I know these beggars."

"That's true," said Bennett.

Davis eyed the range curiously for some time. "There's a spur there that we can work our way up, I think," he said at last, indicating with his hand the spot he meant. The other two, after a short inspection, agreed with him. It was then nearly noon, so the horses were turned out for a couple of hours' spell, a fire lit and the billy boiled.

"What could have led your Dutch sailor up this way?" said Davis as, the meal over, they were enjoying an after-dinner pipe.

"That is what has puzzled me. I have read up everything I could get hold of on the subject of Dutch discovery and can find no record of any ship visiting the Gulf about that date," replied Maxwell.

"There may have been plenty of ships here, of which neither captain nor crew wanted a record kept. Those were the days of the buccaneers," said Bennett.

"Yes, but with the exception of the ship Dampier was on board of, they did not come out of their way to New Holland," returned Maxwell.

"The Bachelor's Delight and the Cygnet were on the west coast, as you say; why not others who had not the luck to be associated with the immortal Dampier?"

"True; but the Dutch were not noted as buccaneers. However, plenty of ships may have been lost in the Gulf of which all record has disappeared. The question is, what brought the man up into this region?" said Davis.

"I firmly believe we shall find the clue to that secret, when we find the ravine. It seems incredible that a shipwrecked or marooned man should have left the sea-coast, whereon was his only hope of salvation and have made south into an unknown land, through such a range as this."

"Well, boys, we'll make a start for it," said Davis, jumping up; and the party were soon in their saddles.

The range proved pretty stiff climbing, and they were so often baulked, and forced to retrace their steps, that it was sundown before they reached the top.

* * * * * * *

It was a desolate outlook for a camp. A rough tableland of spinifex—evidently extending too far for them to attempt to go on and descend the other side before darkness set in—lay before them.

"Nothing for it but to go on and tie the horses up all night," said Bennett. Fortune, however, favoured them; in about a mile they came on a small patch of grass, sufficient for the horses, and as their water-bags were full, they gladly turned out.

For a time the conversation turned on their expectations for the morrow, but gradually it dropped, as the fire died down. One by one the stars in their courses looked down through the openings of the tree-tops on the wanderers sleeping below, and silence, save for the occasional clink of a hobble, reigned supreme until the first flush of dawn.

"Well, Maxwell," said Davis, as they were discussing breakfast, "hear anything from your old Dutch navigator last night?"

"No, but I had some confused sort of dream again about this place; I thought I heard that voice once more telling me to 'go back'. But that, of course, is only natural."

"I think we are close to the spot," remarked Bennett. "When I was after the horses this morning I could see down into the river, and there appeared to be an open pocket there."

Bennett proved right. In half-an-hour's time they were scrambling down the range, and soon stood in an open space that Maxwell at once identified.

Naturally everybody was slightly excited. Although at first inclined to put the story down to hallucination, the subsequent events had certainly shaken this belief in the minds of the two friends. Maxwell silently pointed to the boulder; there was something carved on it, but it was worn and indistinct. Two centuries of weather had almost obliterated whatever marks had been there.

"They were fresh and distinct when I saw them," said Maxwell, in an awed voice.

By diligent scrutiny they made out the inscription that he had repeated, but had they not known it the task would have been most difficult. The words had not been very deeply marked, and the face of the boulder fronting north-west, the full force of the wet seasons had been experienced by the inscription.

"This is a wonderful thing," said Davis. "There can be no doubt as to the age of that."

"Let's go up the ravine and look for the reef and then get back as soon as possible. I don't like this place. I wish I had not come," returned Maxwell.

They left the packhorses feeding about and rode up the gully, taking with them the pick and shovel they had brought. "It was here, I think," said Maxwell, looking around; "but the place seems altered."

"Very likely the creek would change its course slightly in a couple of hundred years, but not much. That looks like an outcrop there."

"This is the place," said Maxwell, eagerly, "I know it now, but it is a little changed."

The three dismounted, and Davis, taking the pick, struck the cap of the reef with the head of it, knocking off some lumps of stone. As he did so a wild "Holloa!" rang up the gully. All started and looked at each other with faces suddenly white and hearts quickly beating. There was something uncanny in such a cry rising out of the surrounding solitude.

"Blacks?" said Bennett, doubtfully. Davis shook his head. Once more the loud shout was raised, apparently coming from the direction of the inscribed rock.

"Let's go and see what it is, anyway," said Davis—and they mounted and rode down the gully again, Bennett, who had picked up a bit of the quartz, putting it into his saddle-pouch as they rode along.

Maxwell had not spoken since the cry had been heard, his face was pale and occasionally he muttered to himself, "Go back, go back!" The packhorses were quietly cropping what scanty grass there was; all seemed peaceful and quiet.

"I believe it was a bird after all; there's a kind of toucan makes a devil of a row—have a look round old man," said Davis to Bennett, and they both rode up and down the bank of the river, leaving Maxwell standing near the rock where he had dismounted. Nothing could be seen, and the two returned and proposed going up the gully again.

"You fellows go and come back again, I want to get out of this—I'm upset," said Maxwell, speaking for the first time in a constrained voice.

Davis glanced at his friend. "Right you are, old man, no wonder you don't feel well; we'll just make sure of the reef and come back. If you want us, fire your pistol; we shan't be far off."

The two rode back to their disturbed work and hastily commenced their examination of the stone. There was no doubt about the richness of the find, and the reef could be traced a good distance without much trouble. They had collected a small heap of specimens to take back, when suddenly the loud "Holloa!" once more came pealing up the gully followed instantly by a fainter cry and two revolver-shots.

Hastily mounting, the two galloped back.

The packhorses, as if startled, were walking along their tracks towards home, followed by Maxwell's horse with the bridle trailing; its rider was stretched on the ground; nothing else was visible.

Jumping from their horses they approached the prostrate man. Both started and stared at each other with terror-stricken eyes. Before them lay a skeleton clad in Maxwell's clothes.

"Are we mad?" cried Davis, aghast with horror.

The fierce sun was above them, the bare mountains around, they could hear the horses clattering up the range as if anxious to leave the accursed place, and before them lay a skeleton with the shrunken skin still adhering to it in places, a corpse that had been rotting for years; that had relapsed into the state it would have been had the former trance been death. Blind terror seized them both, and they mounted to follow the horses when an awful voice came from the fleshless lips: "Stay with me, stop! I may come back; I may—"

Bennett could hear no more, he stuck the spurs in his horse and galloped off. Davis would have followed but he was transfixed with terror at what he saw. The awful object was moving, the outcast spirit was striving desperately to reanimate the body that had suddenly fallen into decay. The watcher was chained to the spot. Once it seemed that the horrible thing was really going to rise, but the struggle was unavailing, with a loud moan of keenest agony and despair that thrilled the listener's brain with terror it fell back silent and motionless. Davis remembered nothing more till he found himself urging his horse up the range. The place has never been revisited.

* * * * * * *

In an asylum for the insane in a southern town there is a patient named Bennett, who is always talking of the wonderful reef he has up North. He has a specimen of quartz, very rich, which he never parts with day or night. He is often visited by a man named Davis, who nursed him through a severe attack of fever out on the Nicholson. The doctors think he may yet recover.

A HAUNT OF THE JINKARRAS

by Ernest Favenc

In May, 1889, the dead body of a man was found on one of the tributaries of the Finke River, in the extreme North of South Australia. The body, by all appearances, had been lying there some months and was accidentally discovered by explorers making a flying survey with camels. Amongst the few effects was a Lett's Diary containing the following narration, which although in many places almost illegible and much weather-stained, has been since, with some trouble, deciphered and transcribed by the surveyor in charge of the party, and forwarded to *THE BULLETIN* for publication.

TRANSCRIBED FROM THE DEAD MAN'S DIARY

March 10, 1888.—Started out this morning with Jackson, the only survivor of a party of three who lost their horses on a dry stage when looking for country—he was found and cared for by the blacks, and finally made his way into the line where I picked him up when out with a repairing-party. Since then I got him a job on the station, and in return he has told me about the ruby-field of which we are now in search; and thanks to the late thunder-storms we have as yet met with no obstacles to our progress. I have great faith in him, but he being a man without any education and naturally taciturn, is not very lively company, and I find myself thrown on to the resource of a diary for amusement.

March 17—Seven days since we left Charlotte Waters, and we are now approaching the country familiar to Jackson during his sojourn with the natives two years ago. He is confident that we shall gain the gorge in the Macdonnell Ranges to-morrow, early.

March 18.—Amongst the ranges, plenty of water, and Jackson has recognised several peaks in the near neighbourhood of the gorge, where he saw the rubies.

March 19.—Camped in Ruby Gorge, as I have named this pass, for we have come straight to the place and found the rubies without any hindrance at all. I have about twenty magnificent stones and hundreds of small ones; one of the stones in particular is almost living fire, and must be of great value. Jackson has no idea of the value of the find, except that it may be worth a few pounds, with which he will be quite satisfied. As there is good feed and water, and we have plenty of rations, will camp here for a day or two and spell the horses before returning.

March 20—Been examining some caves in the ranges. One of them seems to penetrate a great distance—will go to-morrow with Jackson and take candles and examine it.

March 25—Had a terrible experience the last four days. Why on earth did I not go back at once with the rubies? Now I may never get back. Jackson and I started to explore this cave early in the morning. We found nothing extraordinary about it for some time. As usual, there were numbers of bats, and here and there were marks of fire on the rocks, as though the natives had camped there at times. After some searching about, Jackson discovered a passage which we followed down a steep incline for a long distance. As we got on we encountered a strong draught of air and had to be very careful of our candles. Suddenly the passage opened out and we found ourselves in a low chamber in which we could not stand upright. I looked hastily around, and saw a dark figure like a large monkey suddenly spring from a rock and disappear with what sounded like a splash. "What on earth was that?" I said to Jackson. "A jinkarra," he replied, in his slow, stolid way. "I heard about them from the blacks; they live under-ground." "What are they?" I asked. "I couldn't make out," he replied; "the blacks talked about jinkarras, and made signs that they were underground, so I suppose that was one."

We went over to the place where I had seen the figure and, as the air was now comparatively still and fresh, our candles burnt well and we could see plainly. The splash was no illusion, for an underground stream of some size ran through the chamber, and on looking closer, in the sand on the floor of the cavern, were tracks like a human foot.

We sat down and had something to eat. The water was beautifully fresh and icily cold, and I tried to obtain from Jackson all he knew about the jinkarras. It was very little beyond what he had already told me. The natives spoke of them as something, animals or men, he could not make out which, living in the ranges underground. They used to frighten the children by crying out "jinkarra!" to them at night.

The stream that flowed through the cavern was very sluggish and apparently not deep, as I could see the white sand at a distance under the rays of the candle; it disappeared under a rocky arch about two feet above its surface. Strange to say when near this arch I could smell a peculiar pungent smell like something burning, and this odour appeared to come through the arch. I drew Jackson's attention to it and proposed wading down the channel of the stream if not too deep, but he suggested going back to camp first and getting more rations, which, being very reasonable, I agreed to.

It took us too long to get back to camp to think of starting that day, but next morning we got away early and were soon beside the subterranean stream. The water was bitterly cold but not very deep, and we had provided ourselves with stout saplings as poles and had our revolvers and some rations strapped on our shoulders. It was an awful wade through the chill water, our heads nearly touching the slimy top of the arch, our candles throwing a faint, flickering gleam on the surface of the stream; fortunately the bottom was splendid—hard, smooth sand—and after wading for about twenty minutes we suddenly emerged into another cavern, but its extent we could not discern at first for our attention was taken up with other matters.

The air was laden with pungent smoke, the place illuminated with a score of smouldering fires, and tenanted by a crowd of the most hideous beings I ever saw. They espied us in an instant, and flew wildly about, jabbering frantically, until we were nearly deafened. Recovering ourselves we waded out of the water, and tried to approach some of these creatures, but they hid away in the darker corners, and we couldn't lay hands on any of them. As well as we could make out in the murky light they were human beings, but savages of the most degraded type, far below the ordinary Australian blackfellow. They had long arms, shaggy heads of hair, small twinkling eyes, and were very low of stature. They kept up a confused jabber, half whistling, half chattering, and were utterly without clothes, paint, or any ornaments. I approached one of their fires, and found it to consist of a kind of peat or turf; some small bones of vermin were lying around, and a rude club or two. While gazing at these things I suddenly heard a piercing shriek, and, looking up, found that Jackson, by a sudden spring, had succeeded in capturing one of these creatures, who was struggling and uttering terrible yells. I went to his assistance, and together we succeeded in holding him still while we examined him by the light of our candles. The others, meanwhile dropped their clamour and watched us curiously.

Never did I see such a repulsive wretch as our prisoner. Apparently he was a young man about two or three and twenty, only five feet high at the outside, lean, with thin legs and long arms. He was trembling all over, and the perspiration dripped from him. He had scarcely any forehead, and a shaggy mass of hair crowned his head, and grew a long way down his spine. His eyes were small, red and bloodshot; I have often experienced the strong odour emitted by the ordinary blackfellow when heated or excited, but never did I smell anything so offensive as the rank smell emanating from this creature. Suddenly Jackson exclaimed: "Look! look! he's got a tail!" I looked and nearly relaxed my grasp of the brute in surprise. There was no doubt about it, this strange being had about three inches of a monkey-like tail.

"Let's catch another," I said to Jackson after the first emotion of surprise had passed. We looked around after putting our candles upright in the sand. "There's one in that corner," muttered Jackson to me, and as soon as I spotted the one he meant we released our prisoner and made a simultaneous rush at the cowering form. We were successful, and when we dragged our captive to the light we found it to be a woman. Our curiosity was soon satisfied—the tail was the badge of the whole tribe, and we let our second captive go.

My first impulse was to go and rinse my hands in the stream, for the contact had been repulsive to me. Jackson did the same, saying as he did so—"Those fellows I lived with were bad enough, but I never smelt anything like these brutes." I pondered what I should do. I had a great desire to take one of these singular beings back with me, and I thought with pride of the reputation I should gain as their discoverer. Then I reflected that I could always find them again, and it would be better to come back with a larger party after safely disposing of the rubies and securing the ground.

"There's no way out of this place," I said to Jackson.

"Think not?" he replied.

"No," I said, "or these things would have cleared out; they must know every nook and cranny."

"Umph!" he said, as though satisfied; "shall we go back now?"

I was on the point of saying yes, and had I done so all would have been well; but, unfortunately, some motive of infernal curiosity prompted me to say—"No! let us have a look round first." Lighting another candle each, so that we had plenty of light, we wandered round the cave, which was of considerable extent, the unclean inhabitants flitting before us with beast-like cries. Presently we had made a half-circuit of the cave and were approaching the stream, for we could hear a rushing sound as though it plunged over a fall. This noise grew louder, and now I noticed that all the natives had disappeared, and it struck me that they had retreated through the passage we had penetrated, which was now unguarded. Suddenly Jackson, who was ahead, exclaimed that there was a large opening. As he spoke he turned to enter it; I called out to him to be careful but my voice was lost in a cry of alarm as he slipped, stumbled, and with a shriek of horror disappeared from my view. So sudden was the shock, and so awful my surroundings, that I sank down utterly unnerved comprehending but one thing: that I was alone in this gruesome cavern inhabited by strange, unnatural creations.

After a while I pulled myself together and began to look around. Holding my candle aloft I crawled on my stomach to where my companion had disappeared. My hand touched a slippery decline; peering cautiously down I saw that the rocks sloped abruptly downwards and were covered with slime as though under water at times. One step on the treacherous surface and a man's doom was sealed—headlong into the unknown abyss below he was bound to go, and this had been the fate of the unhappy Jackson. As I lay trembling on the edge of this fatal chasm listening for the faintest sound from below, it struck me that the noise of the rushing water was both louder and nearer. I lay and listened. There was no doubt about it—the waters were rising. With a thrill of deadly horror it flashed across me that if the stream rose it would prevent my return as I could not thread the subterranean passage under water. Rising hastily I hurried back to the upper end of the cavern following the edge of the water. A glance assured me I was a prisoner, the water was up to the top of the arch, and the stream much broader than when we entered. The rations and candles we had left carelessly on the sand had disappeared, covered by the rising water. I was alone, with nothing but about a candle and a-half between me and darkness and death.

I blew out the candle, threw myself on the sand and thought. I brought all my courage to bear not to let the prospect daunt me. First, the natives had evidently retreated before the water rose too high, their fires were all out and a dead silence reigned. I had the cavern to myself, this was better than their horrid company. Next, the rising was periodical, and evidently was the cause of the slimy, slippery rock which had robbed me of my only companion. I remembered instances in the interior where lagoons rose and fell at certain times without any visible cause. Then came the thought, for how long would the overflow continue. I had fresh air and plenty of water, I could live days; probably the flood only lasted twelve or twenty-four hours. But an awful fear seized on me. Could I maintain my reason in this worse than Egyptian darkness—a darkness so thick, definite and overpowering that I cannot describe it, truly a darkness that could be felt? I had heard of men who could not stand twenty-four hours in a dark cell, but had clamoured to be taken out. Supposing my reason deserted me, and during some delirious interlude the stream fell and rose again.

These thoughts were too agonising. I rose and paced a step or two on the sand. I made a resolution during that short walk. I had matches—fortunately, with a bushman's instinct, I had put a box in my pouch when we started to investigate the cavern. I had a candle and a-half, and I had, thank Heaven! my watch. I would calculate four hours as nearly as possible, and every four hours I would light my candle and enjoy the luxury of a little light. I stuck to this, and by doing so left that devilish pit with reason. It was sixty hours before the stream fell, and what I suffered during that time no tongue could tell, no brain imagine.

That awful darkness was at times peopled by forms that, for hideous horror, no nightmare could surpass. Invisible, but still palpably present, they surrounded and sought to drive me down the chasm wherein my companion had fallen. The loathsome inhabitants of that cavern came back in fancy and gibbered and whistled around me. I could smell them, feel their sickening touch. If I slept I awoke from, perhaps, a pleasant dream to the stern fact that I was alone in darkness in the depth of the earth. When first I found that the water was receding was perhaps the hardest time of all, for my anxiety to leave the chamber tenanted by such phantoms, was overpowering. But I resisted. I held to my will until I knew I could safely venture, and then waded slowly and determinedly up the stream; up the sloping passage, through the outer-cave, and emerged into the light of day—the blessed glorious light, with a wild shout of joy.

I must have fainted; when I came to myself I was still at the mouth of the cave, but now it was night, the bright, starlit, lonely, silent night of the Australian desert. I felt no hunger nor fear of the future; one delicious sense of rest and relief thrilled my whole being. I lay there watching the dearly-loved Austral constellations in simple, peaceful ecstasy. And then I slept, slept till the sun aroused me, and I arose and took my way to our deserted camp. A few crows arose and cawed defiantly at me, and the leather straps bore the marks of a dingo's teeth, otherwise the camp was untouched. I lit a fire, cooked a meal, ate and rested once more. The reaction had set in after the intense strain I had endured, and I felt myself incapable of thinking or purposing anything.

This state lasted for four and twenty hours—then I awoke to the fact that I had to find the horses, and make my way home alone—for, alas, as I bitterly thought, I was now, through my curiosity, alone, and, worst of all, the cause of my companion's death. Had I come away when he proposed, he would be alive, and I should have escaped the awful experience I have endured.

I have written this down while it is fresh in my memory; to-morrow I start to look for the horses. If I reach the telegraph-line safely I will come back and follow up the discovery of this unknown race, the connecting and long-sought-for link; if not, somebody else may find this and follow up the clue. I have plotted out the course from Charlotte Waters here by dead-reckoning.

March 26th:—No sign of the horses. They have evidently made back. I will make up a light pack and follow them. If I do not overtake them I may be able to get on to the line on foot.

END OF THE DIARY

NOTE—The surveyor, who is well-known in South Australia, adds the following postscript:—

The unfortunate man was identified as an operator on the overland line. He had been in the service a long time, and was very much liked. The facts about picking up Jackson when out with a repairing party have also been verified. The dead man had obtained six months' leave of absence, and it was supposed he had gone down to Adelaide. The tradition of the jinkarras is common among the natives of the Macdonnell Range. I have often heard it. No rubies or anything of value were found on the body. I, of course, made an attempt to get out, but was turned back by the terrible drought then raging. As it is now broken, I am off, and by the time this reaches you shall perhaps be on the spot.

THE BOUNDARY RIDER'S STORY

by Ernest Favenc

THE storm that had been brewing all the afternoon, gathered, towards nightfall, in great black clouds, cleft every now and then by jagged streaks of vivid lightning. Just after dark it burst in a fierce rush of rain and boom and rage of thunder. Blinding as the lightning was, it as only by its assistance that a belated traveller could keep his horse on the bridle-track he was following; for when darkness fell between the flashes, it seemed as though a black pall had been dropped over everything.

With heads bent down, the sodden man and horse plodded on until the rider found himself on a main road into which the track debouched.

"Another mile;" he muttered to himself; "and I'll come to old Mac's." He touched his horse slightly with the spur and glanced nervously round. The travelling now improved, and ere long a dim light proclaimed his approach to some kind of habitation; soon afterwards he pulled up at the verandah of a small bush inn.

"Are you in Mac?" he roared with a voice that outdid the thunder, as he splashed down from his horse into a pool of water, and hastily proceeded to ungirth.

"Who's there?" returned a voice, and the owner of it came out and peered into the darkness.

"Smithson! Lend us a pair of hobbles."

"Jupiter! what are you doing out here such a night as this?" asked Mac as he handed him the hobbles.

"'Cos I'm a fool, that's why," said Smithson as he stooped down and buckled the straps. "Can't go wrong for feed, I suppose?"

"Right up to the back door. Come in and get a change."

Hanging his saddle and bridle on a peg riven into the slab, the late traveller followed his host into the bar. Mac put his head out of the back door and roared to somebody to bring in some tea; then reached down a bottle and placed it, with a glass, before his visitor. Smithson filled out a stiff drink, tossed it off neat, and gave a sigh of satisfaction. Having got a dry shirt and trousers, the traveller proceeded to simultaneously enjoy a good meal and his host's curiosity.

"It's that cursed Chinaman hunted me. The one who cut his throat."

"Did you see him?" asked Mac in an awed voice.

"I did, indeed, with the bandages round his neck just as they found him. I meant to go in to the station and tell the boss he must send out somebody else. When I remembered that you were nearer and came over for a bit of company. Now, don't laugh at a fellow—just you go and stop in my hut for a night or two."

"No fear," returned Mac emphatically.

"Well I thought I didn't care for anything," said the boundary-rider, "but this caps all. You should see—cripes! what's that!" For a long, lugubrious howl sounded outside, followed by the rattling of a chain. Both men forced a very artificial laugh.

"It's Boxer," said Smithson, suddenly illumined. "I left him tied up, but he's got his chain loose and followed me."

A very wet and woe-begone dog came in at his call. Smithson detached the chain from his collar and they sat down again.

"Boxer didn't fancy being left alone," remarked Mac.

"Seems not. It gave me quite a turn when he howled like that. What do you say?" Taking the hint, Mac arose and the two went into the bar.

"All alone to-night?" asked Smithson.

"Yes, the missus is in town; there's only deaf Ben in the kitchen."

"Well, I hope that d——d Chinaman won't follow the dog."

"Don't get talking like that. How did he come to cut his throat? It was before my time."

"The fellow who had the contract for the paddock-fence lived in the hut with two men, and the Chinaman was cooking for them; he was there for over six months. Chris, the contractor, he paid off the other men; and he and the Chinaman stopped for a week longer to finish up some odd jobs. One morning Chris came in to the station as hard as he could split—the Chow had cut his throat the night before. Chris said he wasn't quite dead, and that he had tied up the wound as well as he could. The super and another man went back with him, but when they arrived the Chinkie was as dead as a door-nail. Now, the strange thing was that the stuff Chris had tied round his throat was quite clean; but when they moved the body, with Chris holding the shoulders, the blood commenced to soak through, and turned them all quite faint. All Chris knew about it was that when he awoke in the morning the Chinaman was lying outside with a sheath-knife in his hand and his throat cut."

"And did you see nothing until to-night?"

"No. Just after dark I heard someone calling, and I went to the door and looked out. I can tell you I just did get a fright, for there by the lightning I saw the Chinaman standing, with bloody rags round his neck, and the knife in his hand."

Mac shuddered and passed the bottle.

"Now," said Smithson, "comes the strange part of it. That shout, or coo-ee, I heard, came from some way off, and that there ghost I saw was not looking at me, but listening for that shout, and smiling like a man who was expecting a friend coming."

"What did you do?"

"I slammed the door to, picked up my saddle and bridle and got out of the back window. I knew my old moke was not far off, but I was that scared I left his hobbles where I took them off. I heard Boxer howling as I rode away."

* * * * * * *

It was a beautiful morning after the storm as Smithson rode in to the head station. So bright and cheerful was it that the boundary-rider felt rather ashamed of the yarn he was going to tell and half-inclined to turn back. However, he went on and had an interview with the superintendent. Naturally, he was laughed at, and this, of course, made him stubborn.

"I'll tell you what I'll do," said Morrison, the super, at last. I'll go back with you this afternoon and stop the night with you, and we'll see if we can't quiet the Chinaman."

Smithson agreed, remarking that perhaps it was only on one particular night he walked, as he had never seen him before.

Morrison turned up an old diary and glanced through it. "Oh, that's nothing," he said, pushing it away.

* * * * * * *

The two men rode up to the lonely hut, Morrison slightly ahead. "There's something queer there," he said, pulling up. Smithson stared eagerly; while Boxer, who was with them, sat down on the road and howled dismally.

Recovering themselves, the two rode on. A man was lying in front of the door stretched out in death. Dismounting, they approached and examined him.

"No, no!" cried Smithson, "don't touch him—we mustn't till the police come."

With an impatient gesture Morrison stooped down and turned the dead face up. In the throat was a rude wound, and in the open eyes a terror more than human.

"It's Christy," said the superintendent in a quiet voice.

"The man who employed the Chinaman?" asked Smithson in an unsteady tone.

"Yes. How, in the name of God, did he come here? Tell me

exactly what you saw and heard."

"I was in the doorway, as I told you," said the boundary-rider excitedly, "standing just there, and by the flash of lightning I saw the Chinaman here"—and he indicated the spot.

"He was standing like this"—and he bent forward like a man watching and listening—looking in the direction the cry came from over there."

"And you saw a knife in his hand?"

"Yes, and he was smiling as though expecting somebody he wanted to see badly."

Morrison put his hand on the other's shoulder and pointed to the knife in the hand of the corpse. "Was it that knife?"

"It looks like it," chattered Smithson.

The superintendent glanced about and shook his head. "No tracks to tell tales," he said.

"No, all the storm was on afterwards."

Morrison mused a bit. "Get a sheet of bark," he said, "or one of those sheets of iron there. We must put him inside, and then I'll give you a letter to take in to the police. You can get back with the sergeant by to-morrow morning, and we'll bury him."

"You're not going to stop here?" said Smithson.

"No," returned Morrison. "I'll get over to Mac's."

They lifted the dead man on to the sheet of iron and carried him into his old dwelling-place, Smithson evidently much averse to the job. Morrison tried to close the staring eyes before they put one of Smithson's blankets over the corpse; but the lids were rigid. "Evidently he didn't like the look of where he's gone to," he muttered. The two set out—one to the little township, the other to Mac's pub.

The night was as calm and fine as though thunder were unknown. Morrison mused deeply over the tragic occurrence, trying to recall all he knew of the past and put a common-sense construction on it, but he failed, and only made himself nervous.

"There's one very strange thing about the affair," he said to Mac, when they were discussing it that evening. "When I paid Chris for the contract—over which he lost, by the way—I gave him separate cheques to pay off his men, including one for the Chinaman of about $30. That cheque was not found, and, moreover, it has never been presented to this day."

"What sort of a fellow was Chris?"

"A good fencer, but a stupid fellow, not fit to take contracts. I often wonder if he took the cheque off the body before he came in."

"Then why didn't he present it?"

"That was his idea, no doubt, at first. But I tell you he could scarcely read or write and I suppose after he heard me tell the sergeant that I would give the bank notice and instruct them to watch for the cheque, he got frightened."

"Before that he imagined that one cheque was the same as another, and that you could not trace a particular one?"

"Yes, just about what he would think."

"Perhaps he killed the Chinaman?"

"Perhaps he did," returned Morrison, after a long and thoughtful pause.

By sunrise Morrison and Mac were at the boundary-rider's hut, and soon afterwards the sergeant and Smithson arrived. The examination did not take long, and they prepared to dig a grave.

"Better not bury him alongside the other," said the sergeant.

"No," replied Morrison. "Let's see, we buried him over against that tree; didn't we, sergeant?"

"Yes, and not very deep either. It was dry weather, the ground was hard, and we came upon a big root."

The obsequies were not prolonged. Sewn up in the blanket, the dead man was soon laid in a damp grave. While the others were filling it up, Morrison, still thinking of Mac's remark, strolled over to the spot where the Chinaman slept, not expecting to see any mark of the place left. He started and turned pale.

"Here! Quick! Come here!" he cried.

The men came hastily, the tools still in their hands. The earth over the old grave had been loosened and disturbed.

"My God! he's got up!" murmured Smithson. "I've heard

they can't rest out of their own country."

"Give me a shovel," cried Morrison; and commenced to carefully scrape the earth away. The sergeant assisted him, and they soon came to the skeleton, for nearly everything but the bones was gone.

"What, do you expect to find?" asked the sergeant.

Morrison was carefully brushing the loose dirt off the thing with a bough.

"Look here!" he said.

Clasped in the fleshless hand was the missing cheque

"It wasn't buried with him, I'll swear," said the sergeant.

"And if it had been, it would have decayed long since," answered Morrison.

"He got up and took it from Chris last night. He was bound to get his cheque back," said Mac.

"Well I'm going to pack up my traps," remarked Smithson.

"I'll send down and have this hut shifted," said Morrison. "Although now he's got what he wanted, I don't suppose, he'll get up again."

"By gum, I won't trust him," said the boundary-rider.

CANNABIS INDICA

by Marcus Clarke

Marcus Clarke (1846-1881) is arguably Australia's greatest colonial novelist, justly famous for his novel *His Natural Life*, which was serialised in the *Australian Journal*. He was born in Kensington, London, and hoped for a career in the Foreign Office, but when his father died debt-ridden his uncle arranged his emigration to Australia in 1863. He was a prolific writer for the many literary journals of the day, and wrote several so-called "sensational stories".

Often beset by financial difficulties, Clarke died in penury at the age of thirty-five, leaving his wife and six children destitute. The following strange gothic tale was written as an experiment when Clarke was under the influence of opium. It was first published in the *Colonial Monthly* in February 1868, and was reprinted in Clarke's *Stories* as 'A Hashish Trance'. The doctor attending the experiment wrote, "I have been astonished many times during the writing of what follows, at the extraordinary command of language, and the fitness of expression, possessed by my friend.... There is also a strange consistency in the narrative, and a sort of undercurrent of meaning that is most unusual in opium dreams."

He closed the door and stepped out into the darkness. It was a bleak night. The wind had risen, and howled and cursed as it swept down the narrow street that led to the rooms of the Student Martialis. The spirit of the storm had arisen from his lair in the hills of the Geisberg and Kaiserstuhl, and was flying abroad on some unholy errand. The cold moon was up, and half hidden by the rapidly drifting clouds, she cast a fitful gleam down upon the gabled roofs and quaint turrets of Heidelberg town.

In the upper air the clouds were drifting fast before the gale that rushed after them open-mouthed: but below, the mist and murk hung heavy over the river, and clung, like a funeral sheet, to the skeleton-like bridge that spanned the Neckar with its black arches.

A wild night!—a night when unholy things are abroad, Student Martialis!—a night for Walpurgis revelry and Witch meetings!—a fearsome night! Dull noises came, mixed with the shrill blasts that shrieked and groaned through the ruined Rittersaal in dying cadences, as of some human thing in agony; and, down in the valley of the Neckar horrible horse-laughs died away from among the mists over the river. The moon swam out suddenly from under her mist-shroud, and struck all the dark street into marble whiteness with her brilliant glare. The Student Martialis saw his shadow suddenly grow out on the white pavement as an ebon silhouette of himself. An ungainly shadow it was: tall and distorted, wrapped in a big cloak, that the gusts of wind had blown back into a grotesque semblance to the pinions of some evil bird. A shadow surmounted by a slouched hat, from which the black-blown elf-locks writhed like wounded serpents—a shadow sustained by two long, lean spindle-legs, with huge lumps of feet, that equalled in size those of a giant or wooden-shoed Dutch peasant. In fact, the shadow of the Student Martialis seemed to be a model of Mephistopheles cast into a pair of tongs.

As the Student looked, the moonbeam died away again; and as the monstrous shade was swallowed up in darkness, Martialis thought he distinguished another beside it—a short, dumpy one, that flickered out for a moment and then disappeared.

"Pretty rings, gentlemen; Who'll buy my rings?"

The Student Martialis started back, and as he did so, he came into contact with something—something that was alive, and moved, and croaked.

"Pretty rings, gentlemen. Who'll buy my rings?"

The moon shone out again. There were two shadows now—that of the Student Martialis, and that of an old woman; and the two bobbed and flickered on the white screen of roadway with all the distinctness of figures in a phantasmagoria.

"Go away, woman," said the Student Martialis; and he turned to put her back from him.

Heavens! what a hideous old woman it was! She had put on a big cloak, it would seem, to come out in; but the frolicsome wind had blown it all awry, and left her skinny, withered arms exposed.

Her petticoats, too, were all too short for her sapless old bones, that stood out from a pair of enormous shoes, like the handles from two churns. What a face she had! Puckered into a thousand wrinkles—as many as seem the bark of an old elm tree—and set with two red, sunken, carbuncles of eyes that glowed with a most unnatural fire through the shadows. She laid a hand, shaking with age and palsy, and knotted and gnarled as the root of a pine-tree, upon the arm of the Student Martialis; and extending to him the other, which held a small wicker basket, she croaked, in accents that seemed but half articulated by her blue shrivelled lips.

"Rings—rings! Buy my pretty rings!"

An irresistible feeling of horror came over the Student Martialis. He longed to turn and run, but felt spell-bound with a nameless fear. He looked instinctively down the street for the bright cheerful light that shone from the house that he had just quitted, but it was gone, The street was all still and deserted.

"They have gone home very early," said the Student Martialis.

The moon went out again and he could feel the pressure of the hag's hand tightening on his arm in the darkness, as she piped, with a gruesome senile merriment,

"Pretty rings, gentleman! Buy my rings!"

"Peace, hag, and begone!" cried Martialis. "How came you abroad on such a night as this? I want no rings. Begone!"

The old crone returned, in a foetid whisper, as she crept closer to him, "Buy my rings, pretty gentleman!"

"What do you want for them?" asked the Student, in vain trying to shake off the bony hand that pressed into his flesh. The hag placed her palsied head close to his, and, with a chattering laugh, said, "I sell them dearly to some, but you shall have one cheap, my pretty Student. You shall give me a kiss for one, Student Martialis!"

A kiss! He made an effort to wrench himself free from the horrible presence that stood near him in the darkness, but in vain. His senses reeled, his heart leapt into his mouth with disgust and loathing. Let him only get free!

"Give me one and go, in God's name!" cried the Student Martialis.

He heard a mocking laugh above him, and a window was flung up in the house opposite. A sudden burst of moonlight showed him the street again, and the head of—, the mad Professor, protruded from his window on the second storey.

"Ha! Ha!" laughed the Professor, "courting it at night, my pattern student?"

Martialis shuddered at the laugh and turned away; but the hag placed one lean arm about his neck and glued her mouth, garnished with some three or four yellow teeth-stumps, to his.

The Student Martialis could feel her charnel-house breath, and see her hot, red eyes through the gloom. There was a wild scream from the tortured blast above, echoed by the cry of the Student Martialis, as he forced himself away from the horrible contact.

* * * * * * *

What was this? He was not in Heidelberg streets at all—he

was leaning against a withered elder-tree, close by the Neckar-bank! There was something on his finger—a ring of elder-wood. How it clung to him! He tried to wrench it off, but could not.

The wind howled louder, and the driving clouds obscured the moon. Far away upon the hill yonder, he could see the light of the college faintly twinkling.

"How came I here?" cried the Student Martialis.

He looked hurriedly round—all was darkness and night. The rushing of the swollen stream below him made a dull, continuous noise, the bass of the wild witch song that the wind was playing. The branches of the elder-tree shook and creaked in the blast, and the Student thought he could hear them murmur, "A kiss! A kiss! A kiss!" as they bent towards him—the knotted and gnarled limbs groping about him, as did the hands of the old hag in the Rheingasse.

"God defend me from all harm!" cried the Student Martialis, and ran with a horrible fear at his heart up the road to the town; but as he ran he could hear the creaking branches swaying behind him, and, turning his head, he saw the elder-tree stretching forth its withered limbs, as if to hold him back, and it was no longer an elder-tree, but a horrible travesty of the old woman with the rings.

The mountain of All-Saints, on the other side of the river, loomed vast and black—a shadow among shadows—but the Student could see flames, as if of some summer lightnings, playing round its crest, and shining with the fitful glimmer of corpse lights among the ruins of the old convent. How steep the hill was! Run his best, Martialis could not top it. A nameless something at his heels seemed to drag him back, and the crooked trees, that bristled, white and ghastly, along the roadway bowed their heads to him, and blinding his view of the town lights with a multitude of leaves, whispered, "Stay with us! Stay with us, Student Martialis!" But he heeded them not, for he could feel the Elder-witch gaining on him at every stride. He dropped his cloak—it was too heavy—but he could run no faster. He flung away his hat, but the keen blasts instead of invigorating him with their fresh coldness, screamed in his ears, "A kiss! a kiss! a kiss! for the soul of the Student Martialis!"

There came a sound of footsteps upon his ears, and he heard shouts of laughter. It must be some students returning from the beer-scandal. They came down the hill. Martialis ran faster and faster, till at last he rushed in among them, with scared eyes and white face and open hands, crying, "Save me from the Elder-witch. She has bought my soul with a kiss!"

"Ho! what have we here?" said the foremost student. It was Paolo Sarpi.

"Ha! Martialis, mysterious youth, whither away so late?"

But Martialis could only gasp and cling to his friend's arm, and gesticulate wildly.

The Student laughed, and seizing his arm, led him down the hill, with the rest. Was it his fellow student that led him? He was like him in face and figure; but then, how came he with those fierce eyes, that strange garb, that little cap, and cock's feather?

"It cannot be a masquerade!" said the Student Martialis.

Down the hill they went, whooping, gambolling, and shouting, with a fearsome mad glee, that seemed strange and terrible to the affrighted student.

"Wilt come with us, my bold fly-by-night—we go a long voyage?"

"I will go anywhere with flesh and blood," said the Student Martialis.

A solemn man, whose head was turned looking over his shoulder, said, with the voice of a little child, "Our ship is anchored in the stream yonder."

As he spoke, Martialis saw a huge ship, with all her sails set and full, lying motionless in the most shallow part of the Neckar stream, where there was not anchorage for a cockle-shell.

"Cheerily, ho!" sang out Sarpi; and, in a twinkling, the whole party were on deck. The mighty ship, veering round, ran straight for the Odenwold.

Through the mountains they went. The rocky cliffs seemed to open as they passed in, and the great vessel ran silently through.

Student Martialis saw the lights of the town wax dimmer and dimmer as they entered the vast cleft in the mountain side, and he could hear indistinct mutterings above, below, and around. The whole air seemed alive with sound, and the water-bubbles on the black surface of the water gleamed like the eyes of drowned men.

Flappings of wings, and harsh croaking notes, as of evil birds, were heard in the mist: and amid the continuous roar of the wind, a keener gust than usual would scream in high-pitched accents—"A kiss! a kiss! a kiss! for the soul of the Student Martialis!"

The mountain walls grew wider and wider, the breeze came fresher and more chill; till, at length, with a bound, that, shook her from stem to stern, the ship leapt forth into the open sea. The wild waves were tumbling in from the black midnight ahead, shaking their white mains like a thousand wild horses, and leaping up at the ship with the rage of wolves at their prey. Not a jot of her course did she abate, but with every stitch of canvas set, and swelled by the fierce gale that met the leaping waves in the teeth and hurled them, struggling and hissing, back, held steadily on through the vast flood of surging waters. The seagulls swooped past with low cries of pain and woe, like condemned souls doomed to wander forever in the black abyss of midnight. They looked at the Student Martialis with eyes full of pity. Strange monsters surged up out of the seething waste of waters, and played about the ship. Gigantic shadows of evil things seemed to glide up out of the mist, and to sweep onward and over them into the yawning jaws of darkness; while, ever and anon, the face of the Elder-witch gleamed, white and ghastly, from out the waves, and mocking whispers from the spirits of the night floated past crying, "A kiss! a kiss! a kiss! for the soul of the Student Martialis!"

On a sudden the wind sank, as if struck down by some mighty hand. The billows no longer leapt and spread in sheets of hissing foam. The calm, large moon shone out bright and mellow in the cloudless sky, and the ship rocked peacefully on the long swell of a tropical sea, beneath floods of lustrous moonlight.

* * * * * * *

Martialis stole a look at Paolo Sarpi. He was standing with
one hand on the helm, and the other raised above him. As the
Student looked, lo! it was no longer Paolo Sarpi, but a skeleton
Death who stood there; and who, raising a bony finger to his
lips, piped a shrill whistle.

The whole ship's company were silent and still. Their heads
swung lazily from side to side. They smiled inanely; they leant
against the bulwarks in various attitudes; and as the Student
looked he saw that they were no longer men, but rotting corpses.

The sides of the ship began to swell and grow. Her masts
shot up higher, her deck broadened, and her shining shoulders heaved, as if possessed with life. There was a shout from
below, and instantly the whole vast deck was alive with savage
forms. Dark-browed, red-capped and bearded, they swarmed
up the hatchway, broad as the cathedral square at Milan; and,
with fierce gesticulations, surrounded the terrified student. A
hideous multitude was there. Some gibbered like apes; others,
clad in the vestments of the Egyptian kings, stalked to and fro
in silence, with their fingers on their lips. Some laughed like
hyenas—some grovelled like swine. A woman, one-half of
whose face had been shorn away, took root in the deck, and
her hands and arms grew out into long filaments, that floated
in the air. A burly seaman seized one of the corpse-crew by the
arm, and Martialis laughed as he saw the member come off in
the assailant's hand. How they jumped and danced! Paolo Sarpi
was whirling round like a dervish; and the fat Armenian monk
left his stall in the Bezesteen to offer him a jar of olives. The
mad Professor was there; and, with a wild yell, he flung his
horn-rimmed spectacles overboard, and leapt and capered with
the rest.

* * * * * * *

A lurid smoke burst from below, and tongues of fire ran greedily up from rigging to mast. A hot breath swept over the doomed ship, and the pointed flames leapt and crackled amid the dim shifting smoke-cloud that hung heavily on the thick air. Martialis tried to move from where he stood, but a dread sense of horror weighed down his limbs, and with burning eye-balls and parched tongue he glared speechless into the sea of faces that gibbered at him on all sides. Suddenly, no one knew how, a tall form appeared in the midst, a man naked and bronzed as the Indian Bacchus. He had a crown of white lotus leaves upon his head, and passing one arm round the Student he plunged with him into the deep clear water. They sank down noiselessly into the warm atmosphere of the ocean, and as they sank lower and lower, past coral beds and sparkling diamond reefs, past waving many-coloured sea-weeds, and still, grey forests of petrified sea shrubs, the blaspheming crew shouted, and the crackling fire hissed, "A kiss! a kiss! a kiss! for the soul of the Student Martialis!" They sank lower and lower till the reflection of the burning ship was a watery sun above them, and in an instant, the Student Martialis found himself lying on a grassy bank in the warm sunshine. He was on a hillock in a vast wood. The tall elms made a delicious shade of brown trunks, and the shadows of their emerald leaves, transparent in the sunlight, flickered and danced upon the mossy turf. Mighty oaks towered aloft and shut out the prospect around, save where between an avenue of stems the rich corn-fields sparkled and nodded over the inter-vening ferns. Brown, burnt-up dry ferns were beneath him, and others, fresh and green, clustered around the feet of the forest trees. There was a murmuring sound of insects in the air, and the sweet odours of summer breathed balmily around. The tall foxglove nodded familiarly to him, and the tiny blue-bell peeped out shyly from the long grass with its sweet eyes. In the interstices of the woods, beds of cool, gummy hyacinths spread their rich sheets of blue, and the larks, above in the cloudless ether, sung in a paroxysm of love and delight. Martialis turned to look for his guide. He was gone! and in his place, by his side, was a beautiful woman. The bright locks of her wealth of golden hair half veiled her face, but her dark violet eyes shone through the falling tresses, as the sweet stars shine out amidst the soft grey clouds at eventide.

Martialis looked below. The whole wood-glen was alive with tiny forms. Here a delicate-limbed, roguish elf swung upon a foxglove blossom, and there two more discussed some weighty matter of business beneath an overhanging dockleaf. A band of frolicsome fairies down in the hollow were attacking an owl in her nest with spears of bulrushes; while, upon the pool among the ferns, others sailed their tiny boats of lily leaves, or speared with bulrushes the monstrous dragon flies that settled—brilliants of green and gold—for a moment to warm their huge gauze-wings upon its surface.

The Student Martialis turned, as in a wonder-stricken dream, to his companion. She approached her rosy lips to his, and bending forward until her balmy breath fanned his cheek, said:

"Dost thou not know me, Student Martialis? I am the Spirit of Dreams, and thou art mine by that ring thou wearest."

Martialis looked at the elder-wood ring on his finger. It was no longer wood, but gold, and sparkled with a thousand gems.

"I am thine from henceforth, O Martialis. In the warm sunshine, in the driving storm, in the tempest, and amid the fire, call to me, and I will come to thee—yes, I am thine!" she murmured, in a voice as low and sweet as the cooing of innumerable doves borne by the warm summer breeze over beds of roses. "Let us seal our bridal with this kiss, thou cold student of dead love. By this kiss I claim thee mine, O Student Martialis!"

Martialis looked into her glorious eyes, languid and faint with love. He felt her warm sweet breath strike his cheek as she drew his face down to her lips with her trembling arms. He looked, and a sudden indefinable horror struck him cold and chill as the blast of an east wind, for he saw in the eyes of the siren at his side something that reminded him of the witch-woman of the Rheingasse. He started back, and, with a supreme effort, tore the ring from his finger.

* * * * * *

There was a shrill cry, and then a rush of wind and rain, and the whole forest with its fairy people, faded away behind a storm of blinding rain and driving mist. The face of his temptress changed, and, with a horrible crackling laugh, a lean, withered old woman rose and tottered off into the fog, crying:

"Rings—rings! Who'll buy my pretty rings?"

NORAH AND THE FAIRIES

by Hume Nisbet

Hume Nisbet (1859-1923) was born in Scotland and became an artist, exhibiting at the Royal Scottish Academy and befriending John Ruskin. He visited Australia three times, in 1865-72, 1886 and 1895, and many of his more than forty published volumes draw on his experiences there. He wrote three short story collections with supernatural content, *The Haunted Station and Other Stories* (1894), *Stories Weird and Wonderful* (1900), and *Mistletoe Manor* (1902).

He is best known for the classic Australian ghost story, 'The Haunted Station', which has been often anthologised. The story published here, 'Norah and the Fairies', is a poignant vignette of a little girl lost in the bush from *Stories Weird and Wonderful*.

Over by the East, the pulsating stars resembled a Queensland opal, that most lovely of all gems to the colour lover, full of light and fire, iridescent, yet rarely tender in its filmy softness. The sun was not yet over the misty ranges, but that it was near at hand that intense luminosity, which rendered one particular peak broader than the other peaks, showed. In another moment, that luminous whiteness would seem grey around the superior brightness of that dazzling orb. As yet, however, there was no glitter, but only cool radiance and melting tones.

Spring reigned over bush-land with its countless exquisite

blossom and heath-bells. Varieties of the most delicate pinks, azures, and yellows blended amongst delicious greys, whites, and aesthetic greens. Young leaves vied the bloom of the peach and plum in their tints, with rose-red branches. There was not a shrub without its individual clustering of flowers, not a tree that was not festooned with loveliness, while over all trailed the silvery, dew-laden, gossamer webs of the bush-spider.

A chastened moment that was before the sun burst over the ranges. Opal-grey was the predominant tone, with subdued sparkles of prismatic colours. All the dark shadows of the night had fled, no deep spots broke the silken monotony. It was Australia's most ethereal month, and hour, when she might well compare with the ideal plains of Heaven, where there is no sun, neither is there shadow; but the glory of God fills it with purity.

A moment longer of this divine radiance and silent expectancy, while the little maid at the foot of the ivory-limbed gum-tree, still sleeps on, dreaming about the fairies that have passed from the book under her head into her innocent brain. They have been with her all night, ever since the instant she had sunk, tired out with wanderings, until now. The Snow Queen had been with her, although she had never really seen snow in her life, also the little Sea Maid, although she had never yet seen the sea.

All night the elves, the fairies, the queer big-headed dwarfs and the sharp-nosed but benevolent old god-mothers had been dancing over the young grasses and swinging amongst the spiders' webs. But they were creeping one by one back to their covers and taking their usual places inside the pages of her pillow book. She had seen them plain enough even while she slept, for the big moon had shone all night upon the frolics. The wild cats had watched also the funny beings, no bigger than themselves; therefore they were not the least afraid of these strange visitors to Australia any more than she was herself. The great bull-frog, with his wives and children, came out of the swamp and looked on also with his bulging eyes, grunting approval, while the others went all through the gamut of notes in their surprise.

She knew that she could see quite well, even though her wearied eyelids were fast shut, for didn't she see the laughing jackass sitting on the branch above her, looking down all night at the queer sight, with long beak nodding gravely in his wonderment, and the three feathers on his head standing up? So astonished was this laughing jackass that he hadn't laughed once all through the night, although there had been fun enough to make even a jackdaw tumble off a fence.

She had seen the flying foxes, head downwards, swing themselves backwards and forwards in their jubilation at the sights. The wombats also looked back and forgot to climb an inch higher in their stupid amazement. Only the bush-spiders spun on regardless of everything extraordinary, but they had some excuse for their industry, for there was such a crowd of fairy swingers that the poor spiders were kept busy all night making fresh swings for their little visitors.

Little Norah Westwood had been very hungry when she fell asleep the night before. Her pretty white pinafore and cotton dress were sadly torn also with prickly bushes through which she had brushed.

All the day she had walked, not knowing where she was going, for it is so easy for the most experienced man or woman to get lost in the bush, far less a little girl of eight. Lured away by those wildflowers, she had gone on and on, without looking at first, and afterwards, when she wanted to get home to dinner, she had not been able to.

In Australia, if you walk on, thinking and without watching the direction you are taking in the bush, for half-an-hour, or even less time, and then look up, it is ten chances to one you will be lost. That is if you are not an experienced bushman.

The landscape is as open, almost, as an English park. You can see a good way all round, for the gum-trees appear thinly clad. It seems easy enough to recover your way, and you begin to try it with perfect confidence.

The shape of a gum-tree in the distance strikes you as quite familiar. You go towards it, and when you have reached it you find you are wrong. Then you try again, once, twice, thrice, a dozen times in different directions before the consciousness dawns on you that you are in a maze, out of which you cannot find a way.

The bright sun shines down upon you from a cloudless blue sky. You are in an open shadeless forest, with receding stretches of white-branched gum-trees on every side, and a vast solitude brooding over all.

This sunlit, bare solitude appals you with a mighty fright all at once, and that horror never leaves you until you are discovered; or, failing that, perhaps until you fall down exhausted, athirst, and famishing, to yield up the ghost.

The white, bone-like trunks and branches of the gum-trees all round you remind you only now of the skeletons of men and women who have been lost in this weird solitude before. You run wildly at first, then madly, with shrieks of deadly fear, until your reason leaves you and you fall down and rise no more. Months afterwards perhaps a passing traveller may discover your skeleton, picked anatomically clean by the ants, and perhaps not half-a-dozen miles from where you started.

Little Norah had lost her way, but being a child, and fairy supported, she had none of the horrors that an adult might feel. She had all the faith and reliance of a child in her parents. They would be sure to miss her, they would be sure to look for her, and as they could do everything, they would be sure to find her.

But being a healthy, beef-eating, colonial child, she had missed her dinner and supper dreadfully. That is until she fell asleep.

Then the Fairy God-mother had come out of her book and fed her with grapes and water-melons and such delicious cakes, and all the other fairies had danced to amuse her while she ate the good things.

They were going away now, however, as fast as they could troop into their pictures. The second last to leave her was Cinderella in her ball dress. Now the Snow Queen with a wave of her white arm drifted away like a flash of fire and Norah awoke.

Awoke to find the sun streaming into her eyelids and almost blinding her; to get a glimpse of the laughing jackass, as he shifted from the branch over her head, and flew away seriously and quietly to look after his daily business of catching snakes. There was nothing to laugh over at present, for the events of the night, and she being there all alone, were things for a jackass to think about sedately. By-and-by he might be able to laugh, when he forgot all about that night and watched his natural enemy, the black snake, fall through five hundred feet of air and break his back.

The frogs, wild cats, and flying foxes had also disappeared, and the dew-drops in which the elves had washed were being swiftly licked up by the hot morning sun. Worse than all, Norah's fairy feed seemed to have done her no good, for she was hungrier than ever.

She rose wearily and recommenced her walk of the preceding day through the bushes, picking plenty of lovely flowers until her arms were so full of blossoms that she was forced to drop them and gather a fresh lot.

The midday sun beat fiercely upon her face and shoulders until the heat felt like a heavy load. She wasn't walking fast now, indeed several times she fell and seemed to sleep. Then she would wake up, so hungry, so tired, so thirsty, and stagger on till she fell and slept again.

When the full moon rose that night, and the dew fell gently down and cooled the earth, she was sitting by the side of a water hole in a pretty dell. She was not at all hungry now, and although the water was there she didn't feel thirsty one bit. She was waiting for the fairies to come out of her book, and she had laid it down open before her so that they might have no trouble in getting free.

She had found a nice bed among the bracken ferns that clustered thickly round her. Over the ferns spread the heathbells and blossoms, amongst which already the spiders had begun to spin their swinging threads. Those were for the fairies she knew, so she waited patiently, with her dark eyes shining like stars.

The rabbits came out and sat round on their hind-legs, trimming their long ears with their fore-paws. The little thick furred black-and-white spotted wild cats also came out and played round with each other while they waited for the coming fun.

She saw two wombats and a wallaby climb the tree behind— the tree that was before the silver moon. They climbed until they reached a high fork, and there they sat just under the swinging flying foxes, waiting like spectators in the gallery, for the performance to commence.

The laughing jackass came also after his day's work and sat on a branch, looking this way and that expectantly, and last of all the big and little frogs from the pool.

Then came her friends the fairies; straight out of the pages they all flew, like a flock of cockatoos, and circled round her, Cinderella and her old God-mother, the Fairy Prince and the Sleeping Beauty, now wide-awake and happy; good dwarfs, mermaids, snow-maidens, and every one she had loved, without one wicked elf amongst them.

They fluttered about her on transparent wings, danced merrily over the ferns, and swung like happy children on the spider swings, while all the animals looked on solemnly. Norah watched them also. Watched them with eyes growing bigger and bigger with wonderment, and a strange rapture filling her heart.

Some transformation was taking place in her, she was sure, that would shortly enable her to fly as easily as those radiant creatures who moved around her on those glistening wings. Would she have wings like those pretty elves, all transparent and veined like crochet work, covered over with glitter? They were summer wings, Australian wings, the wings of the lady-bird, whom you pick off the gum-tree like a bit of brown shard and pitch away. Then it all opens up into the lovely tinted silk gauze.

Or would she have wings of white feathers like the cockatoos and the angels? That was what she was thinking about as she watched the dancing with that curious fluttering at her heart.

Then the Snow Queen came over to her with the most lovely silver car, drawn by white horses, and invited her to enter and sit beside her.

This Norah did, and no sooner was she seated, then the magic car rose up, with all the fairy court attending, and flew away, past the moon—right on towards the stars.

THE GHOST MONK

by Rosa Praed

Rosa Praed (1851-1935) is best known for her story 'The Bunyip', which has appeared in many anthologies. She was born in Queensland and grew up on remote stations in the Burnett River District. In 1872 she married an Englishman, Arthur Campbell Praed, and endured three lonely years on an isolated station at Port Curtis. The two had nothing in common and were never happy together.

In 1876 they moved to England where she became a prolific and popular writer, often under the name Mrs. Campbell Praed. She had a great interest in the occult, and many of her novels have a supernatural element, including *The Soul of Countess Adrian* (1891), *The Brother of the Shadow* (1886) and *As a Watch in the Night* (1901). After separating from her husband, she lived with Nancy Harwood, a psychic medium, whom she believed to be the reincarnation of a Roman slave girl, and based the novel *Nyria* (1904), later rewritten as *Soul of Nyria* (1931), on the experience. She wrote three collections of short stories, including the extremely rare *Stubble Before the Wind* (1908), which contains a number of excellent ghost stories, including 'The Ghost-Monk'.

Aunt Felicia used often to tell the story of her friend, Father Canalis, and the ghost-monk of Gontran, and it is given here as she related it:—

I never knew a more delightful person than Father Canalis—Dr. Canalis, I always called him, because not being myself of the Catholic communion, I prefer when it is permissible to use the more secular mode of address. Besides, there was a certain savour of the world about Dr. Canalis. He was in some respects the typical priest of society. Well-bred, highly cultivated, dignified, courteous, and with much knowledge of men and of women, he was indeed a frequent and ever-welcome guest in the houses of many of the great Catholic nobility. Though of foreign extraction, he was to all intents an Englishman, and was for a long time, till his health broke, the head of an important Catholic seminary in London. This position gave him a greater freedom than is usual with the clergy of the Church of Rome. He was a Jesuit, which fact owed perhaps something to his extreme charm of manner, his exquisite tact and his varied social gifts. There was nothing of the ascetic about Dr. Canalis, but he in no sense realised the conventional notion of the Jesuit priest. If there ever lived an earnest, pure-minded and truly religious man, it was my friend Father Canalis.

I call him friend, though I am not as a rule fond of priests; and as my husband belongs to the Roman persuasion, I have had some opportunities of observing the class. Fortunately Gaston is liberal in his views, robust as well as scholarly in his tastes, and has a keen sense of humour. Thus the priests who are his intimate friends are generally men of culture and are interesting apart from their calling.

Dr. Canalis had the reputation of being a proselytist, and it was said that he had made many a convert among a particular order of woman—that which is essentially of London society—the kind of woman who gravitates by temperament towards the Mother Church. I am not that kind of woman; and Dr. Canalis, after one or two conversations in which I frankly stated my objections to his creed, gave up any proselytising notions he might have entertained, and accepted my friendship on another basis. It was these candid talks which made me appreciate the man—his real sincerity, his almost feminine power of sympathy, his toleration of other opinions than his own, and his practical common sense. I met him more than once as a guest during his vacation at the house of a Catholic relative of Gaston's, and so charmed was I with the first sermon I heard him preach in our relative's chapel that afterwards I often went to hear him at the Pro-Cathedral when in London, where his extraordinary eloquence and the poetic grace of his diction caused him to be frequently chosen for the courses of sermons delivered there by popular Catholic divines. It was, therefore, with the greatest satisfaction that I found he was staying at Cannes one winter when my husband and I went out for six weeks' sunshine—a six weeks made memorable ever afterwards by the companionship of Dr. Canalis.

He had been granted leave of absence on account of lung delicacy. He looked worn and transparent, but no serious symptoms had shown themselves, and it was not supposed that he was in real danger. He told us that his doctor's prescription was to live out of doors, to drive as much as possible, to nourish himself with food and to give up work and study for a time. Dr. Canalis was not rich—what good Catholic priest has ever more than suffices for the necessaries of existence?—we saw that he denied himself the drives, which were his greatest pleasure and we, therefore, always made a point of asking him to accompany us on the different expeditions we made in the neighbourhood of Cannes.

One day we begged him to go with us on a rather long excursion to a queer little old-world place in the hills behind Grasse—a place which is almost unknown to the ordinary tourist on the Riviera, and which yet has a history that goes back to the Saracens, for it was once the strong-hold of the most ancient and almost the greatest of the Provençal families. This place is called St Xavier de Gontran.

I noticed that an excited look came over the priest's face, and he smiled with almost a boyish eagerness.

"You are doing me a greater kindness than you could have imagined," he said. "I accept joyfully. I know St Xavier de Gontran," he went on. "I have the most strange and solemn association with the place, which I have not visited for many years. I had an immense longing to go there again. But it is a long expedition, and I cannot now walk over the hills as I used; and, in short, there are difficulties in the way."

We knew what the difficulties were. Father Canalis would have considered it sinful selfishness to waste thirty francs on carriage hire for the gratification of a sentimental desire of his own. I jumped to the conclusion that his association with the place was a sentimental one—he had spoken of it with a hushed drop of his voice—and now I ventured to ask him what the story was. The hesitation of his manner made me feel convicted of an impertinent curiosity.

"I have hardly ever spoken of it," he answered. "I don't think I could do so here"—and he glanced round the crowded drawing-room of the hotel. "Perhaps when we are there I shall be able to tell it you. That experience made a great impression on me. It has to a certain extent influenced my life."

He did tell us the story when we were sitting on a little stone terrace—an abutment of the fortified wall of the old Château of Gontran—after we had gone over the church, had talked to the Curé, had inspected the ancient portraits, and had taken photographs—Gaston and I—of the principal features of interest in this strange human eyrie perched on the Grasse hills.

Father Canalis had left us to this occupation. He had seemed curiously subdued; the hectic in his cheeks glowed. He and the Curé had gone off together. Afterwards, I left Gaston to develop his negatives and strolled through the narrow streets of the village, gleaning such information as I might from the patois of a picturesque crone who sat spinning at the doorway of a ruined house. By and by, I found the church and went in. There I beheld Father Canalis prostrate before the high altar absorbed in an ecstasy of spiritual devotion.

I softly closed the door, for I did not want to disturb him. Gaston was waiting for me in front of the Château. We went down some crumbling steps, and came upon a tiny terrace garden, closed in by a grey, lichen-grown parapet. Below us stretched the beautiful valley of the Siagne, and beyond, the Mediterranean, misty on the horizon. A zigzag path led down the precipitous face of the rock on which the Château was built. To our right was the church—a rather imposing structure, with a tower and a Gothic doorway, and two finely-carved images let into niches on each side of the great oak door. The church and the ruins of the Château and the houses near it showed that Gontran had once been a place of some importance. Gaston and I were speculating on its previous history when the priest joined us. There was upon his face a curious far-away look. He seated himself on a bench in the angle of the parapet and began abruptly—

"I said I would tell you the thing which happened to me here, and which made so great an impression upon me. It was in this very church—"

We begged him to let us hear his story.

"I warn you," he said, with a strange smile, "that it is a ghost-story; and you are now hearing it at first hand."

As nearly as I can remember Dr. Canalis told his story in these words—

"It is about twelve years ago," he said, "before I was appointed to a seminary. I was doing an article on the ecclesiastical history of some of these old Provençal towns, and had come up here to study the inscriptions in the church. I had arranged to stay the night in the Château if my investigations should keep me too late for the walk to Grasse, and the Curé being as I knew absent—he had as well the care of that village yonder"—Dr.Canalis pointed across the valley of the Siagne—"I had gone into the church unnoticed. I had remained there interested in my work till the light failed, and then was suddenly roused from a meditation by the sound of the key turning in the door, and knew that I was locked in. I could make no one hear me, and after a while, reflecting that I might as well sleep in the church as in one of the bare rooms of the Château, I wrapped my cloak round me, and being very tired, was soon fast asleep.

"It must have been after midnight when I awoke with a curious feeling of uneasiness. The moon was shining brightly through the windows, and as I lay, it seemed to me that the wall on the opposite side opened and that the figure of a monk stepped forth and walked along the side-aisle in the direction of the altar. The monk wrung his hands as he moved, and ejaculated in a tone of deep despair: 'Is there no one who will say a mass for my wretched soul?' Then before reaching the altar he turned, walked slowly back to the wall and disappeared.

"I told myself that the apparition was but the illusion of a dream, and once more slept. Again I was awakened by the same feeling of uneasiness, and again the monk stepped forth from the wall and again wrung his hands and repeated his mournful plaint. This time I knew that it was no dream—I got up and kneeled before the altar in prayer and adoration, and then once more laid down and waited till the spectre should for the third time come forth. As the clock struck the third hour the stone melted, as it were, behind the ghost, and it seemed as if the unhappy being were directly addressing his petition to me as he wailed: 'Oh, who will say a mass for my wretched soul?' I got up and went towards him."

"Had you no fear?" asked Gaston.

"None," replied Dr. Canalis, "and I am telling you an absolutely true story. I do not believe that one has any fear of the supernatural, provided that he is conscious of pure motive; at any rate I felt none then. 'I will pray for your soul if it be any comfort to you,' I said; and then I went into the sacristy, of which the door was open, and robed myself while the ghost-monk waited at the steps of the High Altar; and the ghost served me as I performed this strange and solemn requiem mass."

Dr. Canalis paused.

"Then?" exclaimed Gaston.

"The point of the story has yet to come," answered the priest dreamily. "As the monk stood by that part of the wall from which he had appeared, he paused for a moment, and before he disappeared, said in solemn tones—

"'I thank you for having given me peace. There is only one way in which I can show my gratitude. Three days before your death you will see me again.'...

"Don't think me morbidly superstitious," Father Canalis added, "but as I prayed just now at that same spot, the presentiment was borne in upon me that I shall soon receive that promised visit."

He got up as he spoke. "Did you notice," he said, "that space in the wall of the church where the masonry appears to have been lately disturbed? I have been inquiring of the attendant here, and he tells me that a portion of the wall fell away a year or two ago, and that in repairing the place it was discovered to be hollow. A skeleton was found in the recess and also a cup and a platter. It is certain that the ghost-monk who served me at the mass was the spectre of one walled up alive, perhaps centuries ago."

There was a delay in our getting away from St Xavier de Gontran; the drive was long and the way stony, and one of the horses went lame. A mistral had risen, and we reached the hotel long after sunset, chilled to the bone. No one was surprised to learn next day that Dr. Canalis was laid up with an attack of congestion of the lungs. I went to see him a few days later, and I was struck by the change in his appearance and the wonderfully spiritualised expression of his always refined and thoughtful face.

"I am glad that you have come," he said quite cheerfully, "for I shall not see you again. I am glad too that I told you the story of the ghost-monk at Gontran the other day. You know I told you also of the presentiment which came over me that I should soon meet my spectral visitant again. He came last night. I shall die the day after to-morrow."

No reasoning could persuade Father Canalis out of this fixed idea, though the doctors assured him that there was nothing in his condition to give rise to any serious apprehension. Indeed, after an interview with the doctor I felt sure that my friend was labouring under a morbid impression. Nothing could, however, have been less morbid than the way in which he set about arranging his worldly affairs—if, indeed, that term could be applied to the interests of one who was, as regards sordid matters, so unworldly. His presentiment, however, was verified. On the third night after the ghost-monk had appeared to him, he died as quietly as if he had been going to sleep. The doctors could not understand the case; nor can I. I only know that the ghost-story must be true, for Dr. Canalis was incapable of even self-deception.

LUPTON'S GHOST: A MEMORY OF THE EASTERN PACIFIC

by Louis Becke

In his day Louis Becke (1855-1913) was compared with Rudyard Kipling and Robert Louis Stevenson. He was born in Port Macquarie, New South Wales, and educated in Sydney, but left school at fourteen to sail for America. For most of the next twenty-five years he worked as a trader in the Pacific, and his experiences formed the basis of many of his novels and short stories. A chance meeting with Ernest Favenc sparked his writing career; Favenc introduced him to J. F. Archibald the founder of the important Australian literary journal, the *Bulletin*, and Becke began submitting stories set in Australia and the Pacific.

He moved to England in 1896, and subsequently lived in a variety of different countries before returning to Sydney in 1909. He died forgotten and in poverty four years later. Becke wrote several fine supernatural tales, and this, from *The Ebbing of the Tide: South Sea Stories* (1895), is the pick of them.

Along sweeping curve of coast, fringed with tall plumed palms casting wavering shadows on the yellow sand as they sway and swish softly to the breath of the brave trade-wind that whistles through the thickly-verdured hummocks on the weather side of the island, to die away into a soft breath as, after passing through the belt of cocoanuts, it faintly ripples the transparent depths of the lagoon—a broad sheet of blue and silver stretching away from the far distant western line of reef to the smooth, yellow beach at the foot of the palms on the easternmost islet. And here, beneath their lofty crowns, are the brown thatched huts of the people and the home of Lupton the trader.

This is Mururea. And, if it be possible, Mururea surpasses in beauty any other of the "cloud of islands" which, lying on the blue bosom of the Eastern Pacific like the islands of a dream, are called by their people the Paumotu. And these people—it is not of very long ago I speak—are a people unto themselves. Shy and suspicious of strangers, white or brown, and endued with that quick instinct of fear which impels untutored minds to slay, and which we, in our civilised ignorance, call savage treachery, they are yet kind-hearted and hospitable to those who learn their ways and regard their customs. A tall, light-skinned, muscular people, the men with long, straight, black hair, coiled up in a knot at the back, and the women—the descendants of those who sailed with broken Fletcher Christian and his comrades of the *Bounty* in quest of a place where to die—soft-voiced, and with big, timorous eyes.

* * * * * * *

'Twas here that Ben Peese, the handsome, savagely humorous, and voluble colleague of Captain "Bully" Hayes, the modern rover of the South Seas, one day appeared. Lupton, with his son and two natives, were out searching the beach of a little islet for turtles' eggs, when the boy, who had been sent to obtain a few young drinking cocoanuts from a tree some little distance away, called out, "*Te Pahi!*" (a ship). A few minutes passed, and then, outlined against the narrow strip of cocoanuts that grew on the north end of the main islet of the lagoon, Lupton saw the sails of a schooner making for the only opening—a narrow passage on the eastern side.

Now vessels came but rarely to Mururea, for Du Petit Thouars, the French Admiral of the Pacific fleet, had long since closed the group to the Sydney trading ships that once came there for pearl-shell, and Lupton felt uneasy. The vessel belonging to the Tahitian firm for whom he traded was not due for many months. Could the stranger be that wandering Ishmael of the sea—Peese? Only he—or his equally daring and dreaded colleague, Bully Hayes—would dare to sail a vessel of any size in among the coral "mushrooms" that studded the current-swept waters of the dangerous passage.

What did he want? And honest Frank Lupton, a quiet and industrious trader, thought of his store of pearl-shell and felt still more doubtful. And he knew Peese so well, the dapper, handsome little Englishman with the pleasant voice that had in it always a ripple of laughter—the voice and laugh that concealed his tigerish heart and savage vindictiveness. Lupton had children too—sons and daughters—and Peese, who looked upon women as mere articles of merchandise, would have thought no more of carrying off the trader's two pretty daughters than he would of "taking" a cask of oil or a basket of pearl-shell.

* * * * * * *

His anxious face, paling beneath the tropic bronze of twenty years' ocean wanderings, betrayed his feelings to the two natives who were now pulling the boat with all their strength to gain the village, and one—Maora, his wife's brother, a big, light-skinned man, with that keen, hawk-like visage peculiar to the people of the eastern islands of Polynesia, said—

"'Tis an evil day, Farani! No ship but that of the Little Man with the Beard hath ever passed into the lagoon since the great English fighting ship came inside," (he spoke of 1863), "for the reef hath grown and spread out and nearly closed it. Only the Little Bearded Devil would dare it, for he hath been here twice with the Man of the Strong Hand," (Hayes). "And, Farani, listen! 'The hand to the club!'"

They ceased pulling. From the village came the sound of an almost forgotten cry—a signal of danger to the dwellers under the palms—"The hand to the club!"—meaning for the men to arm.

* * * * * *

Lupton hesitated. The natives would, he knew, stand to him to a man if violence to or robbery of him were attempted. But to gain the village he must needs pass close the vessel, and to pass on and not board her would savour of cowardice—and Lupton was an Englishman, and his twenty years' wanderings among the dangerous people of some of the islands of the Paumotu Group had steeled his nerves to meet any danger or emergency. So, without altering the course of the boat, he ran alongside of the vessel which was a brigantine—just as she was bringing to, and looking up, he saw the face he expected.

"How are you, Lupton, my dear fellow?" said Peese, as the trader gained the deck, wringing his hand effusively, as if he were a long-lost brother. "By Heavens! I'm glad to meet a countryman again, and that countryman Frank Lupton. Don't like letting your hand go." And still grasping the trader's rough hand in his, delicate and smooth as a woman's, he beamed upon him with an air of infantile pleasure.

* * * * * *

This was one of Peese's peculiarities—an affectation of absolute affection for any Englishman he met, from the captain of a man-of-war (these, however, he avoided as much as possible), to a poor beachcomber with but a grass girdle round his loins.

"What brings you here, Captain Peese?" said Lupton, bluntly, as his eye sought the village, and saw the half-naked figures of his native following leaving his house in pairs, each carrying between them a square box, and disappearing into the puka scrub. It was his pearl-shell. Màmeri, his wife, had scented danger, and the shell at least was safe, however it befell. Peese's glance followed his, and the handsome little captain laughed, and slapped the gloomy-faced and suspicious trader on the back with an air of *camaraderie*.

"My dear fellow, what an excessively suspicious woman your good Màmeri is! But do not be alarmed. I have not come here to do any business this time, but to land a passenger, and as soon as his traps are on the beach I'm off again to Maga Reva. Such are the exigencies, my dear Lupton, of a trading captain's life in the South Seas, I cannot even spare the time to go on shore with you and enjoy the hospitality of the good Màmeri and your two fair daughters. But come below with me and see my passenger." And he led the way to his cabin.

* * * * * * *

The passenger's appearance, so Lupton told me, "was enough to make a man's blood curdle", so ghastly pale and emaciated was he. He rose as Lupton entered and extended his hand.

"My friend here," said the worthy little Ishmael, bowing and caressing his long silky beard, "is, ah, hum, Mr. Brown. He is, as you will observe, my dear Lupton, in a somewhat weak state of health, and is in search of some retired spot where he may recuperate sufficiently—"

"Don't lie unnecessarily, sir."

Peese bowed affably and smiled, and the stranger addressed Lupton.

"My name is not Brown—'tis of no consequence what it is; but I am, indeed, as you see, in a bad way, with but a few months at most to live. Captain Peese, at my request, put into this lagoon. He has told me that the place is seldom visited by ships, and that the people do not care about strangers. Yet, have you, Mr. Lupton, any objections to my coming ashore here, and living out the rest of my life? I have trade goods sufficient for all requirements, and will in no way interfere with or become a charge upon you."

Lupton considered. His influence with the people of Mururea was such that he could easily overcome their objections to another white man landing; but he had lived so long apart from all white associations that he did not care about having the even monotony of his life disturbed. And then, he thought, it might be some queer game concocted between the sick man and the chattering little sea-hawk that sat beside him stroking and fondling his flowing beard. He was about to refuse when the sunken, eager eyes of "Mr. Brown" met his in an almost appealing look that disarmed him of all further suspicion.

"Very well, sir. The island is as free to you as to me. But, still, I could stop any one else from living here if I wished to do so. But you do look very ill, no mistake about that. And, then, you ain't going to trade against me! And I suppose you'll pass me your word that there isn't any dodge between you and the captain here to bone my shell and clear out?"

For answer the sick man opened a despatch-box that lay on the cabin table, and took from it a bag of money.

"This," he said, "is the sum I agreed to pay Captain Peese to land me on any island of my choice in the Paumotu Archipelago, and this unsigned order here is in his favour on the Maison Brander of Tahiti for a similar sum."

Signing the paper he pushed it with the money over to Peese, and then went on—

"I assure you, Mr. Lupton, that this is the only transaction I have ever had with Captain Peese. I came to him in Tahiti, hearing he was bound to the Paumotu Group. I had never heard of him before, and after to-day I will not, in all human probability, see him again."

"Perfectly correct, my dear sir," said Peese. "And now, as our business is finished, perhaps our dear friend, Lupton, will save me the trouble of lowering a boat by taking you ashore in his own, which is alongside."

Five minutes later and Lupton and the stranger were seated

in the boat.

"Good-bye, my dear Lupton, and *adios* my dear Mr. Brown. I shall ever remember our pleasant relations on board my humble little trading vessel," cried the renowned Peese, who, from former associations, had a way of drifting into the Spanish tongue—and prisons and fetters—which latter he once wore for many a weary day on the cruiser *Hernandez Pizarro* on his way to the gloomy prison of Manilla.

The boat had barely traversed half the distance to the shore ere the brigantine's anchor was hove-up and at her bows, and then Peese, with his usual cool assurance, beat her through the intricate passage and stood out into the long roll of the Pacific.

* * * * * * *

When Lupton, with his "walking bone bag," as he mentally called the stranger, entered his house, Màmeri, his bulky native wife, uttered an exclamation of pity, and placing a chair before him uttered the simple word of welcome *Iorana!* and the daughters, with wonder-lit star-like eyes, knelt beside their father's chair and whispered, "Who is he, Farani?"

And Lupton could only answer, "I don't know, and won't ask. Look to him well."

He never did ask. One afternoon nearly a year afterwards, as Lupton and Trenton, the supercargo of the *Marama*, sat on an old native *marae* at Arupahi, the Village of Four Houses, he told the strange story of his sick guest.

* * * * * * *

The stranger had at first wished to have a house built for himself, but Lupton's quiet place and the shy and reserved natures of his children made him change his intention and ask Lupton for a part of his house. It was given freely—where are there more generous-hearted men than these world-forgotten, isolated traders?—and here the Silent Man, as the people of

Mururea called him, lived out the few months of his life. That last deceptive stage of his insidious disease had given him a fictitious strength. On many occasions, accompanied by the trader's children, he would walk to the north point of the low-lying island, where the cloudy spume of the surge was thickest and where the hollow and resonant crust of the black reef was perforated with countless air-holes, through which the water hissed and roared, and shot high in the air, to fall again in misty spray.

And here, with dreamy eyes, he would sit under the shade of a clump of young cocoanuts, and watch the boil and tumble of the surf, whilst the children played with and chased each other about the clinking sand. Sometimes he would call them to him—Farani the boy, and Teremai and Lorani, the sweet-voiced and tender-eyed girls—and ask them to sing to him; and in their soft semi-Tahitian dialect they would sing the old songs that echoed in the ears of the desperate men of the *Bounty* that fatal dawn when, with bare-headed, defiant Bligh drifting astern in his boat, they headed back for Tahiti and death.

* * * * * * *

Four months had passed when one day the strange white man, with Lupton's children, returned to the village. As they passed in through the doorway with some merry chant upon their lips, they saw a native seated on the matted floor. He was a young man, with straight, handsome features, such as one may see any day in Eastern Polynesia, but the children, with terrified faces, shrank aside as they passed him and went to their father.

The pale face of the Silent Man turned inquiringly to Lupton, who smiled.

"'Tis Màmeri's teaching, you know. She is a Catholic from Magareva, and prays and tells her beads enough to work a whaleship's crew into heaven. But this man is a 'Soul Catcher', and if any one of us here got sick, Màmeri would let the faith she was reared in go to the wall and send for the 'Soul Catcher'.

He's a kind of an all-round prophet, wizard, and general wisdom merchant. Took over the soul-catching business from his father—runs in the family, you know."

"Ah!" said the Silent Man in his low, languid tones, looking at the native, who, the moment he had entered, had bent his eyes to the ground, "and in which of his manifold capacities has he come to see you, Lupton?"

Lupton hesitated a moment, then laughed.

"Well, sir, he says he wants to speak to you. Wants to *pahihi* (talk rot), I suppose. It's his trade, you know. I'd sling him out only that he isn't a bad sort of a fellow—and a bit mad—and Màmeri says he'll quit as soon as he has had his say."

"Let him talk," said the calm, quiet voice; "I like these people, and like to hear them talk—better than I would most white men."

* * * * * * *

Then, with his dark, dilated eyes moving from the pale face of the white man to that of Lupton, the native wizard and Seer of Unseen Things spoke. Then again his eyes sought the ground.

"What does he say?" queried Lupton's guest.

"D— rot," replied the trader, angrily.

"Tell me exactly, if you please. I feel interested."

"Well, he says that he was asleep in his house when his 'spirit voice' awoke him and said"—here Lupton paused and looked at his guest, and then, seeing the faint smile of amused interest on his melancholy features, resumed, in his rough, jocular way—"and said—the 'spirit voice,' you know—that your soul was struggling to get loose, and is going away from you to-night. And the long and short of it is that this young fellow here wants to know if you'll let him save it—keep you from dying, you know. Says he'll do the job for nothing, because you're a good man, and a friend to all the people of Mururea."

"Mr. Brown" put his thin hand across his mouth, and his eyes smiled at Lupton. Then some sudden, violent emotion stirred him, and he spoke with such quick and bitter energy that Lupton half rose from his seat in vague alarm.

"Tell him," he said—"that is, if the language expresses it— that my soul has been in hell these ten years, and its place filled with ruined hopes and black despair," and then he sank back on his couch of mats, and turned his face to the wall.

The Seer of Unseen Things, at a sign from the now angry Lupton, rose to his feet. As he passed the trader he whispered— "Be not angry with me, Farani; art not thou and all thy house dear to me, the Snarer of Souls and Keeper Away of Evil Things? And I can truly make a snare to save the soul of the Silent Man, if he so wishes it." The low, impassioned tones of the wizard's voice showed him to be under strong emotion, and Lupton, with smoothened brow, placed his hand on the native's chest in token of amity.

"Farani," said the wizard, "see'st thou these?" and he pointed to where, in the open doorway, two large white butterflies hovered and fluttered. They were a species but rarely seen in Mururea, and the natives had many curious superstitions regarding them.

"Aye," said the trader, "what of them?"

"Lo, they are the spirits that await the soul of him who sitteth in thy house. One is the soul of a woman, the other of a man; and their bodies are long ago dust in a far-off land. See, Farani, they hover and wait, wait, wait. To-morrow they will be gone, but then another may be with them."

Stopping at the doorway the tall native turned, and again his strange, full black eyes fixed upon the figure of Lupton's guest. Then slowly he untied from a circlet of polished pieces of pearl-shell strung together round his sinewy neck a little round leaf-wrapped bundle. And with quiet assured step he came and stood before the strange white man and extended his hand.

"Take it, O man, with the swift hand and the strong heart, for it is thine."

And then he passed slowly out.

Lupton could only see that as the outside wrappings of fala

leaves fell off they revealed a black substance, when Mr. Brown quickly placed it in the bosom of his shirt.

* * * * * * *

"And sure enough," continued Lupton, knocking the ashes from his pipe out upon the crumbling stones of the old marae, and speaking in, for him, strangely softened tones, "the poor chap did die that night, leastways at *kalaga moa* (cockcrow)," and then he refilled his pipe in silence, gazing the while away out to the North-West Point.

* * * * * * *

"What a curious story!" began the supercargo, after an interval of some minutes, when he saw that Lupton, usually one of the merriest-hearted wanderers that rove to and fro in Polynesia, seemed strangely silent and affected, and had turned his face from him.

He waited in silence till the trader chose to speak again.

Away to the westward, made purple by the sunset haze of the tropics, lay the ever-hovering spume-cloud of the reef of North-West Point—the loved haunt of Lupton's guest—and the muffled boom of the ceaseless surf deepened now and then as some mighty roller tumbled and crashed upon the flat ledges of blackened reef.

* * * * * * *

At last the trader turned again to the supercargo, almost restored to his usual equanimity. "I'm a pretty rough case, Mr—, and not much given to any kind of sentiment or squirming, but I would give half I'm worth to have him back again. He sort of got a pull on my feelin's the first time he ever spoke to me, and as the days went on, I took to him that much that if he'd a wanted to marry my little Teremai I'd have given her to him cheerful. Not that we ever done much talkin', but he'd sit night after night and make me talk, and when I'd spun a good hour's yarn he'd only say, 'Thank you, Lupton, good-night,' and give a smile all round to us, from old Màmeri to the youngest *tama*, and go to bed. And yet he did a thing that'll go hard agin' him, I fear."

"Ah," said Trenton, "and so he told you at the last—I mean his reason for coming to die at Mururea."

"No, he didn't. He only told me something; Peese told me the rest. And he laughed when he told me," and the dark-faced trader struck his hand on his knee. "Peese would laugh if he saw his mother crucified."

"Was Peese back here again, then?" inquired Trenton.

"Yes, two months ago. He hove-to outside, and came ashore in a canoe. Said he wanted to hear how his dear friend Brown was. He only stayed an hour, and then cleared out again."

"Did he die suddenly?" the supercargo asked, his mind still bent on Lupton's strange visitor.

"No. Just before daylight he called me to him—with my boy. He took the boy's hand and said he'd have been glad to have lived after all. He had been happy in a way with me and the children here in Mururea. Then he asked to see Teremai and Lorani. They both cried when they saw he was a goin'—all native-blooded people do that if they cares anything at all about a white man, and sees him dyin'."

"Have you any message, or anything to say in writin', sir?" I says to him.

He didn't answer at once, only took the girls' hands in his, and kisses each of 'em on the face, then he says, "No, Lupton, neither. But send the children away now. I want you to stay with me to the last—which will be soon."

Then he put his hand under his pillow, and took out a tiny little parcel, and held it in his closed hand.

* * * * * * *

"Mr. Lupton, I ask you before God to speak honestly. Have you, or have you not, ever heard of me, and why I came here to die, away from the eyes of men?"

"No, sir," I said. "Before God I know no more of you now than the day I first saw you!"

"Can you, then, tell me if the native soul-doctor who came here last night is a friend of Captain Peese? Did he see Peese when I landed here? Has he talked with him?"

"No. When you came here with Peese, the soul-seer was away at another island. And as for talking with him, how could he? Peese can't speak two words of Paumotu."

He closed his eyes a minute. Then he reached out his hand to me and said. "Look at that; what is it?"

It was the little black thing that the Man Who Sees Beyond gave him, and was a curious affair altogether. "You know what an *aitu taliga* is?" asked Lupton.

"Yes a 'devil's ear'—that's what the natives call fungus."

* * * * * * *

"Well," continued Lupton, "this was a piece of dried fungus, and yet it wasn't a piece of fungus. It was the exact shape of a human heart—just as I've seen a model of it made of wax. That hadn't been its natural shape, but the sides had been brought together and stitched with human hair—by the soul-doctor, of course. I looked at it curiously enough, and gave it back to him. His fingers closed round it again."

"What is it?" he says again.

"It's a model of a human heart," says I, "made of fungus."

"My God," he says, "how could he know?"

Then he didn't say any more, and in another half-hour or so he dies, quiet and gentlemanly like. I looked for the heart with Màmeri in the morning—it was gone.

* * * * * * *

"Well, we buried him. And now look here, Mr—, as sure as I believe there's a God over us, I believe that that native soul-catcher has dealings with the Devil. I had just stowed the poor chap in his coffin and was going to nail it down when the kanaka wizard came in, walks up to me, and says he wants to see the dead man's hand. Just to humour him I lifted off the sheet. The soul-catcher lifted the dead man's hands carefully, and then I'm d—d if he didn't lay that dried heart on his chest and press the hands down over it."

"What's that for?" says I.

"'Tis is the heart of the woman he slew in her sleep. Let it lie with him, so that there may be peace between them at last," and then he glides away without another word.

* * * * * * *

"I let it stay, not thinking much of it at the time. Well, as I was tellin' you, Peese came again. Seeing that I had all my people armed, I treated him well and we had a chat, and then I told him all about 'Mr. Brown's' death and the soul-saver and the dried heart. And then Peese laughs and gives me this news-paper cutting. I brought it with me to show you."

Trenton took the piece of paper and read.

* * * * * * *

"'Lester Mornington made his escape from the State prison at San Quentin (Cal.) last week, and is stated to be now on his way either to Honolulu or Tahiti. It has been ascertained that a vast sum of money has been disbursed in a very systematic manner during the last few weeks to effect his release. Although nearly eight years have elapsed since he committed his terrible crime, the atrocious nature of it will long be remembered. Young, wealthy, respected, and talented, he had been married but half a year when the whole of the Pacific Slope was startled with the intelligence that he had murdered his beautiful young wife, who had, he found, been disloyal to him.

"'Entering the bedroom he shot his sleeping wife through the temples, and then with a keen-edged knife had cut out her still-beating heart. This, enclosed in a small box, he took to the house of the man who had wronged him, and desired him to open it and look at the contents. He did so, and Mornington, barely giving him time to realise the tragedy, and that his perfidy was known, shot him twice, the wounds proving fatal next day. The murderer made good his escape to Mexico, only returning to California a month ago, when he was recognised (although disguised) and captured, and at the time of his escape was within two days of the time of his trial before Judge Crittenden.'"

* * * * * * *

"There's always a woman in these things," said Lupton, as the supercargo gave him back the slip. "Come on."

And he got down from his seat on the wall. "There's Màmeri calling us to *kaikai*—stewed pigeons. She's a bully old cook, worth her weight in Chile dollars."

A COLONIAL BANSHEE
by Fergus Hume

Born in England, Fergus Hume's (1859-1932) family emigrated to New Zealand when he was three. He went to school in Dunedin, studied law in Otago, and was called to the New Zealand bar in 1885, the same year he moved to Melbourne. Famously, he asked a Melbourne bookseller what kind of fiction was selling, and being told that the detective stories of Gaboriau were in vogue, he wrote *The Mystery of a Hansom Cab* (1886). Hume was paid £50 for the outright sale of copyright and subsequently claimed he never received another cent from the book, although it became a great bestseller in England.

He returned to England in 1888 where he continued to write, publishing over 130 books. Several supernatural tales appear in his rare collection *The Dancer in Red* (1906), including this story, a black comedy about a banshee with a broad Irish brogue trying to adjust to 'life' in the colonies.

The average person does not credit the existence of ghosts. He prides himself on believing nothing but his own eyes, and if these deceive him into beholding a genuine ghost he excuses their so doing on the score of hallucination. You cannot convince the average person that there is anything beyond the actualities of this world. Certainly he professes a vague belief in immortality, but his conception is so shadowy, that he never faces it with any degree of confidence. He classes such credulity in the category of 'things we are not meant to understand,' which hazy remark to his mind accounts for all matters in the way of religion. Take away this respectable theological view of the supernatural, and he scoffs at the idea of a phantom world.

I am an average person, a gross, fleshly, stolid, disbelieving St Thomas of the present generation, and in accordance with the fitness of things, should subscribe to the comfortable creed above set forth. I don't. Certainly I was once as materialistic as the average person could desire, but since I saw and conversed with a bona-fide spectre, I have modified my views regarding psychology. She was so convincing that she left me no option, but to believe. There was no getting round her insistence.

It was a female ghost of the Banshee type, and I met her under the most prosaic circumstances. Priding herself on the verity of her ghostly being she needed neither moated grange, nor blue lights to compass her appearance, in fact she somewhat scornfully dispensed with such old-time accessories, and simply convinced me by a short conversation that she was what she pretended to be. The most sceptical would have attested her authenticity on oath, as I do now, and I was the most sceptical of persons—once.

Her name was Bridget. She was an Irish emigrant. I was always under the impression that ghosts, like fairies, could not cross running water save in an egg-shell, but as I met Bridget in New Zealand she must have been an exception to this rule. She, however, made use of a ship in lieu of an egg-shell, and complained bitterly of having been forced to take such a voyage in the interests of her profession. It had a good deal to do with hatred and revenge—she was Irish you see. As the interview was not without interest, I hereby set forth a careful report of the same for the benefit of the Psychical Society. Unless Bridget was a liar, her remarks may throw some light on the mysteries of the spiritual world, and those desiring further information had better apply to the nearest ghost-raiser. I don't want to see her again. One such interview is enough for me.

Queenstown was the scene of this remarkable adventure. I am not referring to the Irish town of that name, but indicate thereby the pretty little sanatorium on Lake Wakitipu in New Zealand. It is amusing how very mixed one's geographical ideas become in the colonies. Here for instance you sail up the Maori christened lake of Wakitipu, stay at Queenstown, the name whereof smacks of Cork, and see from the top of an Antipodean Ben Lomond, the range of the Southern Alps which have nothing to do with Switzerland. It is a trifle confusing at first, but when one gets used to the oddity of the thing it is handy to have spots so widely apart within hailing distance. It is only in Otago that you can go from Queenstown to Ben Lomond in ten minutes.

I was staying in Queenstown for the benefit of my health. Something to do with the lungs I believe, but it is so long ago that I quite forget the exact disease from which I then suffered. Besides, it is not material to this story. It must have been my lungs, however, because the doctor made me climb the lofty peak of Ben Lomond daily for the benefit of them. There I was accustomed to sit for hours among the ice and snow watching the Earnslaw glacier flashing like a mirror in the sunlight, and the snowy range of the Southern Alps standing like fairy lacework against the clear blue of the sky.

When not climbing, I wandered about Queenstown and employed my spare time in dodging the goats. There were a great many goats about the place as the unfinished condition of the town rather favoured their existence. You walked down the main street and in two minutes found yourself among the hills—and goats. You surveyed the palatial hotel of the most approved 'Grand' type and turned round to behold a goat-populated section gaping between a red brick chapel and a corrugated iron store. Or you could arrive in five minutes at the outskirts of the town where the goats abounded among the white pebbles and sparse grass. Sometimes in such a place you met a man, more often a goat. I preferred the former myself as he sometimes invited me to have a drink whereas the goats were all distinctly hostile. They are the most distrustful animals I know.

In common with other visitors, I put up at Farmer's Hotel, where I was exceedingly comfortable. Every evening the steamer from Kingston arrived with fresh cargoes of tourists in search of health and scenery. They found both at Queenstown, which is the most romantic and salubrious place I am acquainted with. A trifle wild and lonely, but one must expect that sort of thing in a virgin solitude. I prefer it myself to an overcrowded play-ground like Switzerland. At Queenstown there is no promenade, no band, no theatre, no casino, no bathing. For this latter the waters of the lake are too cold owing to its being fed by glaciers. When I was there, the principal amusements were riding, driving, climbing, and visiting the cemetery. I didn't care about antici-pating my funeral myself, but many people went there, and told me they enjoyed it greatly. It was so restful. I did not contradict that statement.

Sometimes we drove to Arrowtown and saw the pack horses in long lines climb the track leading to the Macetown reefs. The sight put me wonderfully in mind of Ali Baba and the forty thieves, for in the distance they looked exactly like mules laden with booty. Leaving Arrowtown there was some excitement in regaining Queenstown by the Shotover Bridge. It was a narrow structure with shallow sides which sprang across a tremen-dous abyss in the depths of which swirled a rapid stream. The approach was down an incline, and for the moment it seemed doubtful whether the horses would hit the bull's eye of the bridge, or go over into the chasm. Our Jehu was a wonderful driver, and held his team well together, else I am afraid I would not now be writing this story. I never repeated the experiment. It is a mistake tempting Providence twice.

I conscientiously saw all there was to be seen in company with Nora and Michael. These two young scions of the Maguire family were staying at Farmer's with their ancestral Banshee. I don't think the landlord knew of this addition to his list of guests though Bridget did her best to let him know she was on the premises. She howled, whereon he called the innocent house dog bad names. I am afraid Bridget resented the mistake as a slur on her vocal abilities.

Nora told me all about herself and Michael. They had left Ireland some five years back and taken up their abode in Sydney on account of the brother's health. He, poor fellow, was far gone in consumption, and even the tropical climate of Australia could do but little for his disease. Indeed so much worse did he become, that Nora was advised to try the curative effect of New Zealand air, and for this reason the young couple were staying at Queenstown. When I arrived on the scene they had already been there for some weeks, but Michael did not seem to benefit much by the change. On the contrary, he daily grew weaker and looked more like a shadow than a man.

One day I found her seated by his side in front of the hotel. He had fallen asleep in the warm sunshine, and Nora was dividing her attention between a book and the invalid. When she saw me, however, she softly arose from her seat and joined me in my walk.

"Do you think he looks better to-day, Mr. Durham?" she asked, anxiously.

"Oh, yes!" I replied trying to comfort the poor girl. "I see a decided improvement. If anything can cure him, it will be this air."

"I am afraid the disease has gone too far," she answered with a sigh, "poor boy—to think of his coming all these miles only to find a grave."

"Don't think of such a thing, Miss Maguire."

"I cannot help thinking, Mr. Durham. Since we have been here, twice have I heard the Banshee."

"The what?"

"The Banshee! Did you not hear it wailing last night?"

"I certainly heard a dog howling at the moon."

"It was no dog," said Nora mysteriously, "it was our Banshee."

"My dear Miss Maguire, how can you believe in such rubbish?" I remonstrated in a vexed tone, "there are no such things as ghosts."

"So many people think, but I know there are ghosts."

"Have you ever seen one?"

"No! But I have heard the Banshee cry."

"Nonsense, my dear young lady. Your nerves are out of order with over anxiety. Consult a doctor at once."

"My nerves are not out of order," she replied, doggedly, "I am in perfect health, and thoroughly in earnest. Why, you admit yourself that you heard the cry."

"I heard a dog howling, Miss Maguire. How can you be so superstitious? This is the nineteenth century. Ghosts went out when gas came in."

I took no end of trouble to convince that girl. I promised to lend her a copy of *Abercrombie's Intellectual Powers*, where she would find that ghosts are all humbug. I narrated several instances which had come under my notice of supposititious spectres, which had been thoroughly explained away. A logical person would have been convinced by my arguments. But she was a woman, and therefore not logical. All my talk was on this account so much waste of breath.

"Every old woman in Ireland knows the Maguire Banshee," she said triumphantly, "for generations the death of one of our family has been predicted by its wailing. My father was killed in the hunting field, and I heard it myself crying round the house on the previous night. When my mother died the Banshee wailed three times, and—"

"I don't believe a word of it," I interrupted emphatically, "not one word. The Celtic nature is excitable and prone to super-stition. The howling of a dog, the whistling of the wind, the shrieking of a hinge would account for your Banshee. I am a man of sense, Miss Maguire; I laugh at the idea of such folly. Nothing would convince me of the existence of—"

At that moment I swear I felt a cold breath blowing against my cheek. The afternoon was warm and sunny with little or no wind, but for the moment the unexpected chill struck me dumb.

"What is the matter, Mr. Durham?" asked Nora, alarmed at the expression of my face, "are you ill?"

"Ill? No!" I replied, nervously, "but really you know, ha! ha! I believe you are infecting me with your superstition. I felt a cold breath on my face."

"It's—"

"Now don't say the Banshee, Miss Maguire, because I can't and won't believe such nonsense. My liver is probably out of order, and our conversation about spectres is apt to tell on the nerves. Let us talk of other things. Your family for instance?"

"There is not much to talk about there," said Nora, smiling at what she evidently considered a weak explanation, "my family at one time were rich and numerous. Now we are the only two left, and I don't think Job was poorer than we are!"

"Your estates?"

"Were all sold long ago. My father ran through all that remained of the property, and when he was killed we had nothing but a tumbled down castle, and a few acres of barren bog. We sold this and with the money came out to Sydney. There, through the influence of an old friend, Michael obtained a good Government appointment. Then his health gave way, and we were advised to come on here."

"And what do you intend to do when you go back?" I asked, revolving several philanthropic schemes in my mind.

"I don't know! It is questionable if we do go back. I feel certain that Michael will die here, and then I shall be left alone here with but a few shillings."

"Tut! tut! you must not talk like this," said I blowing my nose to conceal some natural emotion evoked by her story, "the colonial heart is kind! The colonial hand is open. As to your brother, hope for the best!"

"Mr. Durham!" said the girl solemnly, "twice have I heard the Banshee cry—the third time will be fatal."

It was no use arguing against such obstinacy, so I held my tongue, merely remarking that I hoped the Banshee wouldn't wail. Then as it was growing chilly Nora took her brother inside and left me to my own reflections. They were anything but pleasant, for I felt certain that this foolish belief in the Banshee would aid in killing Michael, as surely as would his disease.

To think of such superstition being prevalent nowadays. Here was a well educated young lady living among sensible people, yet she believed in such rubbish as ghosts. It has been proved over and over again that there are no such things. A heavy meal, a tired body, a fanciful mind, and lo, a ghost is created. Dyspepsia and hallucination are the parents of all goblins, which exist but in the imagination of their victims. People who see ghosts should write novels and thus work off their superfluous imagination. No wonder we need school boards, when sensible men can tolerate such humbug. Logic and Arithmetic will cure such morbidity. No student of the exact sciences ever saw a ghost.

The breath of cold air? Well I know that puzzled me, but it might be ascribed to the nerves. The cause I am convinced was internal not external. It was a still sunny day, yet I felt a sensation of cold air on my left cheek. Nerves, or liver only? I am inclined to put it down to the latter, knowing how I suffer from that organ. A liver will make a man believe anything. Perhaps my ghostly interview was the result of a disordered liver, but no—Bridget was too convincing. You can't explain away actualities and though Bridget wasn't exactly an actuality, I certainly can't explain her away.

After that eminently unsatisfactory conversation with Miss Maguire I took a sharp walk to shake the cobwebs out of my brain. Ghost-talk does engender cobwebs in a man's brain, and if you leave them there nobody knows what will happen—but I think Colney Hatch has a good deal to do with the future. Not caring to tend in that direction I walked those ghostly figments out of my memory and sat on a hill top admiring the scenery. The sun was setting and the white peaks were very rosy with his light. It was very beautiful, but very chilly, so not anxious to trouble my lungs with inflammation I returned to the hotel and dinner.

After the meal I went up to my room to put on warmer clothes, and there took place that remarkable visitation of which

I speak. The bedroom was quite dark when I entered, and in place of lighting the candle I stood at the window staring at the wonderful white world without. A stream of moonbeams lay across the floor, and beyond the distant peak flashed the moon herself glimmering like a ghost. The comparison put me in mind of Nora's absurd Banshee story, and the memory made me laugh. To my surprise the laugh was repeated in a thin starved echo. I turned round at the sound and saw a woman standing near the door. I am a modest young man, and the intrusion annoyed me.

"Madame," I said in a dignified tone, "you have mistaken the room. How did you enter?"

"By the keyhole!"

Heavens! what a voice. It was as thin as a whistle. And then she alluded to an entrance by the keyhole. I began to feel alarmed and passed my hand across my eyes to vanish the hallucination.

"Liver!" said I, seeing the figure still there.

"Divil a bit," retorted the lady who seemed a cloudy sort of person. "I'm the Maguire Banshee."

I don't like practical jokes, and thinking Nora was playing one on me ventured to remonstrate. Before I could say a word the figure glided, or rather floated into the stream of moonlight which lay across the floor. Then I saw it was no joke—it was no liver—it was a ghost!

A merciful baldness prevented my hair standing on end, but my flesh creeped, and I shook as though I had the ague. This apparition upset all my preconceived ideas, and reduced me to a sort of moral pulp. I felt a cowardly inclination to run away. The Banshee was between me and the door, and as the window was twenty feet from the ground I could hardly leave that way without becoming a ghost myself. I was therefore compelled to remain, and didn't like the idea.

"Why don't ye offer me a sate?" said the Banshee in an irritable tone, "is it insultin' me ye're afther doin'?"

I pushed forward a seat in great trepidation and she settled on it. I can't say she sat down for she didn't, but simply subsided thereon, like a cloud on a mountain-top. The cold beams of the moon shone full on her face, and the sight did not tend to steady my nerves. I don't want to see another face like it.

It was a grey haggard countenance framed in wild elf locks of tangled red hair. Her mouth was all drawn to one side, and in her eyes dwelt a look of horror. Round her neck hung a fragment of rough rope, and from shoulders to heels streamed a cloudy white robe. The whole appearance of this being was vague and indistinct, the face being the only portion I could see with any degree of clearness. Sitting there in the chilly light, with her filmy dress undulating round her thin form, and her baleful eyes glaring from amid her tangled red hair she was a fearsome object to behold. I shivered and shook and turned away my eyes, but something I knew not what—ever compelled me to look at her again.

I don't think she was a lady Banshee. Her language was too free, and her manners left much to be desired. Still she behaved in a very affable manner for her, and succeeded to a certain extent in dispelling my fear, though I was anything but comfortable during the interview. She spoke throughout in a hoarse broken voice, alternating with a shrill whistling sound. Constant howling had evidently injured her vocal organs.

"So you don't believe in my existence," she said, eyeing me in a malevolent manner.

I began to protest, but she cut me short with a whistling sniff and shifted her mouth to the other side of her face.

"No deceit av ye plase. Didn't ye say oi was an hallucination, ye brutal Saxon?"

"You may be now for all I know," I replied, resenting her rudeness.

She stretched out her arm which elongated itself like a marine telescope, and without moving from her seat clutched me by the wrist with chilly fingers. So cold was her touch that it burnt like fire, and I involuntarily shrieked with pain.

"Whist! ye spalpeen!" she said, contracting her arm again. "Ye'll athtracth attinshun and me reputashun u'll suffer if oi'm discovered in a jintleman's slapin' room.'"

"In that case you had better go away," I suggested, anxious to rid myself of this nightmare.

"Divil a bit," she rejoined, composedly. "Oi've a mind to convarse wid ye about thim Maguires."

"Why can't you leave them alone? It's impossible for a sick man to get sleep while you howl around the house like an insane hurricane."

"Wud ye have me neglect me thrade," said the Banshee, indignantly. "'Tis me juty to wail worse luck. An' as to slapin', Mick Maguire 'ull slape sound enough one av' these days, nivir fear."

"Will he die?"

"Av' coorse he'll die. Haven't oi criedth twice an' ut'll be the third toime this night. It's not wastin' me breath oi am."

"Who are you?"

"Oi'm Bridget."

I laughed at the unsuitability of the name, whereupon the Banshee looked at me fiercely.

"Fwhat's the matter wid the name?"

"It's like a servant girl's."

"An' why not? Wasn't oi that same, sorr. Four hundher years ago oi sarved King Patsey Maguire av' Ulster, the ancister av' the prisint family no less."

"But how did you become a Banshee?"

"Och whirra! whirra! willaloo!" she moaned, rocking herself to and fro, "wasn't oi the pride av' Ulster an' didn't King Maguire hang me bekaze oi'd nivir give up Taddy Donovan?"

"Did he want to marry you himself?"

"How shuld oi know! Maybe he didn't care about Taddy liftin' thim Kerry cows. An' as Taddy wasn't to be tuk, he hanged me, bad luck to him."

"Did that hanging turn you into a Banshee?"

"D'y' see this rope, sorr?" she said touching the fragment, "whin oi died oi tuk the bit wid me as a memory an' swore to haunt thim Maguires for everlastin' till they all died. There's only two now. Whin Mick goes there'ull only be wan. Whin she dies me juty 'ull be ended for ivir."

"But you can't kill them."

"Av' coorse not, but I can warn thim of their sorrows. Oi've croied at their wakes for the last four hundher year in Ould Ireland."

"Why did you come out here?"

"Bekase thim two came. When a Banshee's attached to wan family she has to hould on to thim like the divil. Where they go, she goes, so oi had to imigrate wid the Maguires, bad cess to thim."

"You don't like the colonies?"

"Divil a bit. Oi've not met a single ghost of any consequence here. There's no ruins to haunt an' hathens like yoursilf don't belave in us."

"If you find things so unpleasant, why don't you go back to Ireland?"

"Howshuld oi know? Whin Nora goes back oi'll go back, but where she is I aim. Mick's dying so me only reckinin' on Nora. Maybe she'll die too though," added the Banshee, comfortably, "and thin I can return to me round tower."

"What Round Tower?"

"County Down no less. Me family sate. Once 'twas King Maguire's, now 'tis mine. Oi sit on it in the cove av' the evenin' an' houl."

"Pleasant for your neighbours."

"Iviry one to his juty," replied the Banshee indifferently, "'tis mine to howl an' howl I do."

"Yes! I've heard you!"

"An' sid it was the dog. Oh, oi heard your contimptuous spache."

"Now look here!"

"Oi want nane av' your bullyin' av' you plase. Respict age. Oi'm four hundher year ould."

"Yes! you look it!"

"An' so'd you if ye'd to pass nights howlin' in the open air.

It's sorry oi am that I let ye see a rale live Banshee."

"You're hardly alive. However, I apologise for hurting your feelings. I'm not accustomed to entertain Banshees."

"Maybe that's true. No Saxon has a Banshee."

"And no colony either."

"Wait a few hundred years, sorr. Ye want ruins and family sacrats first. Thin the ghosts 'ull come, but not in your toime."

"I'm not sorry! I don't like ghosts!"

"Maybe ye don't belave in them," said the Banshee, tauntingly, "to-morrow ye'll say 'oive bin dramin'."

"It's not unlikely!"

"Oi'd like to lave some token av' me visit," she said in a meditative tone, "couldn't I lave five black finger marks on your wrist?"

"No thank you," I replied, shrinking back.

"Or turn your hair white?" she added, persuasively.

"Even you couldn't do that. I'm bald!"

"Ah thin! I'll lave the mark of a gory hand on your cranium."

"I'm sure you won't. What's the matter?"

For the Banshee had suddenly shot up as high as the roof.

"Whist!" she said shrilly. "Oi hear his breath failin'."

"Whose breath?"

"Michael's. The cowld sweat is on his brow an' the rattle is in his throat—it's not long he'll live anyhow. I must wail—an' wail. Whirro!"

"Let the man die in peace," I urged anxiously.

"Fwhat? wan av' thim Maguires? Sorra a bit. Ye'll hear me wailin' soon,"

"But—"

"Whist oi tell ye! whist. Oi's goin'. 'Tis not Banshees ye'll scoff at agin oi'm thinkin'."

She spread herself through the room in a cold white mist, and I shrank terrified against the wall. In the white shadow I could see the glare of her fiery eyes like two danger signals. The fog gradually floated out through the open window and the eyes vanished. Then I heard a whistle outside, which I presume was

Bridget's way of saying good-bye. After that I went for some brandy.

The Banshee certainly succeeded in curing my scepticism regarding ghosts. I don't want any further proof that they exist after seeing her. She impressed herself too strongly on my memory. Next time I see an Irish ghost, I would like a dozen or so of my friends to be present at the interview. Now when I hear the average person scoffing at the idea of spectres, as I used to do, I tell him my experience. As a rule he doesn't believe me. Perhaps you can read this story and don't believe it either. But it's true for all that.

When I had succeeded in pulling myself together—no easy task—I hurried at once to Michael's bedroom, but was met at the door by Nora who told me he was asleep. Unwilling to alarm her by a description of the Banshee's visit, I held my peace and went out into the open air. Lighting a cigar, for I thought a smoke would soothe my nerves, I strolled up and down in front of the hotel. In a few minutes a young American who was staying there joined me, and though as a rule I found him a nuisance, yet on this occasion I was not ill-pleased with his company.

It was a bright moonlight night, and far in the distance arose the serrated peaks of the mountains. The iron roofs of the houses around glittered like frosted silver in the light, and here and there on the sullen lake glinted a flake of moonfire. All was wonderfully beautiful and absolutely still. Suddenly there sounded a lone, low wail which shivered pitifully through the air, and died away among the mountains. Then a second, closely followed by a third. I knew what that triple cry meant and stopped short in my walk.

"Dog howling, I guess," said the young American, carelessly.

I heard a whistling sniff near me and turned to see the Banshee glaring at the young man. To him she was invisible, and her speech inaudible.

"A dog howlin'," she said, angrily, "an' I nivir wailed so iligantly before."

"Is he dead?" I asked, breathlessly.

"As a door nail," replied the Banshee and vanished.

"Is who dead?" asked the American thinking I had spoken to him, "that young Irish fellow?—Hark, what is that?"

Another cry, but this time the utterance of a human throat. I hastened towards the hotel, and arrived at the door to meet Nora on the threshold.

"Did you hear it?" she gasped, throwing herself into my arms.

"Yes, I heard it!"

"I told you the third time. Michael is dead."

After that she fainted clean away, which action caused me but little surprise. I was pretty near collapsing myself.

* * * * * * *

Poor Michael was duly buried in the little cemetery under the shadow of the mighty hill. I attended the funeral, did my best to comfort Nora, and in the end supplied her with money to return to her Sydney friends. I presume the Banshee went with her, but of this I am not certain. Sometimes I heard from Nora in the months which followed her brother's death. When I was at Te Aroha in the North Island last Christmas she wrote and told me she was married and had settled for good in Sydney.

This letter set me thinking about the Banshee. By her own showing she could not leave Nora until she died, so as Nora had decided to stay in Australia, I presume, Bridget would also have to remain. From what I heard, Nora is not likely to die for some time so I am afraid Bridget must be very discontented. Here she has no ghostly friends, no Round Tower, and as yet no reason for wailing, so altogether she must be in a bad way.

One consolation she must have. She is the only Banshee in the colonies. None other is genuine.

A STRANGE EXPERIENCE

by A. F. Basset Hull

The son of a coroner and later clerk of the House of Assembly in Tasmania, Arthur Francis Basset Hull (1862-1945) was born in Hobart on 10 Oct 1862. He worked as a public servant for most of his life, firstly in the registry of the Tasmanian Supreme Court, and later, in Sydney, at the General Post Office and the Department of Mines.

Throughout the 1880s, while he was Secretary and Treasurer of the Orpheus Club, he sang and acted in plays and musicals. Hull was three times married, and was once declared bankrupt after being sued for breach of promise of marriage. He wrote fiction, poetry, and short stories, and enjoyed an international reputation in ornithology, natural history and philately. In 1936, he was awarded an MBE for his services to the Royal Zoological Society of New South Wales and the Australian Museum. Hull produced one volume of short stories, *A Strange Experience and Other Stories for Christmas*, published in 1888 by the unfortunately named Propsting and Cockhead.

I will tell you the whole story just as it happened, and I think you will agree with me that there are some occurrences which cannot be explained by any of the hard and fast rules laid down by science for the solution of the apparently mysterious manifestations which occasionally present themselves. Such occurrences may be—in fact, I own they are—somewhat infrequent, but, nevertheless, one will sometimes crop up that defies solution, even by the most enlightened minds of the time. Such a case is the one I am about to relate.

In the summer of the year 1877 a man was condemned to be hanged for having deliberately murdered his wife, to whom he had only been married a few months. I do not define the scene of my story, as the painful circumstances of the case are, even now, too fresh in the minds of many for undue publicity. The names of the actors involved in this tragedy are fictitious ones, given in order the more effectually to conceal the real identity of the unfortunate criminal.

With this preliminary explanation, I shall now proceed to unfold to you all the facts and circumstances of an experience of so awful a nature that now, while writing, I can still feel the effects of the shattering blow given to my system by the unparalleled events of a few days.

As deputy-sheriff it was part of my duty during the temporary absence of one of the clerks of the court to be present at the particular sittings of the Criminal Court at which Robert Caton was tried for the murder of his wife.

Though it happened more than ten years ago, it seems but yesterday that I sat immediately beneath the judge's bench at my desk, which was covered with black cloth and littered with record books, papers, and parchment informations, and went through my duties during the trial of three or four minor cases of perjury and burglary, which were duly disposed of, till, with a somewhat greater degree of interest than usual, I took up an information called Robert Caton, and read that "he, Robert Caton, on the Sixth day of October, in the year of our Lord One thousand eight hundred and seventy seven, feloniously, wilfully, and of his malice aforethought, did kill and murder one Grace Caton."

I put down the document, and for the first time glanced at the prisoner whilst waiting for his plea. A man about forty-two years of age, well built, and evidently in the prime of life; hardly a handsome man, but still with a striking and decidedly pleasing face; he wore a short naval beard, and his close-cropped hair was plentifully silvered with grey. But the most remarkable feature consisted of his eyes, which were of a very deep blue, with a lighter blue ring surrounding the pupil, and although they were at the moment directed above my head towards the judge, I could see that his gaze was calm, steadfast, and searching in the extreme—the sort of gaze one could feel even though one's back were turned towards him.

"Not guilty," he said, in a perfectly quiet and collected manner, "to the charge of murder—it was justifiable homicide."

I hastily recorded his plea on the back of the information, and the case proceeded.

It was a very simple case; the evidence, beyond his own confession that he had committed what he was pleased to style a "justifiable homicide," was clear enough for the jury to bring in a verdict of guilty without leaving the box. His Honour had summed up in a very few words, and the verdict being given, he addressed the prisoner in the usual manner, commenting upon the awful nature of the crime, and asked him if he had anything to say before sentence was passed upon him.

It was at that moment that the first intimation of my strange experience—although at the instant I was unaware that it was such—was given me.

During the pause that followed the judge's remarks, and while the prisoner was evidently preparing to reply, his strange eyes fell upon mine, and, in a second, such a full appreciation of his position flashed upon me, that I seemed to feel myself in the prisoner's place, grasping the railing of the dock, and gazing into the stern face of the judge. I say *seemed*, for the feeling lasted but an instant, and I was once more calmly arranging my papers at my desk, but I now know only too well that it was no seeming, but a stern reality. But I am anticipating somewhat.

"The woman I called my wife proved unfaithful to her vows, so I killed her."

The prisoner made this speech in a straightforward, matter-of-fact way, as if he were stating the most natural punishment of an ordinary offence, and then waited for sentence. The judge put on the black cap, and standing up, said: "Robert Caton, you have been found guilty of the crime of murder, and the circumstances of your crime are such that I cannot hold out to you the slightest hope of mercy. I therefore sentence you that you be taken hence to the place from whence you came, and that you be taken thence, to the place of execution and be there hanged by the neck until your body is dead, and may God have mercy on your soul."

Though most of the spectators in Court could scarcely restrain a shudder of horror, the prisoner accepted his sentence with a calmness which surprised even me, accustomed as I was to the varied emotions exhibited by different criminals.

Some days after the sittings at which Caton had been convicted, seated in my office, I was reading over a letter which ran as follows:—

> Having this day considered in Executive Council the case of Robert Caton, who was on the 6th instant convicted of the wilful murder of his wife, and sentenced to death, I have decided not to interfere with the execution of the sentence.
>
> I have the honour to be, etc.,
>
> (Signed)——————— , Governor.
>
> His Honour the Chief Justice.

Attached to this letter was the small parchment form, the blanks filled in with pen and ink, which stated that "at a session of Oyer and Terminer and general gaol delivery held at—; Robert Caton, convicted of murder, was sentenced to death" and thereby delivered over "the said Robert Caton to the sheriff, to be hanged by the neck until his body was dead."

That, of course, meant that I, as deputy sheriff, was to superintend the judicial murder of this man. Well, there was nothing for it but to set about making the preparations.

The hangman was duly interviewed, and it was arranged that on the last stroke of the hour of eight from the gaol clock I was to take out my watch, and on my snapping the case to, the bolt was to be drawn; a very simple arrangement, and a slight variation from the usual dropping of the handkerchief with which I was wont to make the fatal signal.

The afternoon before the execution was to take place I had been writing out the orders of admission for the reporters and one or two persons who had a morbid desire to "see a man die in his shoes," when a gaol messenger brought me a request from the condemned man that I would visit him before the morrow. This being no very unusual request, I signified my readiness to see the prisoner about eight o'clock that evening, just twelve hours before the time fixed for his execution.

And yet the moment the messenger was gone, I felt an unaccountable dread of the coming interview stealing over me, and regretted strongly having acceded to the prisoner's request, but as I had given my word there was no help for it. All the rest of the afternoon, however, a weight of some impending trouble seemed to hang over me and considerably interfered with the performance of my official routine duties.

Since the day of the trial that momentary feeling of identity with the prisoner—that flash of consciousness that I was actually occupying his position, standing in the dock, and viewing the scene from his point of observation—had haunted me with a persistency that no effort of mine could restrain within bounds, and now, as I looked forward to the meeting with the man with whom I had evidently some strange mesmeric sympathy, this overhanging weight hourly increased, until shortly before eight o'clock, when I left home to visit the gaol, my mind was strung to such a degree of nervous tension that I was a very fit subject for any mesmeric influences which might be brought to bear upon me.

Shortly before eight—and, it being summer, it was still quite light out of doors—I obtained admittance to the gaol, and preceded by the warder, entered the condemned cell.

Caton was sitting at a small table, leaning with his head in his hands, gazing fixedly at the long candle, just lighted, and apparently making a mental calculation as to which would last the longest—himself or the candle.

He did not look up as I entered, but saying to the warder, "Leave us, please," he motioned me to take a seat on the other chair, which, with the table and stretcher, formed the only furniture of the cell.

The moment I was seated, without the slightest preliminary remark or introductory explanation, he rushed into a full and particular account of the crime for which he had been condemned to death, in the following words:—

"As you heard me state in court, I killed my wife because she had proved unfaithful—untrue to her vows before we had been married six months. I will tell you the whole circumstances of the case, calmly and dispassionately, just as they happened, and will leave you to judge whether you would not have acted in precisely the same manner under the same conditions.

"I had lately removed to the suburban cottage where the event happened, and was in the habit of going into business in the city every day, and occasionally, when the press of work detained me late at my office, staying over night and not returning until the next evening.

"I own it was unguarded on my part to leave my newly-made wife so much alone, for she was naturally of a very friendly disposition and fond of society, but I had few personal friends, and so far as I knew she had none; and we had not been long enough in the neighbourhood to become acquainted with the surrounding families. As for myself, I care little about so-called friends—mere acquaintances who generally have some interested motive in calling upon you; who hope in some way to reap benefits from their acquaintanceship with you—so I took very little pains to ingratiate myself with my neighbours, and supplying my wife with plenty of books to read, and music with which to occupy herself during my unavoidable absences, considered that I did my duty towards her; and if she was not satisfied, never did she, by word or sign, give me the slightest cause to suppose that she was otherwise than perfectly happy.

"But enough of this explanation—let me come to the point of my narration.

"One night I unexpectedly returned about eleven o'clock. I had informed my wife that I should be away until the following evening, but the business being less pressing than had at first seemed probable, I was free comparatively early, and returning found a stranger with her under circumstances which left no room for doubt as to her unfaithfulness.

"He was a youth—almost a boy—with a pretty face, a fair, curling moustache, a soft, lisping voice, a gentlemanly manner and appearance, and was very well dressed."

During the whole of this narration, Caton had remained leaning with his elbows on the table and looking straight before him. Never once had he even glanced in my direction, but had quietly proceeded with his story as if he were in reality addressing the candle and not myself. No sign of passion or anger had up to that time shown itself on his countenance. Continuing, he said:—

"You are no doubt surprised at my present calmness in relating this, but I was equally calm during the actual occurrence, and you may perhaps ask why. It was because I seemed to have *gone through it all before*, or rather to have an intuitive preconception of every word to be spoken; of every movement to be made. I could almost have detailed each circumstance that was to happen in anticipation. This feeling added an air of unreality to the whole affair, which perhaps increased my calm and apparently indifferent attitude. To proceed:

"The stranger began to stammer out some apology—to apologise to *me* for the (as he termed it) unfortunate position in which my wife was placed, and begged me not to visit it too hardly upon her, as he was entirely to blame.

"*He* was to blame! Man!" said Caton, clenching the broad flat candlestick in his hands as if it were the object to which he was speaking, and showing for the first time any sign of emotion, "I own nine-tenths of such cases are solely owing to the inherent fault of the woman; the man is but a poor silly fly seduced into the web by the woman. I maintain the opinion, and"—he added with grim humour—"I regret that it is for such a short period that I am able to maintain it; that a woman must go a long way in giving a man unmistakable encouragement before he will attempt to place himself in such a position towards her as this youth evidently held with respect to the woman whom I had so trustingly called my wife.

"I handed the boy his hat and gloves, showed him to the door, and stood there listening to his disjointed apologies and entreaties for my wife's pardon, and finally to what he evidently intended as a burst of heartfelt contrition for his part in the unfortunate affair. I heard him patiently through, feeling only a contemptuous indifference for his apologies, his entreaties, and his regrets; until at last, raising his hat, he passed out of the gate and down the long, deserted road, lying white in the moonlight of that late hour.

"I stood with the half-opened door in my hand for some time, and slowly went over in my mind all the past circumstances connected with my first meeting with the perjured creature who was doubtless apprehensively awaiting my return. The pictures rose up before my mind, one by one, of all our early love and courtship, and finally of the day when, implicitly trusting in her apparent innocence and truth, I had married her and brought her to my home.

"My faith in her had been of such a blind, trusting character, that the shock of this sudden proof of her baseness turned all my feelings to those of the most bitter hatred, a hatred which was solely directed upon her, and which so entirely occupied my thoughts that it left nothing but a contemptuous indifference for the partner of her wickedness.

"'Unpleasantness' the youth had termed the occurrences of the night. Yes, but the most unpleasant duty had yet to be performed.

"I returned to my wife's room. The lamp was burning brightly on the table, and she was lying on the bed, her hands clasped behind her head, and the fair hair, of which I had been so fond, was tossed negligently over the pillow, and over her beautiful false lips a mocking and contemptuous smile was playing.

"I stood looking at her for a few moments, and even in the fullness of my supreme hatred for her baseness I could not help admiring the faultless contour of her neck and arms, and the marble whiteness of her bosom, half hidden by the counterpane.

"'Well,' she said, looking at me coolly with slightly raised eyebrows. 'Well?'

"I did not vouchsafe any reply to her interrogation, and she continued: 'It is all your own fault, you know; you should not have left me so much alone. I had to find some amusement, and poor Fred was the best that offered. By the way, what have you done with the dear boy? I hope you haven't killed him, you look murderous,' and she laughed mockingly.

"Still I did not reply, but clenched my hand over a heavy, brass-handled riding-whip I carried, and advancing to the bed-side struck that false smile from her lips and eyes with one blow that forced the brazen handle into her sin-clouded brain.

"Look!" and he grasped me violently by the shoulder, and for the first time, turning his gaze full into my eyes, "do you not see her fair, cursed face?"

And even as he spoke there arose before me a misty vision of a daintily furnished room and on a snowy white bed lay a woman, whose beautiful forehead was gashed by a hideous wound, from which a dull red stream had flowed, staining the face as if she had shed tears of blood; but on the red lips—redder even than the blood—a mocking curve was still discernible, though the blue-veined lids were hiding the answering smile of the eyes from my sight. *And between me and the vision I could see the long gaol candle, which had hitherto been on the table, far to my left hand.* I had not moved, and yet I was viewing the ghastly picture from the place occupied by the condemned man. I gave a sudden start at this discovery, and like a flash the vision vanished, and once more the candle stood away to my left!

Caton was looking at me with a strange smile. "You can go home, now," he said, "I must take a little rest before to-morrow's excitement."

In a semi-dazed state I went home and sat at my open window all through the long summer night, pondering over the strange interview with the criminal and the stranger vision which I had seen.

Undoubtedly I had viewed that scene of the murder from the place where Caton was sitting. I myself was viewing with *his* eyes, and from his point of observation, the ghastly scene that was photographed with such fearful distinctness on his brain

And now there burst upon me a vivid recollection of that day of the trial, and the momentary consciousness of occupying the prisoner's dock just immediately before the passing of the sentence; the instantaneous mental leap, as it were, from my desk below the judge to the position in which I was facing him; and then did I remember that the prisoner had at that very moment looked directly at me for the first time during his trial. The question then that forced itself upon me was, by what power had he so completely absorbed my personal individuality—my inner consciousness—into his physical body? And also, had there been any reciprocal exchange, did his spiritual being enter my body after mine had dispossessed his of its abode and entered into temporary possession?

I had frequently been present at the exhibition of the powers of different mesmerists, and in looking at the helpless subjects who had performed all kinds of little actions obediently to the will of the mesmerist, while in a kind of trance, had noted that in all cases the subjects on recovery had not the slightest recollection of the occurrences which took place during the period of their being under the influence. I had then come to the conclusion that the body of the subject was actually dispossessed of its personal individuality or consciousness, and was for a time occupied by a portion of the more powerful will of the mesmerist. But this experience of mine, though apparently swayed by somewhat similar laws, yet seemed to go farther; for my consciousness, for the moment driven out of its own habitation by some occult intense sympathy with that of the unfortunate man at once took possession of his body—saw things with his eyes, and while for the moment understanding and appreciating the predominant thoughts in his brain, yet retained sufficient of its own individuality to acquire and bring away with it a permanent recollection of its visit to the strange bodily envelope.

This sympathy being of such an intense nature must necessarily, I concluded, be reciprocal, and consequently during my temporary occupation of Caton's body, my deserted person was filled by the spiritual being of a criminal!

Trying to solve this psychological enigma occupied me until the first yellow light of dawn appeared; and with the morning came the recollection of the unpleasant duty which I had to perform in a few hours.

I threw myself on the outside of my bed and dozed away the time till seven o'clock, when I gave myself a hasty shaking together, and after a cooling plunge in the bath, made my way to the gaol, meeting the warder and chaplain at the door of the condemned cell.

But now, on the very threshold, such a feeling of apprehensive terror came over me that for the moment I was utterly unable to face the prisoner, so, standing in the passage outside, I directed the warder and chaplain to enter and prepare the man for the end.

While there I heard Caton chatting away cheerfully with the Rev. Mr. Francis, but skilfully and most persistently avoiding the slightest reference to religious subjects; though the clergyman constantly returned to the charge and earnestly urged him to think, if only for a moment, of the awful nearness of his end.

But the prisoner merely laughed, apparently with an assumption of amused indifference, and addressing the hangman, asked if his share of the preparations outside had been very heavy, as he looked as if he had been up all night at the work!

At a few minutes before the appointed hour they came out, but without looking at Caton I allowed the others to precede me, and then feeling a little safer when out of the range of Caton's eyes, followed the melancholy procession—melancholy only so far as the attendant officers were concerned—for the principal figure was apparently in the highest spirits, and jokingly asked the hangman if his rope was up to twelve stone!

Arrived at the gallows, the clergyman completed his reading of the service for the dead, and I took my place with the officers, reporters, and other spectators, but all the while persistently kept my face turned away from the prisoner, as I felt a nameless dread of meeting his gaze.

The hangman was proceeding to adjust the black cap, and I was feeling for my watch in order to give the signal agreed upon, all the while struggling against an almost irresistible impulse to look at the prisoner.

The time was passing. Surely the cap must be fixed, I thought, and with the thought I involuntarily glanced up, only to see that something had delayed the hangman's movements—the black cap was only just descending over those blue eyes, when in an instant they met mine with a sudden, flashing glance, *and I was standing on the fatal drop, and the opaque black cloth was shutting out the last view of earth and heaven from my sight!*

The whole horror of the situation burst upon me in one dread shock, and the gaol clock rang out the first stroke of the hour.

Oh, the awful terror of that moment! For it was but a moment, though each of the eight solemn strokes seemed to occupy an age in dying away and making place for the next. Though my body seemed paralysed for the time, my mind was like a whirling panorama of all the chief events of my past life; but, at the last stroke thoughts of the past suddenly ceased, and the terrible present came before me with a redoubled sense of its awfulness. I tried to cry out, but

> 'the lips were cracked, and the jaws were dry
> with the thirst that only in death should die,'

and nothing but an inarticulate murmur escaped me.

With a tension painful in its prolonged strain I then listened for the fatal snap of the watch case. Ah! it came, and simultaneously with it, a slight preliminary click preceded the slipping of the bolt, and with a shuddering start I fell, till a sharp jerk arrested further progress; and then one piercing shaft of agony shot through the brain, followed by a suffocating rush of blood that seemed to flood my consciousness into sudden oblivion.

* * * * * * *

It seemed but a few moments after, that I found myself lying on the cold stones of the gaol yard, with the doctor kneeling over me, holding a glass of brandy and water to my lips, and the other spectators looking on from a little distance. When I had sufficiently recovered to sit up, the doctor remarked—"I thought you had more nerve than that, old man. To think of you fainting at a hanging! Why, you must have assisted at half a dozen before and ought to be used to it by this time. Take my advice and go home to bed; you want a little rest and food."

I went home as he directed, and never since then have I taken my place by those gallows to give the signal which is to launch a fellow creature into eternity, without turning sick with the thought of the time when my own hands, guided by a will not my own, launched my spirit, contained in the body of another, to suffer all the pangs of a momentary death.

A BUSHMAN'S STORY

by Frances Faucett

'A Bushman's Story' survives in a slender, privately printed volume that was published in Sydney in 1886. The author was twenty years old at the time. She attended the Kincoppal-Rose Bay School of The Sacred Heart for girls in Sydney between 1882 and 1886, and was a gifted student, winning the prize for Christian Doctrine and also for Grammar and Composition. Her father was a Justice of the Supreme Court of New South Wales, and her mother died giving birth to her in 1866. There is a note in the school archive that she married and became Mrs. Moran. I have been unable to find out anything more about her and it may be that she published nothing else. The date "December 1882" is appended to the story, and this may have been when the story was written (when Frances was sixteen years old!)—there is a tradition at the school of readings and presentations to mark the end of the school year.

Cobb's Coach had broken down. Only those who have experienced a like calamity can understand the full significance of those words of direful import. The breaking-down of the Mail, generally—in fact almost without exception—implies several hours' improvised camping out, and a long period of waiting and watching for the unhappy passengers. It is rare good fortune if they are delivered from their unhappy position while it is yet daylight; but as Cobb's coaches have a happy facility for disabling themselves at midnight, or there-abouts, this is rarely the case. In the present instance, the coach had "come to a smash" between Nymagee and Narrandera—that is, about one hundred miles from either township—at the pleasing and seasonable hour of nine p.m. on Christmas Eve. A messenger had been despatched to Narrandera for help, but as his horse was tired and the distance considerable, the thought of rescue was still, at half-past ten, only a shadowy probability of the future.

The passengers numbered six: two sturdy bushmen, with the careless, free, and uncivilized air that marks a squatter (a well-to-do squatter), a small party consisting of a gentleman and two young ladies, and an oldish, grey-haired man, with bright, searching eyes. All were occupying themselves in a manner consistent with their station; the young squatters, after ably assisting the driver in extricating his fallen horses from the broken and tangled harness, had retired together to sympathize with each other, and make expressive remarks on the prospect of missing the next train from Narrandera to their destination; the two ladies were trying to make the best of the matter by exploring a little with their brother; the solitary old gentleman had wandered to a little distance, and was surveying the prospect with an absent and preoccupied air.

It was not in the nature of half-a-dozen people, Australian born and bred, to maintain long this dignified isolation. The young men soon joined the exploring party, with whom they had a slight acquaintance, and seating themselves on some convenient rocks, they began to speak of the various Christmases which each had passed in the bush.

"My last Christmas," began the younger of the squatters, "was spent under circumstances rather more unpleasant than even these. My brother and I had been driving stock to an out station where they had a chance of getting some food; the summer had been terrible, and there was neither grass nor water on the home run. When we reached the shanty belonging to the out-station, we found the shepherd departed, fortune knows where, and nothing in the shape of rations in the place, except some flour, a keg of rum, and some raisins. So we determined to be as orthodox as circumstances would allow and make a pudding. We didn't succeed very well, for we forgot to put any water in the pot; but we had nothing else for our Christmas dinner."

The old man had slowly approached the group in a hesitating manner, as one who feared to intrude; the young girls observed this, and turning to him, observed that he had probably passed some adventurous Christmas-time during his life in the bush.

"I don't suppose any of you ever passed such a strange Christmas as I did, some fifteen years ago," said he. "It was a sort of hallucination, probably; I don't know. But whatever it was, I have never lost the recollection of it, which is as strong as if it had happened yesterday. It was up in the Brush Creek district; I was going from our station to one about fifty miles off. I remember thinking it rather hard that I should have to go all this way alone on Christmas Eve, and was not in the best of spirits. Nor was the country through which I had to travel calculated to render one so. It was a perfect specimen of Australian bush—miles on miles of gum trees, still and stately, and silent as death; the stillness was like that of a great cathedral, but there was something weird and uncanny about it. The only sign of life consisted of a grey bird, about the size of a thrush, which now and then startled one by flying suddenly out of a tree, crossing the path I was following, and disappearing again; but without a sound, without a cry, so that if a dead thing could have flown, one might have likened it to this. The silence was so intense, so solemn, that it seemed to *echo* through the vast distance of forest, and to press one down under its grandeur. One felt that one had no right to be there; it was like entering a place inhabited by beings of another world. Involuntarily I checked my horse to a foot-pace; the quiet motion seemed due to the stillness of the place. Suddenly a strange sensation came over me—I began to have an oppressive understanding that this grand quiet was not only there, where I was, but *everywhere*—for miles round—

there was still this great sea of silence. The thought seemed to grow and grow in my mind till I could not stand its immensity; I felt as if I could have sent out my soul in one great cry, yet could not utter a sound. Blindly I rode on, in an agony of awe. Then I saw (as a man in a trance may see an object, without being conscious that he does so) that I was approaching something unlike the rest of the wood. A dull grey light shone among the trees, unlike any light in heaven or earth; as I came near to it I saw that there were shapes in it—domes and towers and mina-rets—like, and yet strangely unlike, any I had ever seen; I went on,—and found myself in a great city—a great still city, with thronged and silent streets—streets with majestic buildings, but having a strange, shadowy appearance. The very people who moved through the ways were not life-like—they glided onward in a hurrying crowd, yet through the town there was no sound of footfall, no voice was raised, everywhere unbroken silence. I left the street I had first entered, and turned to another; it was everywhere the same. Yet there was no peace in this town; the ghostly people hurried past like the wind, with white faces and fixed eyes, as if each had some great end in view; there was no stillness, only an utter absence of sound. I was terribly alone there in the midst of that unearthly city; unnoticed, unseen it seemed, by these men with death-like faces. I tried to speak to one of the passers-by, but my touch was not felt, and my tongue had lost its speech. But I looked in his eyes—they were lifeless and still, yet as I met them I felt a new spirit enter into me; I was drawn irresistibly to join the noiseless crowd. I don't know how I had got off my horse, but I was on my feet, and rushing with a mad eagerness among the noiseless people, I was soon wildly following and striving after some aim, whose every kind was unknown to me; all I knew was that in some misty distance there was something I longed to reach.

"But it seemed quite as a matter of course that I should be thus following after that something—in fact I had no conscious-ness of ever having done anything else, or of having been in any other place all my life. Now the streets and buildings seemed more real—they had no longer their misty, shadowy look; the silent bustle had increased—we seemed to be approaching some great business quarter. Presently the tide of ghosts turned into a street broader and handsomer than the rest, at the end of which was a large mosque-like building of white marble. As the foremost man—or ghost—approached, a large gate in front of it opened, and he entered, followed by the rest, myself among them.

"Now I saw the mystery of this silent city unravelled. It was a city of the dead—they were dead men who walked in its streets—who had raised its stately towers—who sought in this great white dome the objects they had striven to attain all their lives. These objects were here in their own undisguised forms—they filled the building, having vague, strange, but material shapes. I saw that each man recognised that which had been the object of his life; men who had been poets, and had dreamed of and yearned for a higher genius to perfect their work, saw here the genius they had sought for—a beautiful, wonderfully beautiful thing, but slowly burning and consuming the vessel that held it. Some there were who had simply sought for fame—they cared not how, or in what line; perhaps they had attained to it during their lives, perhaps not; but they found it here—the whole place was glorious with it—it was the only light in the building, but it illuminated everything there. Other men had not even known the object of their lives; but to all these was shown that which they had lived for—to some beautiful things, to others such as made them shudder and turn away; but no one left the building without having recognised the especial aim of his life.

"Fresh crowds were coming in, and I went out with the tide of those who had entered with me. I returned to the main street, and having followed it for a little distance, I came to a river. Like all else in the city, the river was dead; it had neither tide nor motion, but lay among the arches of a large bridge that crossed it, a silent, lifeless thing. A strong disgust for the river came over me, and a dread of the dead town and its ghastly citizens.

I resolved to cross this bridge, thinking perhaps, it might lead me away from the place; but no sooner had I set foot on it, than I found myself surrounded by beings infinitely more horrible than anything I had yet met with. They were a sort of ghouls, which rose up from the river, and swarmed the bridge; hideous shapes, and to the touch damp and cold. They laid their hands on me, and tried to retard my progress; but, half frantic, I broke from them, and ran with all the strength I could gather, to the opposite shore.

"The horror of that city, and especially of the bridge, was still strong on my mind, and I ran till my breath failed. Then standing, I looked round. I was in the bush again; it was dark, and I could see the moon just rising through the trees. Looking towards the place where I had left the town, I saw nothing but a thick, impenetrable fog. To my surprise, I found my horse quietly feeding near me; I was rejoiced to see him,—a living creature, belonging to the world of men; and mounting, I hurried onward, and arrived—at 12 o'clock, on Christmas night.

"You can laugh if you like," added the old man—wistfully though, as one who while he cherishes some pet fancy, is yet half ashamed of it. "I daresay it may not strike young minds as it does my old one."

But no one laughed. The story had excited a a weird sensation among its hearers, and for a while there was silence. Presently one of the squatters observed "I've often heard strange things of Brush Creek; I firmly believe the place is haunted. Did you ever pass that way again?"

"No," said the ghost-seer, shortly; " I never did."

The little party gathered more closely together after this; with a feeling of protection in each other's company, which all, however, would have been ashamed to own. Every bush took an unearthly shape, and there was a faint suggestion of ghosts in the moonlight. It was a painful feeling, and, increasing with each half-hour that went by, so strained the nerves of everyone that, at the end of four or five hours, a long faint coo-e-e from some distance caused a general start, as if something unnatural had discovered itself.

He who, by this ghostly tale, had caused this unpleasant state of things, was the first to recover himself.

"That is the signal of our approaching rescue," he said. "Some lucky chance must have favoured our messenger to bring him back so soon."

He was right in his conjecture. The lad had fallen in with a travelling stock and station agent, who had offered him a bush buggy, a strange sort of machine enough, yet sufficient to take on the mails and the six passengers. So, rejoiced at the early termination of their misfortunes, they left the ruins of the coach to night and to the driver, and without further adventure, reached Narrandera.

THE DEATH CHILD

by Guy Boothby

Guy Boothby (1867-1905) is well-known for his supernatural thrillers involving Dr. Nikola, a magician searching for the elixir of life. He was born in Adelaide and became private secretary to the Mayor of Adelaide before settling in England in 1894 to pursue his literary ambitions. Apart from the Dr. Nikola series, he wrote several other supernatural novels, including *Pharos the Egyptian* (1899) and *The Curse of the Snake* (1902). He was also an amateur farmer and dog breeder.

Boothby died from influenza at the age of thirty-seven at his home at Boscombe in Hampshire. His short collections include *Bushigrams* (1897), *Uncle Joe's Legacy and Other Stories* (1902), and *The Lady of the Island* (1904), all of which contain supernatural stories that have been anthologised in recent years. A little-known collection with the unlikely title *For Love of Her* (1905) contains at least three supernatural tales of which the following is the pick of the bunch.

One summer night, about three years after I took to the pearling trade in the Pacific, five of us—John Browdie, a Yorkshireman, standing six feet two in his socks; a Londoner, whom we called the scholar, more on account of his mannerisms than his learning, I fancy; Harry the Digger; Sailor Jim, and myself—sat yarning on the fo'c'sle of the lugger *Waterwitch*, anchored off the New Guinea Coast. It was about the hottest night of the year, and save for the gentle *flip-flap* of the water alongside, and the wear of the cable in the hawse hole, everything was so still that you could even distinguish the sound of the waves breaking on the beach more than two miles away.

The lights of Port Moresby winked at us over our starboard quarter, while away to port shone the riding light of the *Merrie England* Government steamer. The stars shimmered like gold dust strewn across the sky, and, as if to show that there still remained some sort of touch with England, the Great Bear just lifted above the northern horizon.

On three occasions the Yorkshireman had embarked upon the narration of a mysterious story, which we had all heard a dozen times before, setting forth, at interminable length, the adventures of his grandfather at a certain West Riding race meeting; but we invariably managed to stave him off in time.

As the talk slackened he saw his opportunity, and commenced at once—

"Yo' see, n'out would do for gran'fer, but 'e mun see t' Leger run, an' as 'e was a'goin oop t' moor—"

I drummed my foot against the hatch, while the scholar, who had been ashore that afternoon, said hastily from the cable range—

"Do any of you remember the wreck of the *Kate Kearney*?"

The Yorkshireman saw another chance in the silence that followed, and hastened to make the most of it.

"Ho'd tha tongue, lad!" he said, "Wha's t' use o' bringin' that oop now? It's rude to interrupt, and you mun first 'ear tell o' ma gran'fer an'—"

"But what about the *Kate Kearney*?" I asked quickly.

Before the north countryman could get another word in, the scholar had begun his story—

"It is rather a curious story, and it was something that happened to me ashore to-day that made me think of it. First and foremost you must bear in mind that this yarn is not make-believe. At least a dozen men now on their road to—well, never mind where—are convinced of its truth; and all I can say is, if you want further proof, well, you have only to adopt Papuan Lizzie yourself, and see what comes of it.

"She was, or *is* I should say, since she is still very much alive, a New Guinea native from the Lakoli River; fifty miles or so away down there under the moon. 'The Yankee Pirate' (shot last year in the Solomon Group) blackbirded her by mistake, when she was about six years old, in spite of a curse from her infuriated hag of a mother who raced the party down the beach, swearing that whoever had to do with the child would surely die. It was a beautiful curse, so the Yankee told me, and on it the story I'm going to tell you hangs.

"Of course the whole ship's company laughed at the idea of anything happening to them—it would have been strange, if they hadn't—but just mark how perfectly the curse worked out!

"Before I go any further I must explain to you that these things happened at a time when Government agents were unthought of, and when an adult Kanaka landed in Port Mackay meant a solid gain of nearly twenty pounds to the man who brought him over. Legalized slavery it may have been, but the money was there safe and sound nevertheless."

"Lad! I'm jealous tha knaws't too much about yon times," said Browdie with emphasis.

The scholar glanced over the side to where the copper sheathing glittered in the moonlight, and then up at the motionless vane upon the mast-head, before he continued—

"Most of the Kanakas out of that shipment went to the Eureka Sugar Company's plantation on the Pioneer River, and with them went Lizzie. The manager's wife, a kind-hearted soul, took pity on the miserable coffee-coloured little urchin, and allowed her to spend the greater part of her time playing with her own children. Within a week, two of them found their way into the sugar house and were killed in the machinery, and the mother, who saw the accident, is now in a Brisbane lunatic asylum.

"Three months later the company was in liquidation, the

plantation was shut up, and the Kanakas were dispersed to the four winds of heaven. Nobody seemed to want Lizzie, so she passed from hand to hand up the coast, stopping here and there for a few weeks at a time, but always being moved on by the fatalities that followed in her wake. At last she reached Townsville, the capital of the North, as you know its inhabitants grandiloquently term it. Here it looked as if she were going to be allowed to settle down for a while. But the kind lady who was struck by her forlornness and took charge of her, developed typhoid fever in some inexplicable fashion within a month of her arrival, and died a fortnight later, throwing the child upon the world once more. Her executors were at a loss to know what to do with the brat, so they were only too grateful when a kind-hearted gentleman came forward and said that he would take her off their hands, and carry her home to England as a present to his wife. He left Townsville in the mail boat *Carrysfort*, and as the world has good reason to be aware, that ill-fated vessel struck an uncharted rock off Cape York, and went to the bottom in something under three minutes, taking with her every living soul on board save four.

"Papuan Lizzie was one of the four who did not find a watery grave. She was thrown overboard to three Lascars who were clinging to a spar alongside. How it came about it is impossible to say, but the men were never heard of again; Lizzie, however, was picked up by a béche-de-mer schooner a few hours later, and carried to Thursday Island. Unfortunately her fame had preceded her, and it was there that she received for the first time the name of the 'Death Child.' For some days no one would have anything to do with her, and consequently she wandered about the beach as miserable an urchin as could have been found in the whole Western Pacific. Then a zealous missionary, anxious to prove how idle and wicked such suspicions were, gave her a home.

"For nearly six months all went well, and bit by bit the ugly little creature developed an affection for her guardian that was as grotesque as the cause of it was pathetic. He had begun, and would have finished, her education if the curse had not uncoiled itself, and led him to interfere in a drunken street brawl; during which Rhotoma Sam stabbed him to the heart for his pains, and thus deprived Lizzie of another protector.

"After this, for three months or so, the record of her movements is more or less uncertain. I believe she went down to the D'Entrecasteax Group in the trading schooner *Skylark*, and probability is given to the theory by the fact that the Skylark left Port Moresby, and was never heard of again.

"When next I saw her Lizzie was back in Thursday Island, uglier and more impish than ever, and so convinced was everyone of her Satanic association that not a mother's son or daughter would take her in, or befriend her in any way. Consequently she was compelled to live by herself in Tommy Burns' old hut in the gully behind the Chinese Gardens.

"Now, among the multifarious inhabitants of the Island at that time was a former mate of the *Kate Kearney*, the vessel we were speaking of just now, a vindictive sort of a fellow named Benman, who had a great and undying hatred for Captain Edwards, of the same craft. He used to say that the captain had concocted a plot to get him discharged from the company's service, and he vowed that come what might, he would be even with his enemy before many years had passed. The captain, in total ignorance of this hatred and believing that Benman liked him rather than otherwise, wrote in a friendly sort of way, asking him, as a personal favour, to find a suitable black maid for his wife.

"Seeing his way to as devilish piece of mischief as ever was planned, Benman chuckled to himself and began to make enquiries.

"When, a month later, the *Kate Kearney* put in for stores he hunted up Papuan Lizzie and sent her aboard with a polite little note, recommending her, and saying how glad he was to have a chance of being useful to his old friend. Mrs. Edwards, who was an invalid took a great fancy to her new handmaid and as soon as they were at sea, set about completing the education the unfortunate missionary had begun.

"Leaving Thursday Island the *Kate Kearney* sailed on a trading cruise among the Islands. The ship's company included the captain, his mate, a supercargo, an Englishman fresh from home, three Solomon boys, and a half-caste Philippine Islander. Also Papuan Lizzie, who detested lessons or work of any kind, and spent most of her time on the main hatch, huddled up like a native idol, blinking at the sun. Then the curse, which had not made any visible mischief for well-nigh three months, began to think about business once more. On this occasion it took the form of a mutiny.

"One sunny afternoon the *Kate Kearney* lay becalmed off Arurai in the Kingsmills. The sea alongside was as smooth as glass, and almost as transparent, while overhead the spars and rigging stood out double-sized against the azure sky.

"The skipper and mate were pacing the deck, wondering from what quarter they might expect the wind, and talking of things in general. Coming aft they leaned over the taffrail to watch a shark struggle astern.

"Then the half-caste Portuguese, who had been lolling against the wheel with nothing to do, save to hatch mischief and to dream of the spree he intended having when next he got ashore, suddenly received a signal from the fo'c'sle, made up his mind, and drawing a revolver from his belt, shot both men dead. Next moment the vessel, from being an inanimate mass upon the sunlit waters, became surcharged with life. The supercargo, who was below, asleep, alarmed by the noise, ran up the companion ladder, rifle in hand. But the murderer, who had the advantage of him, fired as soon as his head appeared, and the white man fell backwards down the ladder into the cuddy, dead as a doornail, shot through the skull.

By this time the ship was in an uproar. The remainder of the hands made their appearance from their hiding places and set to work to throw the bodies overboard to the sharks they had been watching less than half an hour before. When this was done, the half-caste assumed command. The Englishman was given the chance of serving, or of sharing the fate of his companions. Naturally he chose the former alternative. Mrs. Edwards terminated an interview with the ringleader by throwing herself overboard, while Papuan Lizzie sat on the hatch and cried very bitterly, for she loved her kind benefactress, and would willingly have put a knife into the back of the half-caste, only she was afraid. She was not of course to know that she was the cause of all the trouble.

"For three months the *Rolling Wave*, alias the *Kate Kearney*, did an amazing trade among the Islands. At the end of that time her hold was full to bursting, of pearl shell, copra, tortoiseshell, and dried béche-de-mer.

"Then, quite by chance, for there was no navigator aboard worthy of the name, they reached Ponape, a Spanish settlement of the Caroline Group, and anchored outside the reef. When all was snug the half-caste went ashore, leaving the crew to gamble and quarrel among themselves as they pleased. Though he did not know it, they were hatching another mutiny among themselves, and this time against himself, for they had come to the conclusion that he was carrying things with far too high a hand.

"As soon as he returned, and dusk fell, the Englishman, who was friendly with neither party, seized his opportunity, slipped down the cable, and also made for the shore. It was a long swim, and the sea was running high under a freshening gale.

"Ponape, with its few hundred natives and sprinkling of Spaniards, is not by any means a big place, so he discovered the Governor's residence without very much searching, and poured his thrilling tale of mutiny and murder into that official's ear.

"The Governor immediately ordered out his state army, an officer and ten men, all as zealous as himself, and with great pomp and circumstance issued the command that the schooner *Rolling Wave* should be boarded and seized.

"In spite of the increasing storm, the army put off and eventually got alongside without resistance from the mutineers, who at the time were below. The only visible occupant of the vessel was Papuan Lizzie, who was crying under the lee of the deckhouse aft.

"Having placed sentries at the entrance to the companion ladder, the Governor went below with the balance of his men. He found the ship's company engaged on cut-throat euchre, and you can imagine their astonishment when they saw the soldiers enter.

"They fought like wild cats, but it was only to discover that sheath knives and bare fists are of small avail even against Spanish swords and derelict muskets. Having ironed them, the Commander-in-Chief placed them under a strong guard and then searched the ship.

"While he was occupied in this fashion he forgot to take stock of the weather. When they had come aboard it was working up for a storm; now it was such a night as you seldom see. A cyclone was sweeping down upon the Island, and even the usually placid water inside the reef was white with driven foam. By the time those on board arrived at an understanding of their position, it had torn up the schooner's straining cables, and was racing her along the treacherous line of rocks, at more than racing pace. Eventually she went to pieces close in shore, and out of the eighteen souls aboard her, including the Governor, the soldiers and their prisoners, only two escaped alive. One was the Englishman I have already mentioned, who had accompanied the boarding party to see what happened, the other was Papuan Lizzie, who, strange to relate, was landed high and dry on the beach without scratch or injury. Two days later the Englishman left in a schooner for Tahiti, and for the time being that was the last he saw of that queer little atom we used to call the 'Death Child.'"

Harry the Digger, put down his pipe.

"Hold on, my lad," he said very quietly, "you haven't told us how you learnt these things."

"Well," said the scholar with a quiet chuckle, "it seems to me I should know something about them, considering I was the Englishman who gave the information to the authorities, and who was allowed to live on condition he joined the mutineers."

"A neatly worked out yarn," I continued; "and pray did you ever hear what became of the Death Child after that?"

"She remained in Ponape for upwards of two years, I believe, and then managed to make her way, how I cannot explain, across the Pacific until she reached Port Moresby once more."

"Here?" we cried in astonishment. "You don't mean to say she's in Port Moresby at this moment?"

"Most certainly I do," he replied. "I saw her only to-day when I went ashore. It was my meeting with her that made me think of telling you the story. But you mustn't run away with the notion that she's the same Liz. She's a changed character altogether."

"In what way is she changed?"

"She's grown up and a married woman. You remember Pat Dolson, the man who was in Thursday Island a year or two back, who claimed to have been an Oxford Don, and who had the reputation of being able to drink more mixed liquor at one sitting, and to be able to swear in a greater variety of tongues, than any other white man in the Pacific? You do? Well, then, he's her husband. They were married a month ago."

"Surely you're joking. What on earth made him marry her? Is the man mad?"

"It looks like it, does it not? At any rate, he's gone to pieces now. I never saw such a wreck of a man in my life before. Lives out in the bush among the niggers, dresses in the native style, and if ever I saw a man on the borders of the jumps he was that one. He talked an awful lot of nonsense to me about Fate-Destiny-Powers of Darkness, and goodness only knows what else, mixing it up with Greek and Latin quotations. Said he was bewitched by Liz, and that it was ordained from the first that he should marry her—so how could he help himself? I told him he was a fool for his pains, and that he deserved to come to just the sort of end he prophesied. All the time I was talking Liz sat at the door of the hut, watching me out of half-closed eyes, with that devilish smile of hers upon her face. When I left she stopped me in the bush, and showing all her teeth in a grin, asked me if I didn't think she would make him *'one big all the same first-class wife.*'"

"What did you say?"

"I can't remember exactly, but I fancy I consigned her to the place where wives who make promises before marriage and don't fulfil them afterwards are popularly supposed to go. As it was, she—"

The scholar stopped suddenly, and held up his hand.

"Hark!" he cried. "What was that?"

We sat silent, listening, but all we could hear was the soft murmur of the water alongside, and the gentle creaking of the spars as the tiny vessel rocked at her anchor. Then there was a sound a short distance away on our starboard bow, that made us all leap to our feet like one man. It was the cry of a person in sore distress.

"It's some one drowning!" cried sailor Jim, who was always ready to jump to a conclusion. "I've heard that cry too often not to know it. Here! let's get the boat away at once, or we'll be too late to rescue him."

As he spoke he ran to the davits, but before he could let go the falls the sound reached our ears again, and this time it came from close under the counter.

"Schooner ahoy!" it said. "Take me aboard."

A moment later we were all at the taffrail, craning our necks over the side in an attempt to discover who the man might be, and to render him any assistance that might be in our power.

He did not seem to be in need of so much help as he had led us to believe, for he presently scrambled on board, and having gained the deck shook himself like a Newfoundland dog. He was stark naked, and had long black hair that trailed upon his shoulders. Taken altogether, he did not make a pretty picture.

"Good heavens, Dolson!" cried the scholar with a gasp, as he recognized the man before us. "You don't mean to say it's you? What on earth has brought you out here like this?"

But Dolson only gave a queer sort of grunt, and threw down upon the deck a native basket constructed of some sweet-smelling reed. After that he sat down on the main hatch, and hid his face in his hands. We stood round and watched him, unable to make head or tail of it all. Undoubtedly he was crazy.

"She said she had bewitched me," he began after a pause. "Because I beat her she cursed me only this evening. 'You shall not find your death on land,' says she, 'nor shall you be drowned in water. Your death shall come to you through me, and though I be dead yet shall I be there to see you die.' It's a lie! She *is* dead, it is true, for I killed her myself. But she will not see me die. Of that I am certain.

So absorbed were we in watching him and listening to his ravings, that we entirely failed to notice a canoe which had come softly up alongside, nor the black figure which had made its way aboard over the bows. Had we done so we should probably have warned Dolson, but it was Fate that kept us otherwise employed so that we should not see. An arm went up, and then a poisoned spear came aft, travelling straight for the naked figure seated on the hatch. It caught him full and fair in the chest, between the shoulders, and a few seconds later Dolson was squirming upon the deck, and his murderer had disappeared into the night again. In his agony Dolson chanced to touch the basket he had brought on board with him, and under the impetus thus given to it the contents rolled out, and into the circle of light made by the lantern which some one had thoughtfully brought up from below. To our horror, we discovered that the black ball rolling and bobbing towards the bulwarks was neither more nor less than the head of Papuan Lizzie—the Death Child—severed at the trunk. The eyes were open, and the mouth was set in a diabolical leer. As I noticed this horror, the man whom we called Dolson gave up the ghost, and thus his wife's prophecy came true. He had not died on land, nor was he drowned in water; his death came to him through her agency, and though her body was not present, still her eyes were there, and saw him breathe his last.

And yet there are some people who, having read this story, will say they do not believe in witchcraft, nor will they own that they have any faith in the power of a curse.

THE JEWELLED HAND
by Lionel Sparrow

Lionel Sparrow wrote about two-dozen horror and adventure stories for the *Australian Journal* between 1887 and 1910. He did not publish a book during his lifetime, and he has remained completely forgotten until now. He was born in the tiny Victorian town of Wahgunyah in 1867, the eldest of six children, one of whom died in infancy. He lived most of his life in Linton, Victoria, where he was proprietor of the local newspaper, the *Grenville Standard*. He married Alice Eliza Miller, and they had one son, Geoffrey Sparrow, who became Federal President of the Australian Journalists Association. Lionel died on 9th April 1936.

His horror stories, especially the early ones, were clearly influenced by the 1890s decadents, and show a predilection for torture, mutilation and opium, while his later stories have a strong occult element. I have chosen two stories by Sparrow: 'The Jewelled Hand' was the first story he published in the *Australian Journal* in 1887; the second is one of his last, published in 1907, an unusual vampire story with a Hindu Brahman in the Van Helsing role.

But I swear to you, senors, that you are mistaken—utterly mistaken—in your conviction of my insanity. If I have spoken no word throughout this long tribunal—if I have remained insensible to the questions and demands of you, my judges—it has been solely from horror of my terrible crime, or rather of the appalling circumstances attending the commission and the concealment of that crime. You think I am mad; you cannot conceive, you cannot realise that anyone in the possession of reason could be so utterly lost as to commit such a deed as mine. You search in vain for a motive—for even a *possible* motive—and, finding none, imagining none, you say that I must be mad, and, being mad, you would suffer me to live. But I tell you, senors, life to me now is a horror—death means rest. I prefer death. Therefore I will relate to you, in so succinct and so precise a manner all the details of my fearful crime that you will assuredly end by pronouncing me sane and fit to undergo the direct penalty of the tribunal.

You know that the unfortunate Don Alvaro was my friend—my companion. You know that he was dear to me as a brother—and perhaps dearer than a brother. Yet bear in mind, senors, that I did not *love* him as a brother; for I have never loved a human being. I respected Don Alvaro—respected and admired him—chiefly for the grand, the matchless power of his great mind—and also for the immense knowledge and the wonderful memory he possessed. But that wonderful mind, that resistless will, endeared him to me most. It was but seldom that I saw the full force of this will displayed; it may be—indeed, I believe—that its full force was never displayed until—

But you are impatient, senors; I must speak plainly and precisely, as I promised. Yet, it will be necessary for me to impress upon your mind the vast difference that existed between Don Alvaro and myself. His great power of will rendered all objects easy of attainment; there was nothing he could desire which his will was inadequate to reach; but his desires were few and simple, because his mind was so high and great and powerful—because he used his iron will to govern, not others, but himself. My own character was of a different order; my mind, though intellectual, possessed no force—though it could concentrate itself at times;—it was excessively imaginative, and the gift of a true imagination confers a pleasure which is perennial and exhaustless. This I know, by the memory of my youthful existence. But, many years ago, I experienced an adventure of such a fearful nature—I suffered the torture of such appalling moral horrors—that my nerves were unstrung for ever; and that vivid imagination which had once been a pleasure to me was now twisted and warped out of all semblance to its former self, and I became a prey to the most morbid fancies—I became a slave to the most terrible nervous horrors, frightful conjurings of a diseased imagination. This pitiable state of my mind, increasing with each new day, would, beyond a doubt, have been fatal to my reason, had it not been for the restraining and soothing influence of my friend's society. With this being near me, life became a possibility, and at times even tolerable: I was saved by him from becoming a maniac. Don Alvaro himself, I believe, never suspected the real extent of my nervous malady; my horrible imaginings were unknown to him, as to others. The sensitive soul within me shrank from the thought of another knowing the dread secrets of my wild and perverted imagination. Don Alvaro merely thought that my nerves were weak and easily irritated; his knowledge extended no further than that— so assiduously (though how painfully) did I conceal from him my true state.

Doubtless, senors, you find me circumlocutory and tiring; yet bear with me, for now that I have explained, or tried to explain to you my mental condition, I shall be more able to proceed with my narration of the remarkable circumstances attending my crime and self-conviction.

Once, at night, I was engaged in conversation with my friend. Then it was that the first link of a fatal chain of events was forged.

Don Alvaro was showing me a curious antique vase of glass when suddenly—perhaps on account of some sudden change in the atmosphere—it snapped at its slenderest part, and the upper portion fell to the floor.

"How strange!" exclaimed my friend, "did you not notice,

José, how singularly the top parted from the rest—cleft, as it seemed, by some invisible blow."

"Yes," I replied, my morbid imagination conjuring up a weird simile. "It fell as falls the head of the criminal when severed from the body by the axe of the executioner."

"Ah!" said my friend, "that is a singular way of illustrating the breaking of a vase. But," he added after a long pause, "your metaphor has brought before my mind something I must have read many years ago, for I remember it but dimly—and yet it would doubtless interest you, who revel in the science of physiology."

I listened eagerly, with an intense interest not to be accounted for even by the fact that it was my own especial and favourite study which was concerned in what my friend was about to disclose. I held my breath as Alvaro continued:—

"It was a discussion—an argument—between two notable physicians; and the question was whether for a moment after the head is entirely separated from the body, the faculties of the mind do or do not retain their seat—whether the brain ceases its functions immediately the blow has been struck which severs the neck. One of the disputants, I think, maintained that, so far from any doubt existing, it is impossible for the brain to cease its working *immediately*, unless the executioner blunders in his task. But the other learned man ridiculed the theory, averring that, even if the *brain* did live for a second or two after the neck was severed (which, however, he by no means admitted), most certainly the *consciousness of the mind* could never exist for the merest fraction of a second. Now, my own opinion, José, is that this moment of consciousness after decapitation must necessarily depend on the vitality of the victim, his strength of mind, and the facility with which the headsman accomplishes the work. But I see you are distressed by this frightful reasoning, this terrible speculation. Let us dismiss the subject."

And the subject was dismissed—from *his* mind; from my own it could never—never be driven. There were two reasons why the question should impress my mind so deeply. The first was that my imagination, as you know, had become diseased, perverted, warped, so that such a weird subject could not fail to retain a place within it; the second reason was that the study of physiology, which had in earlier years formed my chief intellectual pleasure, had now grown into a morbid passion—almost a monomania. In my researches—remember this, senors—I spared nothing to ensure success. Hitherto, by wealth, assiduity, daring, and perchance a superior science, I had overcome all difficulties. No means did I consider unscrupulous to attain my end, for that attainment was in me a passion, which I had no will to curb, nor even desire to resist. Doubtless you know, or you have heard of, the great physiological discoveries that I have made. Well, there are others, in the darker and more unknown shades of the science, stupendous, incredible, which I have not ventured to give to an unbelieving world, but which will be found in my cabinet when I am dead.

Senors, I feared, with a deadly fear, the idea which Don Alvaro had promulgated in my mind. I tried to loathe it as horrible, and I tried to ridicule it as absurd, and not worthy of solution. I feared the idea, on account of a terrible, yet indefinable, foreboding of evil which filled my soul. But all my efforts to forget it were futile—and they were worse, in that they increased the horrible suggestiveness of the thought—the irresistible, and at first undefined, longing that seized upon my disordered mind—the gloom of the vistas of terrible speculation through which my sere imagination, delighting in the pursuit of unknown horrors, wandered slowly.

And at length I could deceive myself no longer. No longer could I disguise the fact that what I desired with so ardent, so nervous a desire, was, in dread truth, the solution of that hideous mystery involved in the question which my friend had propagated. I longed with a frenzied, resistless longing that I had never yet known, to satisfy myself whether the power of thought could live, even for one second, after decapitation. Day after day, night after night this terrible longing burnt within me, torturing me like glowing fires.

And now, impelled by the desire, I began gradually to reflect, to plot, to *prepare*.

I started by persuading myself that the thing was impossible, that the end to which my infamously audacious desire urged me was unattainable. And I said—"I will, however, imagine it to be really possible, and I will make the preparations I would make were it possible. It will amuse me, and, perchance, even appease my longing."

And I set about the task.

I procured a long, straight, finely-tempered sword. I rendered the blade, by constant sharpening, keen as the finest razor. Then I enclosed it in a velvet sheath through which the air could not penetrate and locked it securely in a strong bureau. This done I searched among my art-possessions, and found an ebony casket, upon which a great painter had set the seal of his genius. I stood this box against the wall, and measured its height. Half an inch below its summit I made a hole in the wainscoting, in which I fixed a knob, very small, which projected a quarter of an inch, and which the lid of the box, when raised, would press inwards. I now removed two or three planks of the oaken wainscot, disclosing a space sufficient for my purpose. Then—but there is no need to detail so minutely all my proceedings. Suffice it to say that after many days—for I prolonged my task as much as possible—there was in the wall, about eighteen inches above the box, a long, narrow, horizontal slit, concealed by a thin strip of paper, coloured like the oak. And in this narrow aperture, ready to flash forth, the sword was hidden. I had contrived that it should revolve upon a pivot at the hilt, with which was connected a most powerful steel spring. The point of the blade was held in its place by a strong lever, the withdrawal of which would release the spring, and the keen blade would describe a half-circle with resistless force just above the casket. The heavy tapestry of the apartment I had here drawn aside, just sufficiently to be clear of the circuit of the sword. And round about the box were scattered soft cushions, which had all the appearance of having been thrown there carelessly.

All was now prepared.

For what?

Many—many hours I passed in contemplating the deadly engine I had constructed; I pondered long upon my work. The "preparations" which I had said would amuse me and appease my ghastly longing, were now completed, and what was the result? You may guess, senors, I longed more intensely than ever. There was nothing now to do but lure the victim to that chamber of death, induce him to kneel before the casket, and to raise the lid, and so spring the hellish machine. The keen blade would dart forth, describe its flashing circle, and the head would roll softly among the cushions placed there for the purpose of breaking or annulling the force of its fall. I would be present— I would be standing quite close—I would watch the head as it fell—I would fix my eyes upon those of the head, and from their expression I would be able to divine if thought yet reigned within.

And now came the important question of the victim—who was to be the victim?

I swear to you, senors, that at that moment the thought of sacrificing my dearest friend was as far from my mind as it had been a month—a year before. Then whom did I condemn to be the victim of the experiment? I will tell you—and believe me, senors—it was *myself*. Many times before had I contemplated suicide, and now, as I pondered over my plan, it seemed to me that to die for science was glorious—heroic. I had almost decided—would to heaven I *had* decided!—when two difficulties, till then unthought of, presented themselves to my mind, and both were insurmountable. In the first place, unless a witness were present (which was not to be thought of), it would he obviously impossible to leave any record by which science could be apprised of the results. The second difficulty was even more important:—How could I be at all certain, that my power of will was such as to render the theory even possible, if I put that theory into practice by sacrificing myself? I felt that my mind would succumb more easily than that of any average individual. This thought was suggested by the words of Don Alvaro himself:—"I think that this moment of consciousness after decapitation must necessarily depend upon the vitality of the victim, his strength of mind, and the facility with which the headsman accomplishes the work."

Now, among all my acquaintance who possessed the greatest vitality—the greatest will?

Don Alvaro.

I shuddered at the obvious reply.

Yet it was so. It could not be gainsaid. If Don Alvaro became the victim the result of the experiment might be considered as decisive. If *his* mind were extinguished by the stroke of the sword—if his will did not survive decapitation—then the theory fell to the ground. The thing was impossible.

In fact, if the experiment was to he made it must be made upon my dearest friend—a man who trusted, and perhaps even loved me. I felt fear and abhorrence at the thought; yet it was not the idea of punishment in this world or another that made me pause. I could avoid earthly retribution, and in the Christians' hereafter I had no belief. But to lure to his death a man who had been my only friend for many years—who could not think ill of me—whose trust in me was unbounded, to do this clashed with the instincts of old-time chivalry that was in me. Had I been able to procure another victim in the same degree fitted for the experiment, would I than have hesitated an instant? No.

But I swore that Don Alvaro should *not* be sacrificed. Yet how could I prevent it? I could not warn him against myself, and put him on his guard, because I could not confess to him the base treachery to which I had been tempted.

At length I said:—"I will end all. I will seek that rest for which I have so long sighed—I will die. This deadly machine will suffice to accomplish the act."

And with this intention I advanced towards the box, knelt before it, and placed my hands firmly on the lid.

As I was about to raise it a footfall sounded on the threshold. It was a step that I knew.

I sprang up quickly, and confronted Don Alvaro himself, who had entered the room, followed by his little pet monkey, Juan. I had not seen him for a few days, and he greeted me with heartiness, embracing me affectionately, as was his wont. But I could not return that warm embrace.

He was in high spirits, and talked gaily and loud, not noting my own coldness and painful abstraction.

A few minutes after his entrance his glance fell upon the cushions on the floor, and he spoke jestingly of my carelessness. Then, for the first time, he noticed the box, and the painting on the lid struck his artistic eye. He began to admire it.

"Ha!" he exclaimed, "whose work is that? I must know the artist. I seem to recognise the genius of the design." And then he advanced towards the casket. A cold sweat stood on my brow.

"That," I stammered in a choking voice, intending now to warn him of the true character of the casket, "that is—it is—I have been merely amusing myself—the lid—do not—"

"What!" cried Don Alvaro, "did you paint that? Oh, come, José, do not tell me that it is your own work?"

And he sprang forward, fell lightly on his knee before the casket, and looked closely at the painting. And now all things reeled around me. I could not move—still less could I speak. I was conscious that Don Alvaro was saying something, but I heard not his words—only a confused murmur, as of many distant voices. But I could see, and, oh, with what distinctness! My eyes devoured his every movement. I followed his hands as they wandered over the lid, doubtless, in explanation of whatever words he was speaking. I saw them at length rest upon the side of the lid.

And then, of a sudden, there came over me that hellish desire—that ghastly longing. It came with a rush, and I waited—it seemed for hours—waited the *solution of the problem!* Ah, the anguish of suspense! My heart forbore to beat, my eyes almost started from their sockets.

The hands of Don Alvaro began to raise the lid. I suffered a concentrated agony. I wished to cry out to him in warning; I wished to rush forward and drag him from that fatal box; but I could do neither, for the whole action of my being seemed suddenly suspended. And now higher and higher rose the lid—higher, and *still higher*! Great God! Would the stroke never come?

There came at length a sound—a sound that I felt rather than heard—a horrible thrilling *whur-r-s-sh.* It was the rush of the sword in its lightening circuit.

I sprang forward. I saw the head sink to the cushions. The eyes were turned towards me, like the dying eyes of a Caesar. I fixed my own upon them, and I knew by a single glance that in that ghastly object—that in that gory trunkless head—there lived a mind, a will, a thought.

The eyes, at first, had an inquiring light in their gleaming depths. But in a second that had vanished; doubtless the expression of my own made it vanish.

And then their gaze concentrated itself; they burned—they flashed—they dilated; they pierced my inmost soul with their mute but deadly reproach.

And now a most appalling thing happened.

After decapitation, the body had sunk down on the cushions, turning half round with the force of the fell blow, and leaning against the box, almost in a sitting posture.

The eyes of the head, after bending their fierce light upon me for perhaps a second, now seemed, if possible, to flash with a brilliancy yet more intense, as they turned their glance away from my own eyes, and fixed it upon the body.

I followed that deadly glance, and shuddered with a horror for which the world has no name as I beheld what followed.

The right hand of the headless body began to rise!

My limbs tottered—I sank to my knees—but my eyes never left the hand; and it continued to rise, slowly and steadily.

And as it rose—that long white hand, upon which gleamed an opal ring, surrounded with brilliants—as it slowly rose, the forefinger as slowly extended itself, and pointed—pointed straight at my shuddering form.

The headless body pointed at its destroyer!

How long the hand remained uplifted, rigid, motionless, menacing, denouncing, I know not—it seemed for ages.

I could not move—I was transfixed—I was turned to stone, and when at length the hand lost its rigidity gradually, and sank slowly to the side of the headless corpse, I experienced a feeling, not of relief merely, but of a most intense—a most supreme happiness.

The falling of the hand broke the charm that compelled my glance to fix itself upon it, and, looking a last time at the eyes of the head, I saw that they were dark with the shadow of death. That awful will was dead. Only a skull now remained.

A moment after the hand of the headless trunk had ceased to point. I sank into a long and deathlike swoon.

And when consciousness returned, the first faint streaks of dawn were stealing through the lattice of my window.

I sprang to my feet as memory called up the events of the preceding night, and looked round to assure myself that it had not been a hideous nightmare. The objects lying on the cushions told of its appalling reality.

I sank into a couch, and, calm in my despair, I reflected.

The question (in which I now felt no interest) was decided. The will and the mind could not only live after decapitation, but could exert such a power over the body from which it had been separated, as to bring about the terrible result I had witnessed.

The thing had been done, and could not be undone; it only now remained to remove all traces of the body, and to divert suspicion.

I had long since prepared for this exigency. I had the means of so utterly destroying the corpse, that not the faintest trace of it would remain. By a chemical process, known to few, I could consume the body without fuel, without fire, and leave not even the ashes to betray me.

I prepared the acids, etc., which were to be used for this purpose, and subduing as best I could the horror and loathing that could not be suppressed, I set about my fearful task.

To destroy the cushions upon which blood had fallen I used fire. I carefully burnt every ensanguined fragment.

It was necessary that I should divide the body into small fragments, so as to leave no ashes. The head could, however, be consumed whole, and the action of the acids accomplished this in a few minutes When nothing of it remained I felt intense relief. It is the *face* of the dead that most agitates the murderer; the mere trunk had no horrors for me compared with the head.

I then began with the body by severing the right hand. This done, I was about to submit it to the acids, when I suddenly remembered that the garments must be destroyed. The fire was expiring; there must be no delay. I stripped the body and burned every thread of the garments. This work lasted longer than I had calculated on account of the fire being so low, and the absence of fuel wherewith to replenish it. But at last the smallest fragment disappeared, and once more, nervous, agitated, and horribly fatigued, I turned to the body. My mind was becoming more and more confused, but rallying my faculties, I looked round for the hand. I could not see it. Where had I left it? Had I destroyed it? I could not remember. Yet it must be so since the hand was no longer there. I turned to the body.

But I will not weary—I will not disgust you, senors, with the details of my frightful work. At length all was accomplished. There now remained not a trace of that valiant gentleman who a few hours before had been instinct with virile life—not a trace, I thought with a wild exultation.

With what delight did I throw open the door! With what exhilaration did I feel the cool air fan my feverish brow, and saw the sun shining on the calm and silent river!

But as I opened the door yet wider, something passed me with a rush!

It was an animal; it was in truth the little monkey, Juan, which had always evinced a most intense and unaccountable fear of myself. His presence throughout the enactment of that hideous drama I had been unaware of, or had forgotten. Juan, apparently fearing me now more than ever, darted from the door, and flew like lightening from my sight in the direction of his dead master's mansion.

Senors, I need tell you no more. You already know the rest. You know how, tortured by remorse and fearing solitude, I sought society. You know how, on that fatal night, when I and some friends were discussing the strange disappearance of Don Alvaro—you know how the accursed ape suddenly appearing in our midst, sprang upon table, and, with a horrible grin, held before my eyes a ghastly object, at sight of which all were horrified—but none felt a tithe of my own supreme horror.

For, as you know, the hideous thing that the ape held up—the sight of which forced from me that terrible self-conviction— this ghastly object was the hand—the jewelled hand—of Don Alvaro!

And now have I not related all the details of my crime? Have I not accounted for everything?

You are stricken dumb with horror—but do you still think that I am mad? You reply not—you shrink—you shudder—you cannot look upon me! Yet say—do I not merit death?

THE VENGEANCE
OF THE DEAD
by Lionel Sparrow

I.

The disappearance of Martin Calthorpe—"that wonderful man", as his admirers called him, "that arch-impostor," as he was stigmatised by others—was something more than a nine days' wonder, and it has not yet quite faded out of the recollection of those who are attracted or impressed by such mysteries. These will have no difficulty in recalling the circumstances, so far as they were known, of his evanishment. The mystery, however, was so complete that little was left to feed the curiosity of the quidnuncs. When it is stated that he had an appointment with a "client" in his chambers in Brunswick-street on an afternoon of November, 1892, and was waited for in vain, and that he was not seen or heard of afterwards by anyone who could or would admit the fact, the available information (outside of these memoirs) is pretty well exhausted. Some particulars, however, may be added concerning his antecedents preliminary to the well-nigh incredible story of how the mystery was subsequently revealed.

"Professor" Calthorpe was apparently one of those strange beings who, finding themselves possessed of powers outside the cognisance of material science, set about turning them to pecuniary account, without seeking to probe their inner meaning, without realising their legitimate uses. (I say "apparently" for a reason which will be developed later.)

Calthorpe described himself as a hypnotist, a psychometrist, and one or two other "ists"; also as a Clairvoyant. In some or all of these capacities he was remarkably successful, to judge by the number of people who were willing to pay him liberally for whatever services he rendered them. Indeed, the house in Brunswick-street was daily besieged by the many who believe in occult phenomena. The professor had a wife, who was a noted spiritualistic medium, and who also drew a handsome income from her "profession."

It was suggestive of the irony of fate that I, who looked upon such people as Professor and Mrs. Calthorpe as little better than criminal impostors, and their clients as mere gulls, should find my destiny involved with theirs. So, at least, I thought then. Later events have changed my opinions considerably, but they have not increased my respect for the crew who seek to tamper with the mysteries of life and death for their personal profit. However, I must not anticipate.

The professor, as I have said, disappeared. He failed to keep his appointment; and the clients waited in vain. The man of mystic powers was not again seen in his usual sphere of life, and all efforts made to trace him failed. His wife could throw no light upon the mystery—or would not. She seemed greatly agitated—overcome by a sort of terror rather than by natural grief. My friend, Detective Mainspray, who was engaged in the matter, gave me these particulars. Mrs. Calthorpe did not long survive her husband. From the day of his disappearance she gave up her "work," if so it might be called, and fell into a kind of lethargy of horror, like one obsessed, making no effort to arouse herself, though by no means resigning herself to the thought of death. Her bodily vigour (which had been great) declined with remarkable rapidity, but as the end approached a frantic rebellion seemed to rise within her. The final scenes were made memorable by circumstances in the highest degree calculated to unnerve those who witnessed them. I, of course, was not present, but I was told that the dying woman's appearance and demeanour were far from being marked by that tranquillity with which those who are at peace with conscience usually approach the solemn portals of death.

The appalling intensity of her despair shocked the few friends who stood around her death-bed. She seemed to be struggling in the toils of an adversary invisible to them, but only too tangibly present to herself. This death-agony was attributed by some of those who witnessed it to an exaggerated horror of the common fate; the more thoughtful, however, accepted this view with extreme reluctance. Later developments, in which I had part, threw a light upon the mystery. The cause of her death was given as heart disease, accelerated by abnormal neurotic conditions connected with the practice of her "profession" as a medium. A circumstance which greatly puzzled not only her friends, but also the physicians who attended her, was her excessive appetite for rich foods during the last few weeks of her life: this appetite, increasing with a rapid loss of flesh, seemed wholly inexplicable. Those who, knowing the quantities of food she had daily assimilated, looked at last upon a body bloodless and emaciated to an incredible degree, were stricken dumb with wonderment and horror.

II.

Neither the disappearance of Martin Calthorpe nor the death of his wife would have interested me to any considerable degree, but for the fact that I knew my parents to have been acquainted with the man. My father, moody, reticent as he had always been within my memory of him, was not likely to divulge any secrets concerning his past life. Through my friend Mainspray, however, I had glimpses of his early career, which taught me that the book of a man's life may contain pages which it is not wise nor well for a son to turn; and, apart from the bald fact that many years earlier a powerful hatred had been engendered between the two men, through some wrong committed by Calthorpe, I knew little, and sought no further knowledge. When the hypnotist disappeared, however, it became plain to me that my father's gloom had sensibly deepened, and I could not help wondering if this had any connection with the matter. My mother had died only a few months before, after a lingering illness, however, and her death would seem to supply a sufficient and more natural cause for the change observable in the bereaved husband.

My father at first neglected, then finally resigned his business affairs into my charge, and thenceforth lived a very secluded life. I saw but little of him, for he seemed hardly aware at times of my existence. Nothing could exceed, however, the moody intensity of the affection he lavished upon his two daughters, Constance and Winifred. Winnie, the younger, was (if he had any preference) his favourite, for her eyes were startlingly like her mother's. We lived in a rather large house near the St. Kilda-road, about two miles from the city. He owned another house in South Yarra, which should have brought in a substantial sum in rent, but it was out of repair, and, for some reason, he would not allow it to be touched.

Not long after the strange death of Mrs. Calthorpe, my father sought medical advice for our Winnie. We all, Winnie included, were rather surprised, for we could see no cause for alarm in her appearance. Winnie herself protested that she felt well enough, except that she found it rather a bore to cycle or play tennis, and much preferred to go out driving with our friends, the Thorntons, in their new motor car. Old Dr. Gair found nothing the matter with her, except that perhaps she was just a trifle less buxom than a girl of her age and build might be. I think he prescribed some sort of tonic. My father received his optimistic verdict with a gloomy contempt, and it was plain that he was by no means satisfied. The incident passed, and for the time we thought no more about it.

Some weeks later, however, I happened to enter the drawing room, where my sisters were talking, and Winnie was saying—

"No; I can't explain it. And I have such strange dreams, too."

"What sort of dreams, sis?" I asked, lightly; but a glance at her serious face told me that she was in no mood for banter.

"Father seems to have been right, after all," said Connie, in her quiet tones; "Win is getting run down."

I looked at the girl more intently. She was paler than I had ever noticed her to be, and her hands had certainly rather a fragile appearance. She was about eighteen at this time, and should have been flushed with exuberant health. Indeed, a few months before she had been full of a somewhat hoydenish energy and vigour. Now all was changed.

Next week my father took her away to the Blue Mountains. They returned towards the fall of the year, but the girl had not improved. In fact, she had barely held her own. My father called in the best specialists, but they were evidently puzzled by the very simplicity of the case. There was no organic disease, either acute or chronic—no disease of any sort; only a growing weakness, an increasing languor; days darkened by a strange weariness, and nights poisoned by dreams which she would not tell.

To me Winnie was a child—"the baby"; and thus I was on more intimate terms with Connie, who was then in her early twenties. We talked the matter over many times, and discussed the expediency of taking the girl away for a more extended trip.

"It would do you good also, Con," I said; "you're not looking too well."

I said this without attaching much meaning to the words, but Connie gave something of a start.

"Do you think so?" she said; "perhaps I've been worrying about Win. But, really, I don't feel quite myself lately."

This made me look at her closely, and I saw that there was indeed a noticeable change. But the summer had been very trying, and, as she said, the anxiety about Winnie was enough to account for a certain lowering of physical tone.

My father did not fall in with the proposed trip. He only laughed bitterly when it was mooted, and said, in a harsh voice—

"What's the use? There's no hope."

"No hope." I shall never forget the note of tragic despair in those final words. It was as if a fiat had gone forth—as if in some strange way Irrevocable Fate had spoken with his voice.

III.

In these councils of ours Harry Thornton had borne no part. For some reason or other Connie, who had at this time been engaged to him for nearly a year, was unwilling to take him into her confidence in the matter, and as time went on and her own health did not improve, she became even less inclined to talk about it with him.

Thornton was a strange young fellow in many ways. Whilst he was fond of an outdoor life, excelling in all kinds of athletics, I knew him to be equally inclined to intellectual pursuits; in fact, he took up branches of study quite foreign to ordinary taste. Some years before, he had rather startled his friends by becoming the intimate of one Ravana Dâs, a Hindu pundit of the highest caste (Brahmans), and reputed to possess an extraordinary degree of erudition, both Western and Oriental. Thornton made what we chaffingly called a "pilgrimage" to his Eastern friend, and on his return it was plain that he took his "master", as he called him, with intense seriousness. He continued to correspond with this man, whose portrait had an honoured place on the wall of his study. The face was a remarkable one. It was as clearly and delicately cut as a bronze medallion of a proud, yet gentle, expression, and gave one the idea of a learned ascetic. A certain power, also, seemed to breathe from those features. Anyone studying the portrait (which was done in a sepia by an Indian artist) could readily understand the fascination which the man might exercise over impressionable natures.

The Thorntons were wealthy people, and the young man had license to gratify his fancies. But he lived an extremely simple and blameless life, and I knew of no one more eligible as a husband for Connie, whose tastes, moreover, had much in common with his own.

Harry was not long in perceiving Connie's decline in health; and, connecting it, as I imagined, with that of her sister, grew very anxious. One day, after having taken them for an outing in his motor car, he asked me to accompany him to his rooms in the city.

He said little on the way, but once in his 'den' he spoke abruptly of Winnie's illness, which was at this time rapidly progressing.

"What do you think of it?" he asked.

"The doctors advise a complete change of climate," I said, vaguely.

"Humbug!" he muttered.

"It seems the only chance," I said; "but my father has set his face against it. Says there's no hope; but, of course—"

"The girl will die," he said, in a decisive tone. "The only man who could save her is away in the Himalayas, and could not be reached within I don't know how many months."

"You mean—"

"Ravana Dâs—yes. He might do it ... or tell us how."

"Is he a physician, then?"

"More than that. But it is not exactly a physician that is needed, Burford. There is nothing, I think, vitally wrong with Winnie. But there are possibilities that medical science knows nothing of. This vague talk about 'going into a decline' is merely a veil for ignorance."

"Well, old man, it you can supply a better hypothesis, one that we can work on, I shall be very grateful," I said, a trifle ironically.

"I can't do that—yet." he said, "I don't know enough; and what I fear is too awfully improbable to spring upon an old sceptic like yourself ... Tell me," he added abruptly, "did your father know that man Calthorpe, the hypnotist who disappeared about a year ago?"

"Yes—why?" I answered, staring at him in a sort of terror, for which I could not account.

"What was the nature of this acquaintance?" he asked.

"Its nature? Well, I know very little. My father suffered at his hands in some way, and I believe that in a less law abiding country their enmity would have had a tragic ending."

"Burford, your father killed that man!"

"You are mad, my boy—stark, staring mad!"

"Not a bit of it. Oh! if only my master were accessible!"

He stared in a sort of yearning rapture at the portrait on the wall, as if to draw inspiration from it.

"Why do you connect this man Calthorpe with the matter?" I asked. "In the first place, it is not known whether the man is alive or dead."

"Your father's fate is bound up with that man's, Frank," he said, gloomily. "I don't know how. But I can dimly perceive possibilities that horrify me. I did not remark Winnie's extreme weakness till quite lately—unobservant ass that I am! ... After all, I may be mistaken—the thing seems altogether too hideous—too incredible!"

"This is some beastly superstition your precious master has been filling you up with," I said, impatiently. "Winnie is not the first girl who has gone into a decline. I don't see how Hindu philosophers can help her any more than European physicians."

He made no reply. He was apparently absorbed in the face of the Hindu pundit, and did not seem to hear me. I saw no profit in staying longer, so, with an abrupt "Good-night!" to which I got no reply, I left him.

The next day Winnie did not rise till late in the evening; and, after that, not at all. She declined with an accelerated rapidity, and in ten days passed to her long rest. The close of her life was very peaceful; even the dreams, which had been "too dreadful to tell," left her on the seventh day from her decease. She had long intervals of trance-like sleep, from which she brought back vague memories at an indescribable bliss—as though the spirit, impatient of its fleshly tabernacle, could with difficulty be held to earth by the feeble thread of life.

I need not dwell upon our sorrow. That of my father found some doubtful relief in alcohol and drugs; and only the solicitude and devotion of his surviving daughter saved him, for the time, from utter despair.

"For her sake," he said to me, "I will try and keep up; but she also is doomed—my boy—she also is doomed."

"Why do you talk like this?" I demanded.

His eye grew wild. "There are devils," he said, thickly; "or men with devilish arts. You may stab them through and through with knives—you may spatter their brains on the wall with bullets—no use! They come back in the night and mock you; they rob you of your dearest ones ..."

I thought of Thornton's words, and said—

"Had you anything to do with the disappearance of that man Calthorpe?"

He started as if stung then broke into a harsh laugh.

"The devil should claim his own, one would think," he muttered. "But what are you driving at?" he asked, suddenly raising his head and meeting my eye sternly. "What should I know about Calthorpe's disappearance?"

"I had the idea that in some way—hypnotism or something— the man may have had a hand in—"

"Her death? Nonsense, boy! You rave!"

He would say no more.

IV.

By some process of unconscious reasoning, I had evolved the idea that Calthorpe, dead though he was, was exerting a hypnotic power over my sisters, thus striking at my father through his loved ones. It may seem strange that I, a hard-headed man of the world, should have given any attention to such occult hypotheses. But I had lost one beloved sister through a most mysterious malady, and now that malady threatened the other.

Having questioned orthodox science in vain, however, in my extremity, I lent an ear to the suggestions of an alleged knowledge of forces lying outside the range of ordinary experience—a knowledge I had hitherto denied and ridiculed, as the pretension of predatory quacks and impostors. The drowning man catches at straws, and every straw seems a plank of safety.

Connie very soon developed all the symptoms which had marked her sister's decline; and she, too, had mysterious dreams which no argument or persuasion could induce her to disclose, and which evidently filled her with a conviction that she was doomed.

One day she came to me from her father's room, in a state of wild agitation.

"You must watch him," she said. "He is very near madness. I think he will destroy himself."

"What has he said?"

"Oh, his talk is very wild—I can make little of it. He is possessed with the idea of some enemy—someone who is dead. 'I must seek him in his own place,' he keeps on saying; 'I will find him, and drag him down—down!' Oh, the wildest language! It terrifies me."

I soothed her as best I could; and then, obeying some impulse, for which I could not account, I went to Thornton's rooms, though not expecting to see him. I found him there, however, and he greeted me with an intense earnestness.

"I am glad you have come," he said; I have received a communication."

"From whom?"

"My master. He came to me last night, in his—but you would not understand. Let us call it a dream. He knows our trouble, and will help us. That was impressed upon me beyond all doubt. He will help us! Isn't that glorious, Burford?"

"He has left it pretty late," I said, grimly; and I spoke of my father's condition.

"He should be pacified. To pass on to the next plane in his present state would be extremely perilous, unless he was specially guarded."

"I can't follow your ideas, Harry," I said, with some impatience. "But about your friend, Ravana Dâs. You tell me he is away among the Himalayas. How, then, can he help us?"

"He can easily do so, if he be permitted. Though I have the honour to call him master, he is himself a pupil—the disciple of a still higher teacher. Of course, you don't understand these things. But it was made known to me last night that he will help us, and that he will soon be with us."

"What do you call soon? Unless be travels in some impossible airship, I don't see how—And poor Connie is evidently following her sister. She herself seems to feel it. Only to-day—"

A fixed and startled expression on my friend's face froze the words on my lips. He seemed to see or hear something which I could not. Suddenly the look turned to one of supreme joy and peace, and he sank back in his chair like one relieved of all anxiety.

Involuntarily I turned, and saw that there was a stranger in the room. He was near the door, and must of course, have entered thereby, though I had not seen it open. One glance told me that it was the Hindu, the pundit, Ravana Dâs. There were the delicate, finely-carved, ascetic features, with their grave, gentle, yet lofty expression, as of one who knew all that philosophy could teach, and had renounced all that the world could give. To conceive of this man having a single evil thought was impossible. I remembered afterwards that he was dressed in ordinary clothes, such as we wore ourselves; but I did not remark this at the time.

"I am with you, as you see," he said, in a low, musical voice, which seemed just a trifle muffled; "and I will give you what help I can. But time is limited."

"My dear master," said Thornton, with the utmost reverence; "you have saved us all. This is my friend, Mr. Burford."

"Yes. Well? You are troubled about your sister, Mr. Burford; and your father, too? Is it not so?"

His accent was pure enough, but there was a strange intonation or expression difficult to describe. I was completely subdued by the sheer personality of the man, yet I found courage to say—

"You have come here all the way from the Himalayas?"

"Yes. But that is not our present business. There was one

known to you as Martin Calthorpe, whom you suppose to be in some way connected with the death of your younger sister, and the illness of the one still living. Tell me briefly all you know about this man."

I told him the little that I knew, and also what I guessed. His chiselled face remained impassive during my speech. He was silent for some moments; then he turned to Thornton.

"The man is not unknown to us," he said. "He took the darker path many years ago, and developed some powers. By the unbridled use of those powers he finally wrenched away his lower personality from the higher self, and when the time came he passed from earth suddenly. Doubtless he was what you call killed. Being so utterly evil, he found it necessary—you understand."

Thornton sat bolt upright, deadly pale.

"Of course," he stammered: "I—I should have known; but—but these things are so incredible—"

"You were always of the sceptical ones," said Ravana Dâs, with his gentle smile. "This being is happily one of the last of his kind. We must destroy him."

"Destroy him?" I repeated. "But you say he has already been killed!"

"He has been what you call killed. That is probable. Words are misleading. Our task now is to put it out of his power to do further harm; and I think that can be done."

I was silent, pondering these enigmatical words. When I looked up the Hindu had gone. I turned to Thornton, but he grasped my hand, and said—

"Come again to-night, Frank. I promise you the end of all this horror."

I understood that I had to leave, and went away in a confused and dissatisfied state of mind, yet with a growing hope struggling to rise in my heart.

On my return home, I found the house in a commotion. The cause was soon made known to me. My father had shot himself. Connie was prostrated by the shock and could not be seen. A note was handed to me.

"My Dear Frank" (it read),—"I can bear up no longer. I killed that man's body and now I go to find his black soul. If the wretch's own beliefs are correct, I shall meet him in some sphere of troubled or erring spirits, and there our lifelong war shall be renewed. It is my fate. He and I are bound together. He is striking at me through my loved ones, but the end has not yet come. Farewell!"

A madman's letter? So I should have thought, but for the meeting with the Hindu mystic. Now, to my bewildered mind, all things seemed possible. In some strange realm "out of space, out of time"—I pictured two unhappy, crime stained, earthbound spirits, grappling with each other, entangled in an awful conflict for a supremacy that should be eternal.

V.

The requirements of the law having been hastily complied with, I tried to pull myself together for the night's appointment. In a few hours Connie had recovered sufficiently to see me, and I found her, though prostrated in body, calm in mind.

"These are cruel things that have come upon us, Frank," she said, in a tone of gentle resignation, "and I am afraid you will soon be left alone—"

"No, no, Connie!" I said. "It's all unutterably strange, but I have a feeling that something is being done for us even now, when all seems at the blackest. My dearest, you must not lose heart!"

She looked at me strangely. My careless, man-of-the-world attitude in religious matters had often pained her devotional nature, and perhaps she took my words as indicating a reviving trust in the mercy of Providence.

"I feel that I would rather be with dear Winnie," she murmured: "yet I would not like to leave you, Frank."

"Harry wouldn't like to lose you either, sis," I replied, with some faint effort at cheerfulness, at which the ghost of a smile appeared on her pallid lips.

As soon as darkness came I hurried away to Thornton's rooms. He was waiting for me.

"There is work for us to-night, Burford," he said. "My master has traced the whole thing from the beginning."

"An Indian Sherlock Holmes?" I muttered.

"No, nothing of that sort. These men work on different lines—not, perhaps, so very different, though, if the truth were known. He has only to change his centre of consciousness, and read what we call the akashic records—pictures automatically photographed, as it were, upon the ether by all the events that have ever happened—and—But what's the matter? Anything new?"

He had noticed a change in me. I told him of the tragedy at home. Though greatly shocked, he did not seem very much surprised. He read my father's last words with attention.

"It's a great misfortune, old fellow; but don't let these lines disturb you. The vibrations set up by your father's last thoughts will take him into very unpleasant states of consciousness for a time, no doubt; but he will never meet Calthorpe again—that gentleman goes to his own place to-night. And your father will he helped—there is no doubt of that."

"You seem to know all about it," I said wearily. "But where is your master, as you call him?"

"He is here!" said the young man, gravely.

I turned. The Hindu was seated on a chair beside me. This time I was positive that he had not entered by the door, and a moment before the chair had been empty.

"We must go," said Ravana Dâs, ignoring my amazement. My time is precious."

"Come!" said Thornton.

We went into the street and boarded a South Yarra tram, just like a trio of ordinary mortals. The Hindu was silent until Domain-road was reached, then he said to me—

"Whatever happens, friend Burford, you must not let your

nerve desert you. You have a house in a street called Caroline?"

"Caroline-street—yes. But it is empty."

"Assuredly there are no ordinary tenants there. Yet we shall find someone. I think it will he necessary to destroy your house."

"As you please; but it's rather a fine property."

"Property—wealth—all illusion!" muttered Ravana Dâs: and he spoke a few words to Thornton which I did not catch.

We alighted at Park-street, near the gates of the Botanical Gardens, and walked thence to the street in which the house stood. Together we entered the empty house. Thornton produced an electric torch, and we passed along a passage and reached a store-room or pantry, from which we descended some steps into a cellar, the Hindu guiding us. Except for some lumber, the cellar was quite empty.

"Whatever you see," whispered Thornton, "be silent until he speaks!"

The Hindu stood with folded arms gazing intently at the wall opposite the entrance. Several minutes passed in profound silence. Suddenly a brick fell to the floor. It seemed to come from near the top. It was followed by others in quick succession, till in a few moments an opening was made revealing a small, inner cell, from which came the acrid odour of cement mingled with that of long pent-up air. The Hindu, of whom I now stood in the utmost awe, but in nowise feared, signed us to enter.

Raising aloft his torch, Thornton went first, and I followed. There was but one object in the cell, and that was the dead body of a man; and there needed no ghost from the grave to tell me that it was the mortal remains of Martin Calthorpe. It was stretched upon the earthen floor, and stared with glassy eyes at the low, cemented ceiling.

The body was that of a man in the prime of life—a portly, well-nourished body that might have been merely asleep, but for the staring eyes and a bullet-hole in the centre of the forehead. There was not the least appearance of decay—no more than if the man had just been killed. There was even colour in the cheeks. I thought of another corpse lying at my almost desolated home, and a dull, deadly rage began to swell up within my heart.

Then wonder and horror possessed me. How could this body have been preserved so long? Had Calthorpe met his fate so recently? Or had the walling-up of the cell—

"He has been thus a year or more," said Ravana Dâs, answering my thoughts. "But to your work," he added, taking the torch from Harry.

Signing to me, Thornton took the body by the shoulders, a hand under each; I took the ankles, and we essayed to lift it. Harry is an athlete, and my own strength is above the average, but our utmost efforts quite failed to move the corpse.

"It's no use," said the young man, with a gasp, and we fell back, I in a state of speechless amazement.

"Use your blade, then!" said the Hindu.

Thornton drew from under his coat a heavy Goorkha sword, and approached the body, as though that lifeless clay were a living foe. My feeling of hatred had returned, and I set my teeth.

Thornton bent his knee, and aimed a powerful blow at the dead man's neck. To my unutterable horror the blade stopped within a few inches of its mark and flew from the striker's hand. He retreated, dazed.

The Hindu turned to me.

"Take the weapon," he said, calmly. "After all, it is the son who should avenge his father." He gave the torch to Harry, and stood at the feet of the corpse. One glimpse I caught of his bronze features, and it was no longer a living man I saw. It was incarnate Will!

Nerved with a power not my own, I grasped the sword and aimed a deadly blow. It was stopped as before, and my arm tingled as though I had struck a log of wood.

"Again!" cried the Hindu, raising his two hands, and thrusting them forward over the body.

It was like an order to the soldier in battle. I struck; and this time the heavy blade met with no resistance. The head rolled aside, and there gushed from the trunk torrents of rich, red blood, until the body seemed literally to swim in it.

"It is done!" said the voice of Ravana Dâs. "You know the rest. Farewell!"

He was gone.

* * * * * * *

The work of carrying the corpse (which was easily lifted now) to one of the upper rooms was accomplished in silence. Fifteen minutes later we stood amongst a rapidly increasing crowd of people, watching a dense mass of flames spurting from all quarters of the wooden house. The roof fell in, and when it became certain that no part of the building could be saved, we left.

* * * * * * *

It was not yet very late, though it seemed to me that ages had passed since I left home. We returned to Harry's rooms, for I was thirsting for some explanation of the things I had seen.

I was feverish with excitement, but Thornton seemed to have acquired something of his master's self-control; and when we were comfortably seated in his little den, with the pictured, pale-bronze features of the Indian occultist gazing benignantly down upon us, my friend entered into an explanation which, I must confess, only increased my amazement.

"This Calthorpe," he began, "was a man who had given himself up entirely to evil."

"That much seems to be abundantly evident," I interjected.

"You must try and realise, however, what to meant by the absolute rejection of the good in every shape and form. Ordinarily, evil is relative, not absolute—we seldom meet the aristocrat of crime. The fatal grandeur, the awful eminence of a 'Satan' is rarely revealed to us. Had this man been gifted with intellect in proportion to his wickedness, he could easily have made himself a national—ay, even a world-wide scourge."

"Yet he was not of a low type of intellect?"

"Too low to flee to the grander conceptions of crime. What he has accomplished we shall never know, for he wielded powers that enabled him to laugh at human justice, as your friend Detective Mainspray understands it."

"I have heard you say that the development of these occult powers depends on entire purity of thought and deed?"

"The full development—yes. You have seen how easily my master (who is himself only a disciple as yet) overcame by force of will the etheric resistance which Calthorpe was able to interpose between my sword and his precious neck. Yes, occult powers are, at their highest, united with great loftiness of character and nobility of aim; sometimes they are associated, in a limited form, with a grovelling and sordid nature; and, again, as in Calthorpe's case, they are seen in combination with positive malevolence and tendencies of an altogether evil kind. The so-called 'black magicians' of the Middle Ages were, no doubt, men of the stamp of Calthorpe. Such beings, gifted with powers which, though limited on their own plane, are superior to the workings of physical science as commonly known, must possess, as you will see, potentialities for active evil before which the imagination may well stand appalled."

"And this power—whatever it may be—how could this wretch carry it with him to the next world?"

"The power really belongs to the 'next world,' as you call it, and can be more readily exerted there. But let me explain. This man had literally thrown away the immortal part of himself, since he was all evil, and nothing that is evil can live. He was doomed to a sort of slow disintegration—the gradual conscious decay and death of the animal personality that had wilfully wrenched itself away from its immortal essence."

"You mean the soul? And what becomes of that?"

"It rests on its own plane, so to speak, till the time arrives for its next incarnation on earth."

"Very well. Go on."

"We know that Calthorpe was killed. Having some occult knowledge, he was aware that a soulless entity, deprived of its physical vehicle, was doomed to perish. The ordinary man, after the death of the body, remains for a time in a state the Hindus call 'Pretaloka' until his thoughts are entirely freed from earthly concerns. Pretaloka is the scientific fact behind the dogma of purgatory. While living, Calthorpe could, in trance, visit the lower levels of Pretaloka, and roam about there at will—that is, his thought could vibrate in unison with the vibrations of the spirit-matter of those levels, and thus function there."

"But this was only on condition, I understand, that he had a living body to return to?"

"Exactly. Being without a soul to which he could cling, he needed a body as a sort of point of support. Losing his physical life utterly, he would sink by a natural and inevitable law to a lower state even than Pretaloka, there to suffer, as I have said, the horrors of disintegration and decay, ending in the complete annihilation of the human personality."

"But what use could his body be when he was shot dead?"

"The effect of the bullet would be merely to transfer his consciousness to Pretaloka. By occult arts he could preserve his remains from decomposition as long as they were not disturbed. Evidently your father played into his hands by walling up the body in that cell. If he had only thought of destroying it, as we did, by burning down the house, thus severing the magnetic line of communication, so to speak, depended on by Calthorpe for mere existence, that worthy would have gone to his own place almost immediately."

"And that place is—"

"We will not speak of it," said Thornton, with a shiver. "As it was, in order to remain in the state called Pretaloka (for it is not a place), he was compelled to preserve his late vehicle—his body—in a sort of cataleptic trance, and that he could only do so by stealing vitality from the living and transferring it to the corpse."

I shuddered as I recalled the scene in the cell—the torrents of fresh blood.

"Then," I muttered, "this—this creature was nothing but a

vampire?"

"A vampire, indeed—glutting his vengeance and serving his necessity at the same time. Remember how his wife died—she was his first victim; and her fate was the more terrible because she knew what was happening. Calthorpe was a 'black occultist' of inferior powers, or he would probably have been better known to my master, in which case help might have come sooner."

"His powers seem to have been sufficient for his purposes," I said, bitterly.

"Yes. Yet, with a deeper knowledge, he could have dematerialised his body, and removed it to some inaccessible place; and, again with wider powers, he could have kept it alive by extracting the necessary vitality from the physical air, which contains all that is needed for human sustenance. But his fate was decreed, and he himself was the instrument of his own undoing."

"That may be very well, old man, but it doesn't bring back Winnie and the poor, old dad."

"They are far better off where they are, Frank. Religion and occultism agree on that point, as on so many others. The grief of friends for those gone before only harms them, for it attracts their thoughts earthward during their stay in that realm of illusion I have called Pretaloka, and so delays them on their journey heavenward. Thus we should not grieve, but rather, in the words of the poet—

"'Waft the angel on her flight with a paean of old days.'"

"And—and is the creature finally disposed of? Is Connie entirely freed from all further peril?"

"You shall see!" said the young man, his voice vibrating with confidence and joy. "We have slain the cockatrice. Its power for evil is now confined to its own plane. The thing is perishing with its self-created poison. Let us think of it no further."

"One more question," I said. "How did your Indian teacher get here if he were away in the Himalayas only the day before?"

"What we saw was not his physical body at all. The body is the prison of the soul for ordinary mortals. We can see merely what comes before its windows. But the occultist has found the key of his prison, and can emerge from it at pleasure. It is no longer a prison for him—merely a dwelling. In other words, he can project his ego, his soul, his true self—whatever name you choose to give it—out of his body to any place he pleases with the rapidity of thought."

"He seemed a substantial enough body, as far as I could see."

"Doubtless. Thought is creative in a deeper sense than we dream. Science tells us that all the materials that constitute our physical bodies exist in the air we breathe. An advanced occultist can draw thence by the power of will all he needs for a temporary vehicle in which to function; or, if he so prefers he can produce by illusion all that he wishes people to believe they see."

We talked on till daylight neither of us feeling any desire for sleep. Thornton went deeply into his strange teachings, and I heard for the first time a great deal that was wildly incredible; but I had to confess that, if it was madness, there was no lack of method in it.

Early in the morning, feeling the need of fresh air and action, we set out on foot for my home, still discussing the tremendous questions of man's life and destiny.

Arrived at the house, a servant informed us that Connie was in the morning-room, and that breakfast was served there. Somewhat surprised, and forgetting our unwashed and unkempt condition, we entered. Connie was seated at the table, with a liberal repast before her.

She arose hurriedly, a bright flush suffusing her cheeks.

"I—I felt so hungry," she said; "you really must excuse me—"

A rush of terrible memories surged up within my heart, and I fell into a seat, giving way to a fit of hysterical weeping. And Harry, for all his assumed calmness, incontinently joined in my sudden emotion, and the scene was at once ludicrous and tragic. Two strong young men crying like children, and a delicate girl—whom they had helped in a humble degree to rescue from the clutches of a monster—doing her utmost to soothe them.

It was some time before we could join Connie at her breakfast, but when we did I felt that the meal inaugurated a new period of health and happiness for the dear girl and her devoted lover, and formed a peace and resignation such as I had lately despaired of.

THE CAVE

by Beatrice Grimshaw

Beatrice Grimshaw (1871-1953) achieved considerable fame in the first decades of the twentieth century as a writer of novels and travelogues about the South Pacific, where she travelled extensively. Born in Cloona, County Antrim, Ireland, Grimshaw was educated at Caen, Normandy; Victoria College, Belfast; and Bedford College, London. She worked as a journalist in Ireland before embarking on her first expedition to the South Pacific in 1903.

Grimshaw subsequently became a professional traveller and wrote numerous books about her experiences, both non-fiction works and tales of romance and adventure. She spent most of her time in Port Moresby, until she settled in Kelso, near Bathurst, in 1936 where she continued to write until she retired in 1940. Amongst her numerous stories are several tales of supernatural horror, which are worth seeking out. Some are published in *The Beach of Terror and Other Stories* (1931) and *The Valley of Never-Come-Back* (1923), but many are uncollected. 'The Cave' was first published in 1932, and reprinted in the *Avon Fantasy Reader 13*; 'The Forest of Lost Men' was first published in 1934, and reprinted in the *Avon Fantasy Reader 16*.

Over Rafferty's Luck—misnamed—the wind seemed always blowing. Perhaps it did not really blow as much as I imagined. Perhaps, for the first time in my life, I merely had leisure to observe such things, and to be impressed by them.

To see how the long grasses shivered, showing the footmarks of the wind, it strode over them like Peter striding on the sea; as it suddenly failed and sank—like Peter—leaving behind it a flurry of stirred leaflets that made you think of flaws on water.... How, in the tide of the grass, always rising higher against the few doomed buildings, there streamed and wavered, like wonderful seaweeds, long strands of bishop-purple bougainvillea, and *allamanda*, all gold—wreckage of the creepers that used to climb over the roof and wall. How a loose door, in office, or bungalow, would suddenly give itself to the wind, and shut with a thunderous noise, making one think, for a distracted moment, that somebody had returned....

Nobody did. It had not been anticipated that anyone would, when the owners of the bankrupt mine had hired me to stay there. I was to hold the place by doing a little work, while they went afield looking for capital—which they hardly expected to get. There was just enough chance of it, however, to make it worth their while to send me to the island, and leave me there at a negligible salary, with six-months' stores, and the freedom of the whole place, on which there was not so much as a native or a dog. Only myself and the deserted shaft and the rotting bungalow, and the wind that blew continually, complainingly, through the grasses and through the fallen creepers, wine-coloured and gold.

There were these, and something else. There was a shadow on the island: the loom of a strange and eerie story but half-told.

Rafferty's Luck had not failed from the usual causes—not altogether, that is. It had gone through the common history of little, remote mines; supposed at first to be very rich in copper, it had turned out to be a mere pocket, with a problematical vein behind it, that might or might not be worth developing when found.

It had been worked by the partners—there were three—in turns. The island was far out of the track of ships; it had been visited accidentally, by a shipwrecked crew. Three of these had found the copper, and kept silence; and later on, two had gone up to work it.

They had worked it, won enough ore for a good show, and waited confidently for the returning boat. But—when it came, it found only one man. The other had killed himself. Without any reason, he had cut his throat.

The third man took his place, and arranged, as before, that a passing schooner should call. It called within a few days, and found one man. The other, without any reason, had leaped over a precipice, and died.

Upon this, the third went away, and stayed so long that the mine—which was on British territory, and under mining laws—had nearly been forfeited. At the last moment the men now interested in it got me to go and hold the place, while the third partner went to London for capital.

They were candid enough—they told me that the island was under a shadow; and when I asked just what they meant, they said: "Exactly that. Rafferty and Wilder" (the two who had died) "both said something about shadows."

"What?" I asked.

"Nothing that anybody could understand. Rafferty had cut almost through his windpipe, and Wilder's face was smashed in by the fall. As like as not," went on the third partner,—France was his name,—"as like as not, drink had something to do with it; they were neither of them sober men."

"But you are—and you didn't come to any sort of grief?"

"I am—and I didn't."

"Yet you don't feel like staying. You only had a few days of it."

"Haven't I told you I must go and scare up some cash? Are you on, or not?"

"I am on," I said.

"Good. A man with an M.C. and a D.C.M. like you—"

"Hang the M.C. and the D.C.M. I'm going because I'm broke, and because I want to know what it's like to be really alone. As for your shadows, they won't make me jump over cliffs. I take one spot after sundown, never more."

"Good," said France again. He looked at me as if it was in his mind to say something more, but whatever the thing was, he kept it back.... "About the journey," he continued....

Six weeks later I was left at Cave Island by a whaleboat—the last step in a decline that began with an ocean liner, continued through inter-island schooners and trading ketches, and ended in the last ketch's boat, sent off to ferry me through a network of reefs too dangerous for any sizable ship.

"If there is payable ore here," I thought, "small wonder it's been overlooked; God-forsaken and Satan-protected the place is, and out of the way of the world!" And I began to wonder, as the whaleboat stemmed green shallows, making for the hummocky deserted bay that stretched beyond, whether I had done well. I am from Clare; I have seen the dread sea-walls of Moher, and felt, on their high crowns, the "send" of that unknown evil that men of Ireland, for the confounding of strangers, chose to personify as the frightful Phooka. "This too is an evil place," I thought, and on that account, I said a small prayer. Now mind you, it was well done, as you shall afterwards know.

Then we beached, and began unloading my gear; and I was too busy with that, and with carrying most of it up to the bungalow, before dark should fall, to think of anything else. By and by the boat was back at the ship's side, a long way out, and the ship had made sail, and when I looked at her, in the last of the light, and saw her fading away like a ghost that has given its message, and goes back to its tomb, I knew that I was indeed alone—pressed down and running over, I had my wish!

After a day or two, I began to wonder what all the trouble was about, if indeed there had ever been any trouble except drink and the consequences of it. Cave Island was a windy spot, as I have said; not very large or long, only a mile or two at biggest, it was swept by all the winds that blow across the immense, lonely spaces of the central Pacific world, where almost no land is. In the mornings and at nights it was cool; during the day nothing but the wind saved it from most torrid heat. It was a barren place, and full of stones, some of them black and spongy and as big as houses. There was coarse grass, that never seemed to be still, almost as if things unseen ran under it, and kept it moving even in a calm. There were a few flowers that Rafferty had planted in his time, and there was the iron bungalow, and a storing shed, and a shaft with bucket and windlass dangling over, and tools abandoned by the side. For the rest, there was the sun wheeling over the island, at night the myriad unpitying stars, and always sea and sea. So lonely it was, that you could hear yourself breathe; out of the wind, you could listen to your heart beating. When you got up in the morning you took the burden of yourself upon your shoulders, and carried it, growing heavier and heavier, all day; even at night, it was with you in your dreams. Yet I liked this, as one likes all strong, violent experience. Solitude is violent; it is delicious, it is hateful; and as surely as a snake unwatched can strike, so it can maim or kill....

What do you know, you who think that solitude is a locked room in a city, or a garden with the neighbours shut away?

A week or so went past. Every day I went to the workings, did a job with pick and shovel; wrote in my diary what I had done, and for the rest, was free. I liked to be free. Not since the war—and certainly not in it—had I been my own man; if I was not filling one of the blind-alley jobs that confront the untrained, hardly educated man of near forty, I was harder at work than ever, hunting another.

But if I was free, I was not at ease. I could see, after the first few days, that there was not much in the mine—worse, that there was never likely to be. I had worked copper before, and I judged that the worst of it was better than the best of this, once the surface show had been removed. In fact, it was nothing but a pocket. And how was a mere pocket going to give me a brick bungalow with an arched veranda, in Bondi or Coogee, and a garden behind it and a little touring-car, and a tobacconist's business somewhere near the surf beaches, to keep all going; and in the garden, behind the windowpanes of the bungalow, in a long chair on the veranda, at the wheel of the car, or swimming brown and bonny through the surf—always there, in my heart and in my life, the girl of my hopeless dreams.

No, I had not told France all the truth. He is a good fellow, but one does not give him confidences. Being broke was nothing new to me; being alone, the spice of it, the strangeness, I could have done without. But Rafferty's Luck offered the one and only chance I had of making my dream come true, and I would have taken it if it had led halfway to hell.

Instead, it seemed to lead to nothing.

I was so disappointed, so sore against France—whom I now perceived to be engaged in the familiar trick of unloading a hopeless venture upon a public too far away to understand—that I set my teeth, and resolved to hunt the island from coast to coast—to comb it through for a better show, and if found, to take that show myself. I don't know that this was moral; I only know I was prepared to do it.

By this time, I had forgotten all about the "shadow," and the suicides. Men who have roughed it, who own little, are not particularly shocked at suicide, or sudden death of any kind. You must have much to lose before you shudder at the passing breath of the storm that has swept another from his hold on life, and that will one day sweep you too.

So I did not think about Rafferty, or about Wilder—until the day when I found the cave; and after that it all began.

I had been prospecting over the summit of the island, without much success. On this day, I went down to the beach, and began patiently to circle the whole place, resolving, literally, to leave no stone unturned in the search for something better than Rafferty's Luck. It takes longer to walk all around an island than you'd think, even if the island is no more than a mile or two across. I spent all day upon the job, eating a biscuit for dinner, and drinking, once or twice, from the little streams that ran out of the crevices. If any of them had tasted ill I should have been glad; but they were all fresh as milk, no tinge of metal in them.

Toward sunset I came upon something that I hadn't noticed before—a cave. It was at the foot of an immense wall of rock; you could not have seen it from above, and the only way of reaching it was the way by which I had come, a painful climb along the narrow glacis of stones on the windward side. The beach and the anchorage were of course on the lee side. Ships wouldn't, for their lives, come up to windward; I was therefore almost sure that nobody, save myself, had seen or visited the cave.

That pleased me—you know how it is. I was glad that I had brought my torch with me—a costly big five-cell, like a search-light, that She had sent me when I sailed; she hadn't sixpence to rub against sixpence, but she would have given her head away—and so would I; that was why we both were poor, and likely to remain so....

I had a good look at the cave. It was very high; seventy or eighty feet at least. It was not quite so wide, but it seemed to run a good way back. The cold stream of wind that came out of it had a curious smell; I could not describe it to myself, otherwise than by saying that the smell seemed very old. I stood in the archway, in that stream of slightly tainted wind, examining the rocks about the mouth of the cave. There was not much daylight left now, but I could see, plainly enough, that here was small hope of a better find. I kept the torch in my hand as I went on into the interior of the cave; time enough, I thought, to turn it on when I had to; there were no spare batteries on the island.

By and by I began to go backwards; that is, I went on a little way, and then turned to look at the ground I had passed, lit up by the stream of light from the entrance. Coral, old and crumbling underfoot; limestone; a vein of conglomerate. Nowhere any sign of what I sought. It was getting darker; the cave, arching high above me, seemed to veer a little to one side, and the long slip of blue daylight was almost gone. Now, with half-a-dozen steps, I lost it altogether; I stood in complete darkness, with the cool wind streaming about me, and that strange, aged smell, now decidedly stronger.

"Time for the light," I thought. Something made me swallow in my throat, made me press my foremost foot tight to the ground, because it seemed, oddly enough, to have developed a will of its own; it wanted to move back, and the backward foot wanted to swing on its toe and turn round....I will swear I was not afraid—but somehow my feet were.

I snapped on the light, and swung it ahead. It showed a narrow range of rock wall on each side, a block of velvet darkness ahead, and in the midst of the darkness, low down, two circles of shining bluish green. Eyes—but what eyes! They were the size of dinner-plates! They did not move, they only looked; and I was entirely sure that they saw me. If they had been high up, I do not think I should have minded them—much. But they were, as I have said, low down, and that was somehow horrible. Lurking. Treacherous....

I had shot crocodiles by night, discovering them exactly as I had discovered this unnamed monster, by the shine of their eyes in torchlight. But I had had a sporting-rifle to do it with, and knew what I was shooting at. Now I was totally unarmed; the futile shotgun I had brought with me for stray pot-hunting, was up at the bungalow. I had not the vaguest idea what this creature might be, but I knew what was the only thing to do under the circumstances, and I did it: I ran away.

Nothing stirred. Nothing followed me. When I reached the outer arch of the cave, all glorious with sea and sunset, there was not a sound anywhere but the lifting crash and send of the waves upon the broken beach. I stood for a moment looking at the magnificent sky that paled and darkened while one could quickly have counted a hundred. "I shall have to come back," was my thought, "with a charge of dynamite, and a bit of fuse. Shotgun just as much use as a pea-shooter." I told myself these things, but now that I was out of the cave, I could not for the life of me believe in what I had seen. "It wasn't the sort of smell it ought to have been," I said aloud weakly, and kicked the stones about aimlessly with my foot. Something rolled. I looked at it, and it was a skull.

"Peter Riordan," I said, "this is not your lucky day." And I picked up the skull. There were bones with it, all loose and lying about. "I can make a guess what happened to Mr. Bones!" I said, peering through swiftly falling twilight at the skull. It was like a shock of cold water to see that it was old beyond computing— almost fossilized, dark and mossy with the passage of incalculable time. As for the bones, they crackled like pie-crust when I put my foot on them. I could see where they had fallen out of the rock; they must have lain there buried, for a long time.

"I don't understand," I thought. "Things don't fit together. This is a hell of an island." It seemed good to me to climb the cliff as fast as I could, making for the solid walls of the bungalow, and leaving behind me in the inhospitable twilight those queer bones now unburied, and the cave, and the immense green eyes that did not move.

The bungalow was a good way off; in order to reach it, I had to cross the empty rolling downs on the top of the island, with their long grass that never was still, and their heaps of hummocks of black stone. By this time it was so late that I could only see the stones as lumps of indefinite darkness. Some of them were big even by daylight; by night they looked immense. They were queerly shaped, too; once, when I paused to get breath (for I can assure you I was going hard) I noticed that the biggest one in sight looked exactly like the rounded hind-quarters of an elephant, only no elephant ever was so big.

I leaned against a boulder, and mopped my face. There was a rather warm wind blowing; it brought with it the sort of scents that one expects by night—the dark-green smell of grass wet with dew, the curious singeing odour of baked stones gradually giving out their heat, little sharp smells of rat and iguana, out hunting. And something else....

"Peter Riordan," I said, "you quit imagining things that aren't there. Rafferty did, and Wilder did." And I propped myself against the stone, and took out a cigarette.

It was never lighted. Just as I was feeling in my matchbox, I looked at the giant boulder again, and as I hope for heaven, I saw it walk away. That is, it did not walk—it hobbled, lurching against the sky.

For obvious reasons I didn't light the cigarette, but I put it into my mouth, and chewed it; that was better than nothing. "We aren't going to be stampeded," I said (but noiselessly, you may believe). "We are going to see this through." And, being as wise as I was brave—perhaps a little wiser—I got inside a sort of pill-box of loose stones, and peered out through the openings. By this time it was as dark as the inside of a cow; you could only see stars and stars, and the ink-black blots made against them by one thing and another. And the great black thing that wasn't a boulder, and wasn't an elephant, went lurching and lumbering, smashing through Orion, wiping Scorpio off the sky, putting out the Pointers where the Cross was waiting to come up; it seemed to swing all over the universe.

"It's chasing something," I thought.

It was. One could see it tack and turn with incredible swift-ness, swinging behind it something that might have been legs and might have been a tail. Clearly, it was hunting, like the rats and the iguanas, and now I could see—or thought I could see—the thing it hunted: Something very small, compared with the enormous bulk of the beast; something that dodged in and out of the stones, running for its life. A little, upright thing with a round head, that scuttled madly, squeaked as it ran.

Or had I fancied the squeak? The whole amazing drama was so silent that I could not be sure. It seemed to me that if there had been a cry, a queer thin cry, I had heard it inside my head, not outside. I can't explain more clearly, but there are those who will understand. At any rate, I was sure the thing had cried, and that it had cause. The end was approaching.

There was another frantic doubling, another swing around of the immense hobbling beast, and then the little creature simply was not—and the enormous shadow had swept to the edge of the cliff and over, and was gone.

I felt my forehead wet. My breath was coming as quickly as if it had been I who had squeaked and doubled there, out among the night-black grasses and the stones.... The shadow! They who died had seen shadows.

"But," I found myself saying argumentatively, to the silent stars, "I am real, and that wasn't. It's like things in a dream, when you know the railway engine can't run over you, because it isn't really there."

Something obscuredly answered: "Rafferty is dead, and Wilder is dead. Death is real."

I got out of the pill-box. "I shall say the multiplication table all the way home," I told myself. And I did. But when I had got home to the bungalow, I said something else—I said a prayer. "Perhaps they didn't," I thought. Then I went in, and cooked my supper. It was quite a good supper, and I slept very well.

Next morning nothing seemed more impossible than the things that, I was assured, had not happened last night. All the same, I decided to go and have another look at the cave, with plenty of dynamite, and the shotgun, for what that might be worth. I could not forget that Beth, who would give her head away—and who had given her heart—was waiting for that brick house, and that little car, and those Sunday mornings on the surf beaches. And I was resolved that she should not miss them.

It was now about ten days since I landed, and I began, for the first time, to count the days that remained. France would have to reach London, find a simpleton who would finance his venture (I knew he'd do it—he could have squeezed money out of a concrete pillar), return to Australia, and make his way to the island. Six weeks; three weeks; six weeks; three or four weeks. Nineteen in all. And I had put one week and a half behind me. There remained seventeen and a half. Four months and a half. A hundred and twenty-two days, if I succeeded in keeping my senses. If I did not, it was a hundred and twenty-two minus x.

I could see the x in front of me; a black, threatening thing, big as a garage door. But I defied it. "You won't get me," I said. "I'm bound for Bondi and the brick bungalow." And, whistling

"Barnacle Bill" to keep my spirits up, I began to cut lead piping into slugs. "Ought to have brought a rifle," I thought, "but never mind; I can do something with these, and a bit of dynamite and a fuse."

It took me about fifteen minutes to cut up the slugs. When I raised my eyes from the table on which I was working, I saw, through the window of the cottage, a steamer—a small trading-boat with a black and white funnel. She was out in the road-stead, and she was just preparing to let go anchor.

I let off a shout; you should hear a Clare man do it!

"X, I've got you," I cried. "Dead as a doornail—stabbed with your own beastly minus!" And I sent the lead pipe flying across the floor. I just had to make a noise.

In the roadstead, the little steamer was making a terrible row with her roaring anchor-chains, and a whaleboat was rapidly being lowered. Within ten minutes, France and I were shaking hands.

"Never went to London at all," he told me at the top of his voice. "Got the whole lump of expenses right in Sydney, from two or three splendid chaps who were staying at my hotel. Loads of money. Country fellows."

"They would be," I thought, remembering France's local reputation.

"Brought the machinery up with me. Brought a geologist. Get a start, get a nice report, go down again and float the company."

"Leaving me in charge?"

"That's right."

"It isn't—not by a mile! France," I said, looking him straight in the eyes,—he had candid, jolly blue eyes, the little beggar, and he had a smile under his toothbrush moustache that would have wiled cash out of a New York customs-officer,—"France, I don't like this affair of yours any too well, and I'd prefer to be out of it." For I knew, now, that the little car and the Sundays in the surf would have to come by some other road.

"Got the wind up?" he asked, cocking his hat on one side of his head, and looking at me impertinently.

"I don't know about that," I said,—and indeed I did not know; it was a puzzling matter—"but I do know that there isn't enough payable copper here to sheet a yacht."

"Oh, you're no expert," he said easily. "Let me introduce Mr. Rattray Smith, our geologist. Mr. Peter Riordan."

"Why not a mining engineer?" I asked curtly, glancing with some distaste at the academic-looking youth who had followed France out of the boat.

"Came too high," explained France with a charming smile. "Smith knows copper when he sees it."

"I reckon he knows which side his bread is buttered on," I commented, without troubling to lower my voice over-much. I simply could not stand that geologist; he was such a half-baked looking creature, fairly smelling of chalk and blackboards.

"Quite," was France's answer. "And he's got all sorts of degrees; look lovely on a prospectus."

"Maybe," was all I answered. I heard afterwards that Smith's degrees were more showy than practical, from our point of view—B.Sc., F.G.S., and something else that I forget; palae-ontology was his special game, and he knew next to nothing about metals. France had got him cheap because he had been ill, and needed a change. France, it appeared, meant to make full use of Mr. Rattray Smith's shining degrees in the forthcoming prospectus; meantime, as he somewhat coarsely put it to me, he intended to "stuff the blighter up for all he was worth."

"You go and take him for a walk," he said to me now. "Show him the workings, and help him with his notes. I've got to see the machinery ashore."

I didn't want to see that machinery land; I knew only too well what it would be—old, tired stuff that had been dumped on half-a-dozen wharves, for the deluding of share-holders, in many places; stuff never meant to be used, only to be charged at four times its value in expense accounts....I took Smith to the workings; showed him the ore, lowered him down the shaft, displayed the various tunnels. I said not a word. He could delude himself if he liked; I meant to have no hand in it.

Perhaps he was not such a fool as he looked; perhaps, I cynically told myself, he was more knave than fool. At all events, he said very little, and took only a few notes. I began to like him better, in spite of his horn-rimmed glasses and his academic bleat.

"Look here," I said, as we were returning to the house. "I've been all over the damned island, and I'll eat any payable stuff you find."

"All over?" he said, cocking one currant-coloured eye at me through his glasses.

I began to think he might not be such a fool as he looked. Clearly he had sensed a certain reserve that lay behind my speech.

"Well," I said, not caring enough about him to mince words, "there's a warren of caves down on the wind'ard side of the island and I tried to investigate the biggest one the other day."

"What did you find? Any indications?" he squeaked.

"Couldn't tell you. I was stopped by a beast. Nightmare beast, with eyes as big as plates. Hadn't a gun with me, but I meant to have a go at it later on."

"But that's—but that's most—" he began to stammer eagerly.

France, who had gone to the house for a drink, looked out of the window, and interrupted me.

"What's this about beasts, and why are you making slugs for your silly old shotgun?" he demanded.

I told him.

"You've got 'em too," was his only comment.

This, for some reason or other, made me desperate.

"That's not the whole of it," I said. "Last night I saw a thing as big as six elephants chasing a little thing in the dark."

"You would," he said. "Have a hair of the dog that bit you, and take some bromide when you're going to bed."

"Look here—will you come down to the cave yourself?" I pleaded.

"With all that machinery to land, and the ship bound to clear before sun-down? Not much."

"Very well. Will you come for a walk on the top of the island after dark?"

"Oh, yes," he said, casually. "Never saw anything when I was here for a fortnight, and don't expect to now. But I'll come."

"Was it moonlight when you were here?" I shouted after him as he started for the beach.

"What's that to—Yes, I reckon it was."

Rattray Smith began deliberately: "The influence of light on all these phenomena—"

"What d'ye mean?" I asked. "Are you a spiritualist? Surely you couldn't be."

"In the excellent company of Sir William Crookes and Sir Oliver Lodge, I certainly could," he answered. "I suppose you think that the modern man of science is necessarily sceptic, like his—his—"

"I think he believes either a darn' sight too little, or a devilish sight too much, if you ask me," I said. "But wait till tonight."

We waited. And after dark, we all went up to the top of the island and posted ourselves in the "pill-box." There was an enormous sky of stars above us; all round us the faintly smelling, feebly rustling grasses, and standing up among them, big as cottages and railway cars, were the silhouetted shapes of gigantic rocks.

I had thought we might have hours to wait, and after all might see nothing; but I was wrong. We had not been in the pill-box ten minutes, before a whole mass of stars before us went suddenly black. It was just over the biggest of the cottage-sized rocks, and I had a nasty idea that the rock itself—or what we had thought to be rock—was part of the rising mass.

Have you ever seen an innocent stick turn into a serpent, a log in a river show sudden crocodile-eyes and swim away?

If you have, then you will know how I felt.

Up went the monster, half across the sky; and now it began to lurch and hirple with that strange movement I had noted before, covering immense areas of ground with every lurch. I heard Rattray Smith draw in his breath with a sort of whistling noise.

"I don't think it'll touch us," I whispered, with my lips on his ear. "Keep quiet."

"Man," he said. "Oh, man!" and seemed to choke.

France kept quite still.

I smelled the queer smell of it, not the sort of smell it should have been; strangely old and non-pungent. I saw a small shadow, round-headed, come out of nowhere and scuttle away. I saw the great shadow hunting it. Smith saw too; for some extraordinary reason, he was crying, in broken, half-suppressed sobs.

"I don't reckon it can—" I began, in a cautious whisper. He interrupted.

"Man," he said, "You—you—don't know. I've seen discarnate spirits; I've seen—I—No matter. This is beyond everything one ever—*Woop!*"

They were out of the pill-box, like rats breaking cover, and I after them, going I didn't know where. I had seen what they had—and even though I didn't believe it, I ran. The big shadow had turned toward us, suddenly rearing itself up, up, until it stood a hundred feet high among the stars. It leaned a little forward, like something listening; it was semi-erect, and in its enormous forepaws it held a small dark thing that kicked and then was still.

"I—I—" stuttered Rattray Smith as we ran. "Discarnate dinosaur—spirits if they get angry—Where's the house?"

"Wrong way," I panted, seizing his elbow. I had caught a pale grey glimmer in front of us, and realized we were heading for the sea. We stopped and looked back. Something immense rocked heavily against the stars, coming up with appalling swiftness. I saw that it was between us and the bungalow. Not that that mattered; by its size, it could have cracked the bungalow like a nut—and that it meant, for sport or for spite, to drive us over the cliff. I knew—I don't know how—that it was powerless to treat us as it had treated the little black ghost of prehistoric man, in that strange reproduction of an age-old drama, but that it was an evil thing, and would harm us all it could. And I knew too, in the same swift enlightening moment, why one man of the two who died had fallen over the cliff, and why another had slain himself. The last had not been able to endure this terrible rending of the veil....

"Smith," I panted, "stand your ground; you'll break your neck. It can't harm us. It's only the fear."

"Discarnate spirits—" he babbled. I did not heed him. I was busy doing what the soldier did for Joan of Arc, in her evil moment—making a Cross of two sticks, with a stem of grass twisted round them. I held it in my hand, and I said—no matter what. Those who know will know.

By ever so little, the giant shadow missed us, lurched forward and with one toppling leap, went down the cliff.

"Come on," I shouted to Smith and France, though I could not see the latter. "I've got my torch and a plug of dynamite; we'll see the whole thing through."

"What are you going to do?" squeaked Rattray Smith.

"Put out those eyes in the cave," I shouted. I was exhilarated, above myself—as one used to be in the war. I scrambled down the cliff in the transparent dark, feeling my way; slightly surprised, but not much, to hear Smith coming after, I found the cave.

We stood for a minute gaining breath, and looking about us. There was nothing to be seen anywhere; nothing to be heard but the steady slapping of waves on the beach.

"I'm with you," declared Smith squeakily. "As a palaeontologist—"

"A which?" I said. "Don't trip over those bones, and don't stop to pick them up now!"—for he was stooping down and fumbling. I added, without quite knowing what I meant, "The dinosaur's ghost didn't have eyes." But he seemed to know; he said: "That makes it all the more—" I did not hear the rest; we were too busy picking our way.

Round the corner, we stopped. The eyes were there. Low down, unmoving, unwinking in the ray of the torch as I threw it on. Big as plates; blue-green, glittering—

"Hold the torch while I fix this," I whispered. Smith took it;

his hand was unsteady, but I could not blame him for that. I bit off my fuse as short as I dared; lit it, and tossed the plug....

There was a boom that almost cracked our ear-drums; immediately after, stones and dirt came smashing down in such quantity that we found ourselves staggering wildly, bruised and cut, beneath a hundred blows.

"Are you hurt?" I called to Smith.

"Bring your damned torch here," was his only reply.

I came forward, and found him on hands and knees in the midst of an amazing raffle of half-fossilized bones; some of them were as big as the masts of a ship, though partly smashed by the explosion. Almost falling loose from the cliff above our heads was the most astounding skull I had ever dreamed of, a thing far bigger than an elephant's, with huge eye-sockets set well forward, and the tusky jaws of a tiger. Behind the eye-sockets, as I waved the torch, shone a mass of something vivid, greenish blue.

"Oh, God," cried Smith—who didn't believe in God,— "you've broken up the finest dinosaur skeleton in the world!"

I was too busy to trouble about him. I had climbed a little way up, and was scraping at the mass of iridescent, green-blue crystals in which the skull was set; which, through uncounted ages, had sifted down through various openings, filling the huge orbits of the eyes, so that they gleamed in the light as if alive.

"I'd break up my grandmother's skeleton," I told him joyously, "if it was bedded in copper pyrites. We've found the paying stuff at last!" It was not the dark roof of the cave that I saw, as I said that, not the glittering pyrites, or the amazing great bones, or the scrambling, complaining figure of Smith, on the floor of the cave. It was St. Mary's in Sydney, on a summer morning, with a white figure coming up the aisle "on her father's arm"—to me!

Rattray Smith, I understand, has written a great deal for different scientific magazines about the curious happenings on Cave Island. In one, he told the story of the great skeleton; how it was found, and where, and how put together again. He doesn't say what he got for it, but I believe that was something to write home about; good dinosaurs come high, with or without incredible ghost stories attached. The spiritualistic magazines simply ate up his account of the prehistoric ghost and its sinister activities. Especially did they seem to like his conclusions about the skeleton acting as a sort of medium, or jumping-off point, for the apparition. He may have been right or wrong there; at all events, it is certain that after the removal of the bones, no one engaged in working the mines ever saw or heard anything remarkable.

France? We found him in the bungalow, drunk, and under a bed. He says, and maintains, that we were all in the same condition. A man must save his face.

THE FOREST OF LOST MEN

by Beatrice Grimshaw

I don't mind talking to you (he said)—you've been in the big bush yourself, and you know.

It's those new chums I can't stand, the fellows out from Home that knows it all before they ever set foot on a coral beach. They know everything, and they believe nothing; if you tell them anything that couldn't have happened at four o'clock in the afternoon in the Strand, London, they think right off you're "having the loan of them."

It was one of that kind that went up the Kikiramu with me the year after the war; he couldn't learn anything, he thought—but the Kikiramu learned him.

His name was Harlow, a nice fellow enough, if he hadn't been so sure and certain that human knowledge began and ended with what they stuff down their throats in lectures. Cambridge, he was—science of some sort; one of the lost chicks of them exploring expeditions that come out every year in the dry, to find what no one's ever found before. And maybe some of them does find it, those who get fever and die; but the rest of 'em never finds much beyond the last plantation in the hills, where they can get a drink.

And they spend their money, and go home, them who can; but the rest stops, and sometimes it's bad for them. I've known one to sit down in an armchair in broad daylight in front of a hotel and blow his brains out with a revolver that was bought but not paid for at the store.

Harlow hadn't got to that yet; he had a bit left, and he was all on to gamble and make it more, like they do in the books about Monty Carlo. I'd been south with a good shammy *(to Sydney with a lot of gold)*, and I was back, broke. Where there's gold in New Normandy—and it isn't an island proper, but a country of itself, so gold takes finding—I'll find it. I've lived that way, cleaning up a thousand or so a year, but spent it as quick as it came, ever since the Second Jubilee.

Well, we got together, and went up the Kikiramu, mates. You know how it is when you're mates with a man; you've got to find the best in him, and he in you; and you've got to stick, no matter what happens. I could tell you things—but you've lived in the bush yourself: you know....

After we'd had a week together on the river, crawling up and camping among the alligators in the mud, and being bit by sand-flies and mosquitoes about all the time, though sometimes worse, I got to like Harlow quite a bit, because all the time I was learning him, and it's natural.

I learned him to "crack hardy" when it rained on us twelve inches in six hours, and the flour got melted, and the bed-sacks, so that you could have wrung a horse's ration of water out of them. And when we walked so far the first day we landed that we ached too much to sleep, but by four o'clock we had to be up and on, for a worse day! Things like that. It done him so much good, you wouldn't believe.

But for all I was making him over, I couldn't get him to change his mind about the things and people in the bush, which he knew nothing of any more than a monkey knows about mathematics. Of course, he let on he knew everything.

We got to the field, which was at the bottom of a river gorge thousands of feet deep, and I staked claims for both, and we set our boys to work getting down to the wash. There was unknown tribes about us in the bush, which was a hundred or two feet high, and as thick as hairs on a new hair-brush. I didn't take any notice of them, and they took none of us, except sometimes when they came and pegged spears among us, themselves hid so that you couldn't see 'em. I'd fire a shot at random, and let it go. But Harlow, he was keen as terriers after rats, about those useless heathen. Keener than he was after the gold. Most of the work was done by me, in fact; as soon as he knew (for I was fool enough to tell him) that the Lakalakas was unknown to whites, you couldn't hold him.

"Let them alone, and they'll let you alone," I told him, one night when we were sitting together as far away from the boys' camp-fires as we could get, fighting mosquitoes over a little smoke of our own. "If once you get them snake-headed," I told him, "they'll show their spite—catch a boy and roast him alive on a stick, maybe. They're used to being shot at," I told him, but don't you go trying to find any of their villages, not if you value your life, and want to keep your signed-on labour."

He said, sitting there over the smoke, with his face dirty, but white under the dirt, and his eyes as big and blue as a girl's full of that sort of ginger that one likes to see: "The name of science," says he, "is sacred," says he. "If I don't come to the claim tomorrow," he says, "you'll know I've gone to look."

He didn't come. That was the best day we'd had so far; it was Saturday, and I cleaned up, and it ran about a hundred ounces for the week; so, if you understand, I was pretty busy, and pretty well pleased, and hadn't much thought left for young Harlow. I reckoned he'd be all right.

When he came back, he dropped like a pig when you club it, right in the doorway of the tent. "I'm done," he said. "But oh, Tim Monahan," says he, "I'm so happy I could die this minute!"

Then he told me what he'd seen. He had that sort of beginner's luck makes a man lift gold out of a creek first time he tries, and maybe never again. He'd found what no one else had found,—a village of the Lakalakas—and they hadn't killed him for doing it. They were more or less pigmy, he told me, not the size of a boy of twelve, but bunches of muscle, and all naked except for boar-tusks and shells; and they had spears all carved and painted, like the ones they use to peg at us in the dark. He danced before them and sang, to show it was peace, and they were that pleased they took him by the hand, and led him to the men's house, which was full of all manner of queer things—heads and dried guts, among them. And it was too dark for photos, but he said, when he went away, "I'll come back," and made signs about returning.

"What do you think of it?" says he.

"I don't think," says I. "I've enough to do looking after two teams of boys and two men's claims, without taking time off to think."

"I'm sorry," says he, all grieved. "I didn't—I'm afraid I've not been exactly playing the game; but after I've got my photos," says he, "it'll be all right." And he went to sleep.

I called up my head boy by and by, a wicked young savage that I liked quite a bit, and he knew it, and would tell me things.

"What do you reckon they let him go for?" I said. "I remember a mate of mine when the Wakaka field brake out, that was taken and eat alive for less—eat by bits, cutting off what they wanted. And I went through a village for it, afterward.... What do you reckon?"

The boy said, straight away: "They think him mad."

"Oh!" says I. I understand. Savages won't kill a madman. But they will do queer things to him, if he gets across their hawser, in a way of speaking.

The boy stood up in the firelight, with the smoke curling round him like he was some picture of a heathen god in the clouds; a fine chap he was, clean as bronze, and clever in his own way; and it came to me then, how little we knew about any of them, after all.

"The Lakalakas," he said, "are very great sorcerers."

I didn't laugh, at that; nor you wouldn't. You know....

"Well," said I, passing him out a fig of tobacco, to keep him going, "what sort do they do?"

He said something then that I can't translate; it was a native word meaning something like enchantment, putting spells on you; but, if you get me, it had to do with your surroundings too, and the way they was related to you.

"Oh," says I at once, "you mean the cursed forest."

He didn't say any more; he bit the fig of tobacco, and moved away, and I knew he meant: "You've got enough for your money." So I shut up.

But I thought a bit that night in spite of what I'd said about thinking; and in the morning I said to my mate: "You've got a nice little locket hanging on your watch-chain."

"If I have," said he, "whose business is—"

"I'm not asking what's in it," I said. "I lay she's a bonzer little lassie, anyhow. I reckon you'd better think about her, and think twice, before you set out after them Lakalaka men again. You got away once," says I, "and I reckon they won't kill you; but—"

"You mind your mining," he says, "and I'll attend to my science."

Well, I don't believe in interfering with people's fancies, even with the best intentions; many a man has spoiled a nice profile doing it. So I said no more. But I noticed him opening up the locket, later on that night, and looking hard at what was inside. If I happened to be walking behind him just at that moment, it was no fault of mine; and if I had a girl with that kind of hair that shows gold even in a photo, and eyes like hers, I wouldn't mind anybody taking a look.... She was handsome enough, too—I don't mean Harlow's lass. But she couldn't do with the mining; women are that way. And gold-mining, you never know how the years go.... I pay a bloke in Sydney to keep a few flowers on her grave, but most like he drinks the money...

Well, I'm sorry; this isn't my yarn. I meant to say, that Harlow was as near as nothing to taking my advice, and keeping off of the Lakalakas. But he didn't. And next day he went out, and didn't come back.

When he'd been away a day and a night, I started after him. I took two or three carriers with me, loaded no more than thirty pounds apiece, because I thought there was maybe going to be work. One of them was the boy I'd been talking to; Hanua was his name.

"If you see one of the Lakalaka dogs," says I, "sing out."

For though you never see one of the tribe unless they wanted, the dogs gave them away sometimes, coming and going for a drink, or looking at you out of the bush; small black dogs they were, that never made a noise, and didn't look natural nor real. Like the ghosts of dogs that have died and gone to hell, I used to think.

To walk through that country, it's like an ant going up and down the teeth of a comb. We climbed till the sweat ran off us like rain off a roof, and we went down sliding, and climbing again; and so it went on all morning till about one o'clock, when I called a halt, and got out the food.

* * * * * * *

While we were eating our tin and biscuit, Hanua, sitting near me, caught me by the arm and pointed. The small wicked face of a black dog was looking out of the bush, just where you couldn't have taken two steps without cutting your way. I think it smelled the tinned meat, but it would come no nearer, not even when I threw a bit at it. It just lifted its lips and cursed us, like, and then it wasn't there.

But now I knew the Lakalakas was following us.

So did the carriers; and before I had time to do anything but pull my revolver out of my belt, not even time to threaten them with it, they had dropped their loads and was away. You can't follow a naked native into the bush. In two minutes, with hardly as much noise as would wake a sleeping cat, they had got down the side of the nearest gully, and was running along the stones at the bottom; and that was all I ever saw of them again. Or anyone else.... What? I don't know, and I don't want to think; some of them was decent boys enough.

Hanua, he finished chewing the wad of meat and biscuit he had in his mouth, and then he says: "You-me go look, suppose you die, me die." And he wiped his mouth with the back of his hand, and stood up. And I clapped him on the shoulder, and I says: "Suppose no die, you live with me."

It was up and down again after that, up and down fit to break the heart of a goat or any army mule, only neither one of them could have gone where we were going. And hot. And there was snakes; I trod on a tiger snake, and he just missed me; and one of them pythons swung out of a tree, yards of him, at Hanua, but Hanua slashed his head off with his clearing-knife, and never looked behind. We didn't have any time to spare; we were making for the village in the hills, and wanted to get there before dark, always provided the Lakalakas didn't spear us first.

Why they did not, considering they must have been following all the time, was what I didn't understand, and didn't much like. We saw no more of them, nor their dogs. And when we come, after an hour or more, on a bit of flat ground, the relief was that wonderful that I could have laid down and slept, just where I was.

It was thick with forest, bigger and blacker than any I had seen before. I couldn't remember the like of the trees, not exactly; they had red papery trunks, that bled like arms and legs when you hit them; and their leaves, a good way up, were long and thin like worms. A kind of fir-tree, maybe, but I didn't know it. It smelled bad in there, the sort of smell there is in a butcher's shop on a hot day; but there was nothing to account for it—it seemed just to be in the air. The bush ropes that tangled everything together, and that you had to cut through, same as in other places, wasn't like common bush ropes, not plain brown and green; but they was spotted red, and dirtied up with white, as if some one'd been spilling blood and brains on them.... What? Oh, yes, you do see that sort of thing in the bush, but not that much of it.

I stood on the edge of it all looking in, and I didn't like the look of it, but it was on the line I'd marked out with the compass, and we couldn't afford to waste time. So in we went, and Hanua, he pulled a long breath or two through his teeth, and said nothing, but I knew what he thought.

"Come on, old son," I says, clapping his shoulder. "It can't take us ten minutes to go through, judging by the lie of the hills and the river, and I don't hold with that heathen rubbish, anyhow." For you see, there was chat about that place, though no other white man had ever seen it; and they said that it was cursed, in a way, and that when you got in, you couldn't get out again.

* * * * * *

You may believe me or you may not, but I've looked up the place since, and there isn't room for it, anywhere, unless in a spot that's no more than half a mile across. Judging, that is, by the lie of the river, which we did map out careful, and did know—rivers with gold in them gets mapped out soon and good. I tell you, there's no room for it—but all the same, the boy and I walked all afternoon, and we didn't get across it. The compass was no good; I reckoned there must be an outcrop of ironstone somewhere about, though I can't say I seen it. We blazed the way as we went, and we didn't come back on any of our blazes.

When it came near dark, we undid the bit of tarpaulin that we carried instead of a tent, and we didn't light any fire, because of the Lakalakas. And Hanua and me, we sat down beside one another, because I reckoned he was a man, for all he was a naked savage, and we talked a bit, quiet, in his own native talk.

He says: "This is the Forest of Lost Men."

I says: "I've heard of it, but I don't understand. What is it?"

He says: "The sorcerers of the Lakalakas are greater than any other sorcerers, and they have put spells, big spells, on this place, and it goes for miles and miles. And it isn't really there, more than a little bit of it," he says: "but once you get into it, you go on walking and walking, and you walk till maybe you die."

"*Koi-koi!*" says I, which is what you say in the Islands, when you mean damn nonsense.

"No *koi-koi*," he says, and sits with his head on his hand.

We never slept; it wasn't a place to sleep in. There was queer noises, like children crying, but there weren't no children there. You weren't quite sure if you was there yourself; but all the same you knew, worse luck, that you was nowhere else. When the light came, late, through all those trees, we up and ate a bit. And we walked. And we walked. Like they used to do in Flanders, when the roads was a thousand miles long before a halt. And we walked.

And that night we slept a little, but we were hungry, because the food was near gone. And next day we walked. And we walked. And there was almost nothing left to eat, and no water except what we licked off the leaves of the trees in the early morning. And all the time it was the dark trees with the wormy leaves, and the bush ropes spotted dirty white and red. There was no footmarks, nor anything of that kind; but we found a bit of necktie stuck on a thorn, and it was blue with stripes, the colour of Harlow's school tie, which he thought a lot of. So we knew we were on the right track, if that was any good to anyone, we being all in the same box now.

End of the next day, Hanua says: "They been following us somewhere outside this place," he says; "and when we drop, they'll come in. The sorcerers will come and take us away," he says, "and even the dogs will be full tonight," he says.

All of a sudden I gave a whoop. "The dogs!" I says. You see, I'd got an idea. I was a cattle-hand once in the Northern Territory, and it learns you to be quick. Or dead.

"I reckon," I says, talking to myself for a bit, "that you can't enchant a dog. If there's such a thing as enchantment. Because," I says to myself, "you must have a soul for them games, and a dog he has no soul."

* * * * * * *

We'd kept one little bit of meat for the last, and I took it, and used the last of the matches to make fire with. And I hung the meat before the fire on a scrap of bark fibre, and I cut myself a length of small bush rope, tough as a whip. And I waited.

It was near half an hour before the thing I was waiting for, happened. Just as the light was beginning to go, at the time those dogs come out to get a drink in the rivers, and hunt food in the bush,—because their masters they don't feed them, except when there's plenty of roast enemy about, just then, I saw a small black wicked face looking out of the bush, and a small black snout working up and down, at the smell of the cooking meat.

Hanua, he didn't move no more than one of the trees, and I stayed quiet. The dog put out its head, and half its body, and then it stopped. But that was enough for me; I had the loop of the bush creeper around its body, from twenty feet away, before you could wink,—and it kicking like a roped bullock, more than you'd think that anything ten times its size could have done.

We got the tarpaulin over it in a minute, and it bit right through it like it was an alligator, and near took a piece out of me. It did get a bite at Hanua, before we had the rope knotted safe around its neck, and let it go.

We kept hold of that rope the way a drowning man keeps hold of the life-line they throw him from the beach. And we followed the dog, where it went. And in ten minutes—you may call me a liar if you like, because it don't make any difference to me—we were out of the wood, and it was only a black patch of trees behind us, looking not much bigger than you could throw a stone across.

We cut the line, and let the little devil of a dog go; and Hanua, he burned his arm with a firestick, to take the poison out. And we got back to the camp, I don't just know how, for it came on dark in no time at all, and the compass was still cronk—is to this day.

Afterwards we had all the men on the field out looking, and maybe we found the wood that was cursed, and maybe we didn't; there was nothing to tell us. If we did, it wasn't working, for nobody got lost. But I reckon we never came across it at all.

We didn't find Harlow, either. Only the other half of his necktie, floating down the river, miles away....

What? Oh, no, they don't kill lunatics; and they didn't kill him. He turned up again, like his necktie. It was in Sydney, a year after, and no one knows to this day what he saw, or how he got down to the coast again. The yarn he pitched—and he quite believed it—was that he had looked for the Lakalaka villages, didn't find any, never saw the tribes at all, and had an attack of fever in the bush that took away his memory.

I don't know about fever. Something did; that's sure. The less you know about those matters, the better; I'd sell a lot of what I remember, for half of nothing with the tail cut off.

I sent his share of the gold we won. It was after that that he got married, to the girl in the locket.... Me? No. The bush has got me, and you know what that is.

THE CAVE OF THE INVISIBLE

by James Francis Dwyer

James Francis Dwyer (1874-1952) was born in Camden Park, New South Wales. His father was a gifted storyteller and this probably influenced Dwyer to write. In 1899, while working in a post office, he was convicted of forgery and sentenced to seven years prison. While in prison he contributed verse and short stories to the *Bulletin*. Dwyer was released in 1902 and left Australia altogether in 1906, travelling widely in the United States, Asia and Africa. He became a prolific novelist and short story writer, most of them tales of mystery and adventure in the Haggard tradition. His short story collection, *Breath of the Jungle* (1915), contains a number of supernatural tales, many of them involving Hochdorf, the German naturalist. The following tale, an unusual ghost story, was first published in *Bluebook* in April 1939.

Jan Kromhout, the big Dutch naturalist, lowered himself into a huge rattan chair and looked out across the green swath of palms and canarium trees. Kromhout's camp, in which I was a guest, was close to the village of Brajonolon, in central Java; and from the terrace of the bungalow we could see the great Temple of Bororboedoer. In splendid majesty it rose before us;

the mighty Tjandi Bororboedoer, "Shrine of the Many Buddhas."

Not as large as the monuments of Angkor Wat, Ajanta and Alara, the Temple of Bororboedoer is considered more beautiful in architectural design. Its carvings, still intact after twelve hundred years, brings thousands of tourists to stare at the bas-reliefs. Those bas-reliefs, if placed in a straight line, would extend for more than three miles. Here was the centre of Buddhist influence in java in the Sixth Century....

"Belief is a strange thing," said Kromhout, his eyes upon the temple. "There are many places throughout the world where the atmosphere has been charged with a definite spiritual quality put into it by the reverence of believers. Buddhism in Java is dead— Mohammedanism has throttled it; but a blind person who came close to this sanctuary would sense the awe and mystery that is still here. Still here after centuries have passed. *Ja.* Into the mixture of oxygen, hydrogen and carbon-dioxide has filtered a spiritual compound that does not react to the instruments of the scientists. It is Faith.

"Do you know that argon, one of the constituents of the atmosphere, was only discovered forty years ago? It is present in seven or eight parts to a thousand in the air we breathe; but we did not know it was there till Lord Rayleigh and Sir William Ramsay discovered it toward the end of the last century. That discovery makes me hopeful. Sometimes—sometimes I think that in the days to come, we might have instruments so delicate that we could measure the spiritual intensity of places like this temple. Measure the degree of faith, of hope, of longing for a better world. I would like to measure the holy dreams that fill the Oude Kerk in Amsterdam, that was built in about 1300, or the air of St. Paul's and St. Peter's, or that place in the Mosque of Saint Sophia at Stamboul that is called 'The Holy Wisdom.'"

For a long interval the big naturalist remained quiet; then with a strange eagerness in his voice he went on: "If such an instrument were perfected, one might also be able to measure the devilish quality of places. Of demon-filled places that I have visited in the Malay."

In silence we sat and stared at Tjandi Borborboedoer. The sun had set; and a soft rose tint spread slowly over the porous trachyte and lava blocks of which the temple is constructed. This tint deepened to a gorgeous crimson, changed to a dark red; then with a fierce suddenness the tropic night plunged upon the building and blotted it out.

Filled with black gloom now were the interminable galleries with their two hundred scenes of Buddha's spiritual experiences. Invisible were the thrilling bas-reliefs beginning with that of Mâya, the mother of Buddha, watching the white elephant descending on a lotus flower from heaven to symbolize the conception of her son, and ending with the last thrilling scenes that show the weapons of the Prince of Darkness turning into flower petals as they fall upon the head of the saint.

From the soft dusk came the voice of Jan Kromhout. The great Buddhist sanctuary seemed to be nearer now. It was, I thought, squatting just beyond the row of flame trees whose red flowers perfumed the night.

"At times," said the big Dutchman, "the East frightens me. I become the victim of terrors. Then I pack my things and take a trip home to Amsterdam, so that I can get my courage back. There is sanity in Holland. Much sanity. I am nearer to God when I put my feet on Kalver Straat. I go and sit in the Oude Kerk, and those stained-glass windows of the Lady Chapel make me feel clean and good. There is a lot of faith in stained glass. And I go to the Ryks Museum and look at the fine pictures by Frans Hals and Rembrandt and Rubens, and so I cure myself. *Ja, ja.* I cure myself.

"Five years ago I went back to see my sister and her husband. I stayed a month; then the East came in the night and whispered to me. I thought that the whimperings of little animals came up to my room from the Leidsche Kade. My sister cried and begged me to stay, but I could not.

"On the ship that brought me to Batavia, I made friends with a strange man. He was a Russian named Andrey Ilyin, and he was an archaeologist. He was but thirty-four years of age, and he was big and strong and bold-looking. And he was a dreamer. A great dreamer. Some one has said that there is no rest for the man who is both a dreamer and a man of action, and this Russian was of that type. He knew the East. He thought it the cradle of life, the home of all the mysteries. He had many ideas that were disturbing; and in the hot, heavy nights crossing the Indian Ocean we stayed up on deck and argued till the dawn.

"He put forward theories that were not supported by scientific evidence; but that lack of evidence did not trouble him. *Neen.* He just jumped across the gulfs, and when you asked him how he got to the other side, he laughed. He thought that scientists lacked imagination, that they spent too much time building bridges instead of hopping mentally to the other side. It may be so. Dreamers see many things.

"One of his theories I had big cause to remember. I will never forget it. He thought that longevity was a matter of breathing the same atmosphere that we had started to breathe. That life depended on the constancy of the atmosphere. You see, we did not know what the atmosphere was composed of, till Cavendish made his tests at the end of the Seventeenth Century. And Cavendish did not know of argon and of other substances.

"'The atmosphere we are breathing is not the same as the Pleistocene or the Neolithic man breathed,' said Ilyin. 'It is not the atmosphere in which the mammoth and the dinosaur lived. We know nothing of its composition in those days. A change in it might have killed them off. Then again the longevity of Methuselah might be accounted for by the air he breathed. Some special brand.'

"Sometimes he made me laugh; sometimes he puzzled me. When we were near Tandjong Priok, he told me the reason of his visit. He was searching for old atmosphere! *Old. Ja, oud!* Atmosphere that had not changed for hundreds of years. Air which was the same air that blew over the Malay in the days when King Asoka sent a piece of Buddha's body to Java as propaganda for Buddhism. They were good propagandists in those days.

"'How can you find such a place?' I asked Ilyin.

"'There might be an old temple bottled up and forgotten,' he said. 'You know how wine gets better with age? If I found such a place, the atmosphere might have improved.'

"I said good-bye to that Russian at Tandjong Priok. I was not sorry. He talked too much. We Dutch say, *Der gaan veel woorden in een zak.* Many words go to one sack."

Kromhout rose from his chair as a soft whimper came from within the bungalow. The black ape was on the point of becoming a mother, and the big naturalist went inside to comfort her. I could hear his voice assuring her that he was close by, and that no harm could befall her.

Returning to the veranda he took up his story. "I went here and there in my business of collecting specimens. I made a trip to Samarinda in Dutch Borneo, and I went from there to Makassar and on to the little San Miguel group in the Sulu Sea. Now and then I thought of that Russian and his theories. It was not easy to forget him. Ideas that are a little crazy stay in our heads when we forget matters that are founded on common-sense.

"I came back to Batavia, and I got a commission which took me to the volcanic country near Padjagalan. It is bad. The sulphur fumes and the carbonic gas kill birds and animals that are fool enough to stay around. It is a little piece of country that looks as if it might blow up at any moment, when some of the old volcanoes start their fires again.

"I had been there two weeks when that Russian fellow Ilyin walked into my camp. 'It is old *Tête-de-Fromage!*' he cried. 'Old *Tête-de-Fromage* who will not be convinced!'

"He told me that he was camped some fifteen miles away, and that he was quite happy and contented. 'I heard that a Dutchman was trapping here, and I thought it might be you,' he said. 'I'm pleased because I wanted to tell you something. You remember our talks about atmosphere? Well, I have found proof of what I said to you on the ship.'

"'What have you found?' I asked.

"He grinned at me. 'I have found a place where the air is six hundred years old,' he said. 'Six hundred years old, and pure.'

"'Pure?' I asked.

"'That is what I said, Dutchman,' he answered. 'Dry and pure. It has been bottled up for centuries. Six centuries or more. There has been no opening except one small door that is not used once in a century. The things living there, toads and lichen, die immediately when in contact with modern air.'

"'You mean that they are killed by the light?' I said.

"'No, by the air,' said Ilyin. 'I have moved them in the night. It is the air that kills them.'

"I sat silent, waiting for Ilyin to tell me more, and he did. 'There is something else about this place,' he said. 'Something extraordinary: the Past is there.'

"'How?' I snapped.

"'In the atmosphere,' he said quietly. 'The air of the place is impregnated with old memories. It has clung to them. They have been held in a sort of atmospheric solution because there has been no fresh air to disturb them. At times—at times you can feel and see enough to reconstruct what happened there.'

"'*Ja*,' I said, 'I know all about those spots. They are not good. They are vicious. If you go trying to reconstruct events that have happened here six hundred years ago, you will get yourself into the crazy house, and the Dutch will ship you back to Russia.'

"'Imagination,' said that fellow, 'is one of the greatest gifts of God. The straight back-heads of the Dutch and the Germans make it impossible for them to carry the gift. If you feel inclined to come over and visit me, I will show you all the proof that you want.'

"Of Course I was curious to know what that fellow had found. My skin prickled with curiosity. He had given me directions; and three days after his visit, I went along the jungle path that led to his camp. That part of Java has many old temples. Quite close are the ruins of Brambaran, which was a Brahman temple dedicated to Vishnu and Siva. I found that Ilyin's camp was alongside a small temple so completely covered with crawling vines that you might pass it, thinking it was a green hill.

"Ilyin grinned when he saw me. 'I knew you would come,' he said; 'I have been watching the road for three days. Cheese and mysteries are great things to attract Dutch naturalists. Tell me, Kromhout, why you people put caraway seeds in your cheese?'

"'To make fools ask the reason,' I snapped. 'Where is your old atmosphere that you were bragging about?'

"'You must not approach it in that spirit,' said Ilyin. 'You see, there are reasons. I am not the owner or the real discoverer. I will introduce you, but if you please, try to look as if you believed, even if you lack the imagination to see beyond your nose.'

"I was annoyed, but I had come to see what I could see, so I followed Ilyin through the jungle till we came to a thatched hut. In the hut were an old man and a girl of about eighteen. First I will tell of the man. He was a Sundanese; and when I saw him, he was what is called *latah*. His eyes were glazed and his nostrils distended. I did not like the look of him.

"The girl—*Ach!* the girl was something that the gods of the jungle had made to peep at. She was just meeting womanhood. Her skin was of beaten gold, and all the dreams of the world were in her big frightened eyes. Eyes like the little musk deer that spoke to you, saying, 'Do not harm me; I am nice and innocent and I will be good.' *Ja*, they were wonderful eyes. And she had little teeth so white and beautiful that you wished that she could get annoyed and bite you with them. And she was dressed as she should be dressed. She had a six-foot strip of scarlet silk wound tightly around her waist, then thrown loosely across her bosom and over one of her shoulders. Sometimes that sash slipped from her shoulder, or maybe the little devils of the jungle pulled it away. In her left nostril she had a small ruby that winked at you as much as to say: 'Wouldn't you like my job?'

"Ilyin spoke to the Sundanese, but that fellow was in dreamland and did not hear. The girl answered for him. She said we could not visit the temple that day. The man was *latah*; I would have to wait. That Russian tried to bully her, but she would not give way, although she was afraid of Ilyin, who was big and strong and did not think much of women. When that scarlet sash slipped from the girl's shoulder, Ilyin would grin like a tiger that meets a young antelope.

"'Dutchman, you must stick around,' he said. 'It will be worth it. You will know things after you have seen what I have seen.'

"For three days we waited. And we argued a lot. When I spoke of Hanne's *'Handbuch der Klimatologie'* or Woeikof's *'Die Klimate der Erde,'* that Russian would laugh at me. 'All the fellows that have written about climate and atmosphere write of them in relation to health and industry and crops,' he said. 'Not one of the idiots writes about the relation of climate to the soul. They tell how altitude affects the circulation and respiration of the body, and how winds are bad for persons with certain complaints, but they say nothing of the effect of places on the vital principle, on the spirit. Look at this place! Wouldn't the atmosphere of this spot transform a man? Wouldn't it get into his blood?'

"'If the damned leeches left him any blood!' I snapped. There was a strange quality around that place, but I would not let that Russian bully me. There is something that you say in the United States. *Ja!* That is it: you say 'I am from Missouri.' Well, I was from Amsterdam, and I wanted to be shown too."

Again the black ape called to the naturalist. Kromhout hoisted himself from the chair and hurried to comfort her. As I listened, I detected a whispering accompaniment to his words. Other small captives knew of the condition of the black ape, and were troubled.

"On the fourth day that Sundanese got over his bout with hashish," continued Kromhout, as he returned. "He did not like me. He said the place was *kramat*; that meant it was too sacred and magical for me to put my big feet inside it. Ilyin swore at him. At last the Sundanese gave way.

"First we entered the temple proper. That was only an antechamber to the real place. But we entered quick, so that not much fresh air could get in, and that no old air could escape. It was quite dark, but the Sundanese took my hand and led me. I would sooner have had the little hand of the girl, but that Russian had grabbed her as a guide.

"'Why not a flashlight?' I asked.

"'There is no need for one,' said Ilyin. 'There is light in the vault where we are going.'

"That puzzled me, but I said nothing. We came to the far end of the temple and climbed down a stone stairway. I could see nothing, but I understood that we were in front of a stone doorway. Ilyin spoke to me. 'It is necessary to enter quick,' he said. 'When the old man pulls the lever, the stone will swing back. It will be light then. Sava, the girl, will go first, then you, then I and the old man. But move quick! *Poskorēe! Poskorēe!*' He was all excited.

"I could not understand how it would be light when the stone door opened, but I said nothing. Then the door swung back, and I found that Ilyin had spoken the truth. Through the lighted space hopped the girl; I stumbled after her, and after me came Ilyin and the old man.

"We were twenty feet underground, and there was no opening to that vault except the door through which we had come, but the place was illuminated. It was lit up like a phosphorescent sea. I thought for a moment that the light came from millions of fireflies, or the luminous beetles of the *Lampyridae* that are related to glow-worms. I was wrong. The light came from a type of lichen that I had never seen. A variety of *Lecanora calacarea* that is mentioned by Engler and Prantl in their book *'Die natürlichen Pflanzenfamilien.'* It sweats in the dark places where it grows, and its sweat is phosphorescent.

"That lichen covered the walls and the roof of that big vault— covered them like a silver tapestry. Lichen is strange stuff. Some day when the world dies, the lichen will make a death shroud. *Ja, ja.* And it will be very pretty. The blue-green algae, the red and yellow *Agyrium*, and the phosphorescent *Lecanora* that covered the walls and roof of that great vault. Lichen is the beard of death.

"After I got over the shock from that growing stuff, I noticed the air. It was heavy, very heavy. It was so thick that you thought you could chew it, but it was not unpleasant. Not at all. It was soothing. Have you ever tried opium? *Neen?* Well, the air of that place brought to me the nice loosening of the nerves that you get after the first whiffs of an opium pipe. It rubbed against my face like an invisible kitten. It touched my hands and my bare calves. It got into my hair and tickled my scalp. It had the ways of a bazaar woman. Now and then I swung round with the belief that some one had touched me with a finger on the back of the neck.

"There were small toads hopping about on the stone floor of the vault—the jerboa type of toad, with long legs. Ilyin, the old man, and the girl Sava took care not to step on the toads; and when the girl saw that I did not take much care, she spoke to the Russian, and he whispered to me: 'Please be careful,' he said; 'the old man will get annoyed if you squash them.'

"'Why?' I asked.

"'The old man speaks to them,' said Ilyin. 'When he wants to show me something extraordinary, he tells them to keep close to the wall so that they will not he trodden on by the others.'

"'What others?' I snapped.

"'You'll see,' he grinned. 'You'll see, Dutchman.'

"He was full of mystery, was that fellow. It was bubbling out of him. And the air that had fingers, and the phosphorescent lichen, were the hypodermic syringes with which he tried to squirt it into my system.

"We walked the length of that place. It was enormous. The pillars were beautifully carved with figures of birds and monkeys, and at the bottom of each pillar was a square stone box like those at Brambanan, that are filled with the dust of the dead. We did not speak. The only sounds were the *slap slap* of the toads as their bellies hit the floor. It was not nice. The only sweet thing in that place was the girl. I thought she was afraid of that vault—quite a lot afraid of it.

"We came out from that place in the same manner as we went in—slipping quickly through the door at the bottom of the stairs. For an hour or so I felt that I had been drugged; then I was myself again, and able to argue with that Russian. I had to admit that the air was curious, but more I would not admit.

"'You have no imagination!' cried Ilyin. 'The French named you Dutch well when they called you *Têtes-de-Fromage*. Cheese-heads you are! You could not feel the Past in that place?'

"'I felt the air, and I heard the jerboa toads,' I said. 'Not more than that. It is good to have belief, but it is not good to have too much of it. That is the way to madness.'

"'Wait around,' said the Russian; 'you will see what you will see. The girl has promised me.'

"He smacked his lips when he spoke of that girl. There are two nations that strut when they speak of women—the Germans and the Russians; but the Russian has more charm. He is more dashing. He is a little mad, and women like madmen.

"I wanted to go away from that place, but I could not. It held me there because I felt that something would happen, something big. Have you noticed that lots of tragedies have been photographed? Those photographers have been there with the machines aiming at the spot where an automobile turns over, or some racehorse falls down, or that Balkan king is shot. You think it is luck? It is not. The man with the camera sensed the accident before it happened. That is what makes the good press photographer. Sometime I will tell you a story about that business of sensing a smash.

"Each day I would see that Russian stalking the girl. *Ja*, stalking her like a black panther stalking a mouse deer. Whenever I saw the flash of her scarlet sarong in the jungle, I would see Ilyin close to her. And I would watch her eyes and watch those of the Russian. The fear was growing greater in hers; in his was the belief that he would conquer. He would pull his moustaches and brag about the girls that had loved him in Moscow when he was at the university. He made me sick with his talk.

"'You had better watch that old man,' I said to him.

"'Pooh!' he cried. 'He is nothing. The girl—ah, the girl is something precious. Do you know, Kromhout, that she believes she is a reincarnation from other days. She speaks as if she was around here when things were happening.'

"'Then she will know too much for you,' I snapped.

"'No woman knows too much for me,' said that fool. 'At the university they called me "Little Andrey, the Fisher of Souls." She will be mine very soon.'

"Men are fools. We Dutch say: 'Roasted pigeons do not fly through the air.' It is a good proverb.

"One morning I saw that old Sundanese creeping through the jungle on his hands and knees. I could not see Ilyin or the girl, but I guessed that old man was hunting for them.

"That afternoon Ilyin was very gay. He sang little Russian songs that were all about girls who loved very much and who were willing to kill themselves for fellows. He sang them in his own language, but he translated them for me. I thought them foolish. Dutch girls would not do the things that those songs told of. Not much. Dutch girls keep their feet on the ground very hard.

"'Tonight, Kromhout,' said Ilyin, 'something might happen. It has been a big day for me. Sava loves me. *Da!* She loves me a lot. And she has promised me that she will make old sulky Mokhan put on a show tonight to celebrate our love-pact. In that vault we might see the Past.'"

The naturalist paused in his narrative. He sat silent in his big chair. I thought he might be marshalling the events of that evening of long ago, putting them in order, shaping them so that they could be intelligible. Or perhaps he thought that the pause might let the caressing fingers of the Malayan night bring to my mind the capacity for belief. Belief in the strange tale that he wished to unfold.

"It happened as that Russian thought it would happen," he said, and his voice was lowered as if afraid that the Tjandi Bororboedoer, squatting out in the thick darkness, might be annoyed at hearing him tell of the secrets of the long-buried past. "The girl persuaded the old man to put on a big show. *Ja*, a big show. And he did!

"When we climbed down into that vault, I thought the lichen was more phosphorescent than the first time. It might have been just fancy. I don't know. Perhaps I was excited. The air was that air that had fingers which tickled the back of my neck and rubbed my scalp.

"The Russian did not know what was going to happen. I do not think the girl knew. It was just the business of the old man. He was not *latah* now. He was alive. His black eyes were sparkling, and at times I thought there was a grin of delight on his face.

"We had walked about twenty paces when the noise started. *Ja*, the noise. It started at the far end of the vault, some hundred feet from where we were standing; and it came creeping toward us, eating up the silence. Eating up the silence like a great invisible mouth. It was funny. At first it was not a great noise. It was soft and rather soothing, but as it crept nearer and nearer, it became louder. Much louder.

"Now and then it would stop for a few seconds—stop as if it had been throttled. And all our eyes were turned to the spot where it had halted. Do you understand? We knew, although we could see nothing, that it had a certain point. It was near this or that carved pillar that supported the roof. A noise made by something that we could not see. Moving and stop moving and stopping.

"It grew louder. Much louder. New noises joined up with it. Noises that I could not place, noises that had been lost to the world when that temple went out of business. There was a devilish rumble that seemed to be the backbone of the clamour. It came at intervals. It seemed to shake the temple. And it carried a poisonous fear with it. Drums of hell was that noise. *Ja*, drums of hell!

"When that big queer noise came, I thought the veins in my head would burst. It led the others to a sort of crescendo; then it snapped off quick so that it hurt your head. And you could see nothing. Nothing at all. In that vast underground vault there was only the old man, Ilyin, the girl and myself. *Ja*, and the toads. Those toads were banked now inches high around the walls and around the pillars. They were afraid—those toads. Possibly they saw things that we did not see. That *bufo-jerboa* is clever. Very clever.

"Closer and closer came that racket. Bulging its way toward us! I leaned forward, pop-eyed and sweating, in an effort to see something. I have heard all the noises of the jungle, but I have never heard noises like those. They were devilish. They were beyond the intelligence of man. They woke memories of things that were snaky and shiny, things of the past when the bull-roarer struck fear into the hearts of those who heard it.

"In the bones of our ears are echoes that have been asleep for hundreds of years. Frightening echoes. They are in the cells of our brains. They are part of us. We collected them in our climb out of the dark womb of the world. This civilization of ours is a small thing. It is of yesterday. It is the thin scum of conceit that we have placed upon the terrors of other days. And when we are frightened, that scum that is civilization, that is modernity, that is law and order and smugness and silly pomp and humbug, is broken by those memories that are mostly hooked up with sounds.

"They come out of the depths. The beat of the tom-toms, the clang of the devil-gongs, the hiss of big serpents, the whirring of the wings of vampires and pterodactyls. *Ach!* This memory of ours is a terrible thing—for the subconscious is filled with sounds. There is stored the bellow of the mammoth and the sound made by the slime dripping from the scaly legs of the plesiosaurus!

"Now, years after, I can hear those sounds of that vault when the world is quiet. I will always hear them. They are in my flesh, in my bones, in my blood. They are a fear-poison that has got into my body through my ears.

"I wished to run, but I could not. My legs had lost their

power. They were boneless, and I was afraid that I would fall to the floor. The noise had swung a little to the left of us, and for that I was glad. You bet I was. If it had swept over us, I would have died from fear.

"The old man, the girl and the Russian did what I did—turned their heads to follow the sound. It was now surging between two great pillars of the vault, surging through them like a cataract of clamour!

"It was then that the girl cried out. She shrieked and pointed. Pointed at nothing that we could see, but something that was plain to her. Something or somebody. Somebody, I think. *Ja*, I am sure that she saw some one, at that instant.

"She shrieked again, and sprang forward; but that Russian was not going to let her get into that racket of noise. He grabbed hold of her waist and tried to hold her. He was strong, as I have told you; but she wished to touch something in the stream of noise. She was slippery like a snake. Her sarong was almost torn from her body as she wrestled; then as she leaped forward again, she and the Russian were in that frightening river of noise. They were in it! We knew!

"That Russian was six feet and a little bit. He weighed two hundred pounds, and he had muscles of steel. But his size and his weight did not matter much then. They were nothing to the forces that were around him. Nothing at all. Something picked him up. For an instant he was held horizontally at about three feet from the floor; then he was jerked head high and thrown across the vault, thrown across with such force that he struck the wall some twenty feet away. Struck it and dropped to the floor.

"That noise stopped then. Stopped with a suddenness that made me think I had become deaf. We did not move till we heard the *slap-slap* of the toads as they moved away from the walls and the pillars. It was comforting to hear those jerboa toads moving about.

"I went over to the Russian. He was quite dead. His head had struck the wall, and his skull was fractured. I remembered his face for a long time. There was fear on it. A great fear. I have often wondered if he saw what it was that picked him up and tossed him across the vault....

"*Ja*, there was an inquiry. The Dutch were angry about that business. They sent a magistrate from Djokja, and police came from Soerakarta. I told what I had seen and heard, and those police grinned. They were stupid fellows who could not believe anything unless they saw it with their little piggy eyes. And the fat magistrate from Djokja was so stuffed with *rystaefel* that there was no room for imagination.

"The girl would not speak. She was a little frightening. That fat magistrate asked her if the Russian had seduced her; and she looked at him in a way that gave him cold shivers. She did not like that question.

"The old man would not say much. When the magistrate asked him what had made the noise in the vault, he gave a funny answer. He said: 'They are the dead, that the years have eaten their bodies, but whose souls walk.'

"The police ruined that vault. They smashed down a part of the wall, and all that phosphorescent *Lecanora calacarea* shrivelled in an instant when it met the air of the day. And those jerboa toads turned over on their backs and died with little croaks. It was a pity. I would have liked that some big man, some scientist of the order of Regnault or Angus Smith, should study the air of that chamber. Now it is too late."

The big Dutchman rose and went within the bungalow.

I sat silently looking out across the dark stretch to where Tjandi Bororboedoer, "Shrine of the Many Buddhas," rose imperially. That foolish idea that the temple had moved closer to hear Kromhout's narrative was still upon me. I was a little afraid.

The big Dutchman reappeared. "The black ape has got a little one," he said, and his voice was soft with tenderness. "Come and look at it. She thinks it is the most wonderful baby ape that the Malay Archipelago has ever seen."

WHERE THE
BUTTERFLIES COME FROM
by William Hay

The following strange fantasy, another little girl lost tale, was penned by William Hay (1875-1945), an Adelaide-born, Cambridge educated writer. He was deeply disturbed by the mysterious disappearance in 1909 of the ship taking his mother and sister to Europe, and he subsequently moved to Tasmania. He was a painstaking writer and his output was small; he wrote half a dozen novels and a single collection of short stories called *An Australian Rip Van Winkle and Other Stories* (1921), from which this story comes.

The range of hills behind the city of Adelaide is, much of it, almost bare of scrub and tree, and in the winter these lofty cones and ovals are covered with a smooth green grass, and rise one over the other in the distance, as round and pleasant as a giant's pleasure-links. Deep in the pathless range, as most people know, are strange, remote valleys and cul-de-sacs, where the sheep feed on the grassy sheer, and outlaws from our Black Forest are said to have made a last stand in former times, while here and there, far up on the sloping bosoms, little cobweb paths wind round and about: perhaps, before the days of mountain roads, the way the early legislator rode his forty miles to the Governor's Ball or Parliament House. In any case the paths were well worn enough, for in many a man sinks well up his calf in the little creepers and weeds that choke them now.

Down in a close valley, in a cot on the Waterfall Road, lived little Isbel Yawkins. Perhaps you would remember that year, after the drought, when the butterflies were so troublesome. *Troublesome*, we repeat, because many were convinced they killed the flowers in the gardens where they fluttered and crowded, though it was impossible to make quite certain, because, flying in orange companies from flower to flower, and settling for so short a time on this and that, it was not easy to be discovered if their long tongues wrought any damage, or the flower died of something else. Often, that year, Isbel was within an ace of settling this vexed question, but just as she trotted near enough to see the butterfly's face, it lifted orange wings and floated by. Some people, it may be recollected, said you ought to "kill all you could catch," which was not a difficult matter, for they seemed so stupid in the hot air and hung about in nines and tens. Indeed, I heard it said, many grown gardeners killed as many as they conveniently could. Little Isbel, however, was never able to catch any but the dead ones that lay beneath on the ground, and these she was glad enough to secrete for her own.

Nobody else seemed much interested in the butterflies—at least nothing like so interested as was little Isbel. Her too oft-repeated questions on their way of existence, why they were so silent, and where they nested in the evening, produced confessions of absolute ignorance or answers most immature and vague. "Accursed caterpillars which just come from nowhere and go with the blessed rain," was hardly satisfying to a person surrounded daily by these indestructible and lively presences, and no one liked the brilliant things to be trifled with as, "Bugs with angels' wings," or treated jokingly as, "sorts of giddy mosquitoes that have given up housekeeping"; nor, indeed, was she permanently oppressed by mere cross remarks, as "they were bits of doomed vanity without sense enough to make a hole to die in." To Isbel their enchantment was born anew each sunny morning, and decked her short and homely hours, like the gardens where they swam and swayed, with bright and restless mystery.

It seems to have been owing to a remark of Mr. Yawkins' brother—a sort of sailor when he was not helping with the potatoes—that there was the trouble in the family. Mr. Yawkins' brother was sometimes very talkative, and, generally, it was thought, rather a giddy sort of young man. It was vaguely wondered how so giddy-minded a man could trust himself upon the masts and shrouds. Some of the things he related—well!— an elephant or an acrobat couldn't have endured so much worry, and even grown people privately agreed that they didn't believe all his remarks, though politeness might keep them sitting silent longer than you would have expected. Nevertheless, Isbel found him as agreeable a pass-the-time-o'day acquaintance as you might meet in a parsley-walk. To come upon him down by the creek, where the mint smelt strong enough to knock you down, and the soil was black as a coffin, sometimes resulted in a little fish swimming in a glycerine bottle, a geranium-breasted robin on a fork, a frog, or a remark of considerable witchery. Even with Isbel, Mr. Yawkins' brother was never unready with a word, and this was how it occurred that the former, with her interminable butterflies, got that particular reply after the numerous others he had made her. "Where the butterflies come from?" returned he, with a thoughtful gravity, as if the idea was still rather curious to him; "Where the butterflies come from? Look, I'll tell you where they come from, Lizzie! See yonder, up on that great, green balloon" (pointing at one of the hillsides hanging over them), "there's a little path running up and around, till it rounds the corner—well, you chivvy aloft up there, and you follow under where the white cloud is, away and away till it stops ... ah, there you'll find 'em sleeping in the trees like pretty birds."

Now Isbel had been nearly up to the lower part of this path before, when she was accompanying some goats that had a kid. So when a great longing took possession of her, to see all the butterflies asleep in their nests, it did not take her more than a night and a day to decide she would go again. She chose Friday, because Mrs. Yawkins had gone to town after some boots. As it happened, Mr. Yawkins' brother was also absent, having had a slight coolness with Mr. Yawkins on the subject of the sea-shells that hang underneath ships, and had gone for the night to the Black Hill. And Mr. Yawkins had taken his lunch along, and did not come up the garden, till he heard Mrs. Yawkins call his name in her rather shrill voice, and when he did, there she was dead-tired and bewildered, and that Isbel nowhere that she could find.

As for little Isbel, in pursuit of her pretty fancy, she had trotted up the hill till her form looked like a small moving stone in the grass, and then she found the path and trotted away. You could hardly have seen her head as she went along. She trotted along the path, and trotted along the path, and trotted along the path, till just round the corner, there was a single hollow tree, in which quite a grown man might have found shelter from the storm. Here somewhat to her bewilderment, the path, as they say it is with life itself, instead of mounting on towards the hill-top, began to descend again, and, though the descent was very gradual, still it was not quite the arrangement she expected. Though a little daunted, she was soon reassured by the "rattle" of some wattle-birds, and three great blasts from the quarries, which made her feel quite at home, and on she went round the hill. At the next bend, she came on a number of black lambs' tails hanging from varnished walking-sticks, which she could not know were just grass-trees, and they made her think of goblin things. Only a little further down, however, was a tiny grass valley, all shut in by towering slopes, in the middle of which was a single great gum-tree. Little Isbel stood awed on the precipitous path-edge, at the sight of this great tree, which was lush and full-leaved with the beautiful soil in which it grew. From ground to summit and from side to side, every leaf was hung with clusters of orange butterflies, till the whole tree was a moving orange yellow in the fading light; so plentiful they were, it seemed as if all the butterflies in the world were clustering there; so thick they hung there was hardly a leaf to be seen for their yellow wings; while others yet, as if they could not find nesting room, or were too happy to sleep, floated rejoicing above the rest in the delicate air.

* * * * * * *

Poor Mr. Yawkins went up the road nearly to the waterfalls looking for Isbel, and then down the road to the electric-tram terminus, but he did not see her anywhere, nor had any of the neighbours seen her, not even Mrs. Allnutt, who lived at the first bridge, and generally knew where anybody was. He and Mrs. Yawkins and that hurried about all night looking for Isbel, and next morning in the dawn they were still hurrying somewhere, but they could not think where the child had taken herself. Mr. Yawkins' brother came back to dinner at twelve, and he talked a good drop when they told him Isbel was gone away, and followed them about (very aggravating of him it was) just behind them, Mr. Yawkins one way, and Mrs. Yawkins another, bothering them, when they did not want to talk, with all sorts of inquiries. But suddenly he threw up his hands into the air, and gave a wild screech; and when they turned, quite distracted with him, he was running up the mountain behind the kitchen door, shouting to them to scurry up aloft, for he was pretty certain now where the pretty was run to.

Mr. Yawkins soon closed up behind his brother, and quickly learned the stuff he'd been telling Isbel about the butterfly path, and Mrs. Yawkins hurried after them as quickly as she could, shouting at them in her rather shrill voice, and being shouted back at, but she never quite caught up with the others. She was in the brown dress she preferred to wear, with darkish plain hair, and she followed them just as she was, with her sleeves a little up her arms.

You would be surprised how long it took the three, who were in such hot haste, to ascend to the path, and then along to the corner, and so, past the hollow tree, down—down to where the great gum was shimmering in the sun-light, even now alive with butterflies. Mr. Yawkins' brother was struck a'back with the sight, and stood staring at it almost as amazed as Isbel had been, but Mr. Yawkins pushed roughly by him, looking this way and that after his lost one, while Mrs. Yawkins came up and began to call the child's name in a voice rather thoughtlessly loud.

Little Isbel must have slipped in her pleasure at finding all the butterflies, for they found her lying below the path in the valley, her face on her arm, which was stained with blood. About her head, attracted perhaps by the colour of her hair, fluttered two or three of the pretty creatures she had come to see, and one was actually settled on the wayward strands. Mr. Yawkins carried her home, with his wife stumbling and hurrying just behind his arm and now and again reaching forward and touching the child, and behind them came Mr. Yawkins' brother, talking endlessly and excitedly.

THE VAMPIRE

by W. W. Lamble

W. W. Lamble was a pseudonym of the Australian poet Hugh McCrae (1876-1958). McCrae was born in Melbourne, the son of the poet George Gordon McCrae, and went to school at Hawthorn Grammar School and grew up around his father's literary circle. In 1896, after the publication of his first poem in *The Bulletin*, he abandoned his apprenticeship as an architect to take up full time writing. He always struggled as a writer, and he worked at times as an actor and as a decoder in the Censor's Office.

Although not fashionable today, his poetry was highly influential and he remains an important figure in Australian literature. 'The Vampire', a vignette on a familiar theme, appeared in *The Bulletin* in November 1901.

How well I remember my first love,—with her stuffed busks and her stuffed hair! We did not meet in the summer, nor in the green grass near running water, but in winter,—under the pale glare of gas, in the wet street and among people.

She was complexionless, her face so bleached that her black eyes and red lips positively glared; yet she had a silky fascination for me. And her smooth, evil hands brought not only flesh into contact, but mind.

She said she was hungry. I had just drawn my month's earnings, and we went arm-in-arm to a little green-curtained restaurant. It was sufficiently evil-looking,—the gas low, and the solitary waiter unobstreperous.

I was drunk. The fumes of the cheap Burgundy started an orchestra in my ears, and swelled the veins of my brain. The wind lifted the blind and blew my cigarettes in a whirring covey off the table. I stooped to pick them up, but the blood-strings in my throat stood out,—and the room darkened to my eyes. The waiter noiselessly came to my assistance, replacing them on a plate and retaining a few slyly up his sleeve. But I said nothing, only looking at Marguerite and her long, folded fingers.

She ordered some oysters and, when they had come, I watched her squeeze a lemon-quarter into the shells and over the firm fish.

I seemed to be in a garden with Marguerite. The garden was full of lilies—tall, white lilies without a speck or mark; and everywhere amongst them were blue flies, trumpeting and buzzing with pleasure. Here and there a rich bee, with powdered legs, swayed on a flower, like a jewel in snow. The air was warm and soft as down, while the rounded sound of bubbling water poppled in the moss, between the bars of lily-stalks. A delicious sweetness of earth and honey mounted to my brain. I watched a butterfly, winged in old-gold and grey, as he flickered on a red tile under the steady shadow of a fern.

Gradually I grew aware of the subtle electrical hand upon my wrist—then of the eyes that made my mind hers,—nay, my very soul. The small, piercing eyes, whose pupils diminished and enlarged, and enlarged and diminished, like the flame of a dying lamp. And every time the pupils diminished, they seemed to me two miser hands that gripped my brain and squeezed myself from me, like a water from cloth, opening only to grip again.

But the woman, in the body, was tall, and breasted like a young girl; her back was straight as an arrow, and her neck reared white as a rock-wave carrying the magnificent head on its summit. She had a broad brow, but somewhat slanting; a long, slight nose, an eagerly insolent mouth, and the eyes I have spoken of. Her hair, where it was loose, shimmered and shook as though over a heat-mist.

Presently she lifted her hands from my wrists, and I felt her fingers thrill through my temples, as she drew me towards her and kissed me on the lips. A song seemed to set up in the garden, and the lilies shot up like stars, swayed in the sky, meeting in an arch, and crossed in stormy rushes over our heads. The noise of the water rose clamorously, and a flight of coloured birds brushed my shoulder. A soft sensation went over the whole of my skin, like the dropping of a delicate veil.

And still she drew me closer.

I tried to resist, but, as in a nightmare, my arms remained limp and paralysed. Neither could I cry out. All at once, in the midst of a million kisses, she drew back her head, and, with a gasping laugh, pushed her red lips at my throat and bit me deep, even to blood.

In vain I beat her about the face, and plucked at her cheeks. She hung like a dog. With horrible little laughs and gurgles she greeted my impotent rage.

I put both hands to her forehead, and made to thrust her from me; but again my muscles failed. And she bit deeper.

Then the lilies withered down from the skies and lay stained and yellow on the earth. The butterfly lost its old-gold, and its wings and whole form broadened into a bat's. The soft ripple of the water changed to the purring of a flame, and bale fires leapt from every corner.

Still the woman tore at my throat.

My breath shortened, and I felt as though my skull were contracting and injuring my brain. Spasm after spasm shot through my head. Goaded to madness, I hurled my tormenter away, and as she returned to me, bloody-mouthed, I saw that she too had changed. Her eyes had sunk, her teeth were old and wasted to an appearance of cloves; her nose seemed flattened, and her hair thin. Her face was almost simian.

My strength failed me, and I staggered on my feet.

"Marguerite," I cried. "Woman! Devil! Vampire!"

And I fell clean to the ground, like a tree in a storm.

A great coldness rushed upon me, and an icy breath fanned my forehead. I could feel a pair of hands beneath my arm-pits. I was smothering. There was a bandage round my mouth.

I opened my eyes. There were stars—thousands of them—blinking and blinking, but below, turbid and swollen, lay the river without a light for miles.

The hands withdrew suddenly; and a man darted from me, fleeing up the steep stoned bank. It was the waiter of the restaurant. The bandage dropped off my jaw, and I could now understand the sweet scent of my garden dream.

My pockets were empty as the day when my clothes were made; that was a foregone conclusion.

Marguerite never again crossed my path. Yet I know that green-curtained restaurant, and some day I shall see her standing in the doorway. If she beckons, I must go to her.

Because I dare not refuse.

HALLOWE'EN

by Dulcie Deamer

Dulcie Deamer (1890-1972) was a New Zealander who became a well-known figure in Sydney Bohemian society in the 1920s and 1930s. In 1907 she won first prize in a literary competition with a highly imaginative Stone Age story, which was illustrated by Norman Lindsay. Later she wrote: "Even at that tender age I loved blood, murder and violence." She wrote several historical novels and a collection of fantastic historical tales, *In the Beginning: Six Studies of the Stone Age and Other Stories* (1909), from which the following story is taken.

Hevar sat up—not suddenly, but with a cat-like movement, that left the weight of the woollen coverlet still on her knees. The close, shuttered darkness was difficult to draw breath in, and there was a smell of clothing. On her left side rose the loud, nasal breathing of a man, flavoured with the fermented drink of his last meal, and his nearness was witnessed by the coarse, human odour of one whose skin is never touched by water, and who has grown warm between blankets. A masculine odour with a hint of milch cattle and manure in it. It was on the stroke of midnight, and Hevar was more awake that at high noon. She drew up her knees listening, and from the bed foot came the wordless moan of a sleeping child. Then, very far away, a long, long howl was lifted, nearing and nearing until it seemed to touch the shutter and whimper at it, nose against the fastening. The child cried out in its sleep, half-sobbing, and beat with its fists. Hevar's nostrils widened. "It is time, it is time," said a sharp voice within her, and she got out of bed, slipping her pillow stuffed with hen's feathers into the place where she had lain, that it might kept the warmth of her body. Again the child struck the sides of its carved wooden chest. Hevar felt as it were cords that drew her, and she yielded to them with gladness. She went surely with no feeling hands, treading only on her spread toes after the manner of a cat. The door opened and was latched. Then she lit a taper of yellow wax, and set it in a candlestick on the floor. The airless room was empty, with many shelves, and bunches of dried sage hung from a rafter. Hevar unbolted the hinged shutter, and hooked it back. A square of cold darkness looked in, but there was no wind, and the taper burned steadfastly on the stone floor. It was the midnight of Hallowe'en. Standing in the centre of the room, she loosened her white night-shift. It slipped to her breast, to her waist, to her knees, and lay around her feet. Hevar glanced once at the shadowy corners; then she laughed soundlessly with a show of teeth. The metal cross she took quickly from her neck, and laid it under her right heel, and the heavy, dark plaits were shaken loose. Dipping her fingers in a jar, she began to moisten her body from the head to the feet. The jar held poisonous liquid, distilled from the leaves of rue, foxgloves, hemlock and monk's head. As she rubbed herself, the place where the chrism of baptism had marked her forehead burned as though a red coal were held to it. But when the poison touched it, the burning ceased. Then she put out the taper, and in the darkness belted herself with a girdle cut from the hide of a black wolf, into whom a devil had entered. Immediately she was gripped with strong shuddering; the girdle held about her like a cincture of fire, and the sight behind her eyes seemed to go out. She had a muffled sensation of sinking, sinking, sinking, to a place that is beneath the bottom of all bottomless things—a something less than the span betwixt hell and heaven, but far enough. There was light—but the light was black, if such might be—and the uneasiness of great activity. A flame, dark as the smoke of burning pine logs, went upward, and those that served moved in it, coming and going. Something was said, and she saw an inverted cross... Then her eyelids lifted, and she knew that the sight of the flesh had returned to her.

Hevar the she-wolf stepped from the circle of a dropped night-shift. The nature of the darkness had changed, and she could see easily the tokens of mice by the wall-chinks. She crouched, sprang through the window-place, and alighted on silent feet. Some tiny thing that bore a green glow-worm light ran, threading the thin grass by the house wall. A number of fat, velvet-backed spiders, having drawn a single thread from the eaves to the gateway post, filled in a planned design of wheel-shaped openwork, and hung a dew-drop to each silvery spoke. Immediately a flight of midgets on wings transparent as diamonds and shot with greenish sheen, alit on the stretched thread, dancing the length of it, while three death-watches ticked in concert, keeping some sort of time. Hevar could see these happenings, and the thatched sheds of the steading, and the tops of the orchard of plum trees as though it were full day. And the night was awake and busy. A waft from the sheep pen, where ewes on the verge of early lambing were folded, stirred the hair on Hevar's spine, and sent an anticipating quiver to the tip of her bushy, inward-curving tail. She padded through the gateway, where the farm-gate swung on its hinges. On the gate sat a black impet with its forked tail over its shoulder. It pointed at her, and began to whirl round and round the top bar. The dog that was tied by the fold-fence lay close with eyes of fear, and his mane stood up. When the fold bleated with one voice and pushed hither and thither, and crowded foolishly from side to side, it was as though he did not hear... Hevar the she-wolf tore at the bloody gullet of the last just-killed ewe. In either of her lives there was no pleasure like this throat-ripping, this worrying of warm wool. Her open mouth grinned, and the tongue flickered between the white dog-teeth. The dead ewes lay everywhere on the fold floor, and the thick blood crawling to the centre had sunk, leaving the imprint of a dark cross.

Hevar the woman was wont to take feeble lambs into her lap, giving them milk from a heated pipkin.... "Look up-up-up!" sang the house kobold, from the sloped thatch of the hen-roost. "To-morrow you will weep because a wolf—a wolf, huh! has been in the sheep-fold. Till cockcrow, and I—I—I will tweak the rooster's longest tail feather, and tickle him with a barley straw. Huh!" Below, two flames of evil fire moved in the sheep-pen. Then a shadow leaped back into the mystery from which it had come.

Hevar stole down by a field edge, her belly low in the sweet, soaked grass. A mild glow lay on the face of the field, as though the patient, hidden earth were breathing, and the breath was luminous. Twice a great owl skimmed the grass-heads with some semi-human, prick-eared, slit-eyed atomie hunched between the motionless wings. Where the soil turned peaty and rich-smelling, and the grass coarse and mixed with reeds, a row of pollard willows slanted outward over the widening of a mill-brook that had scooped itself a mysterious depth. Grass-green fire flickered on the water, and the nixy of the hole, lividly pale as the undersides of some fishes, with full blue lips, and great soulless whitish eyes, had risen to below her woman's breast, and was plucking at the almost sunken body of a man. The water-fire dripped from her hair in which little eels were knotted, and all over the pool phosphorescent bubbles rose and burst. The she-wolf crossed a shallow matted with cress and mint. In the flat meads many stooping figures moved, gathering and gathering. A woman, with her apron filled with poisonous meadow saffron, was culling fool's parsley. A huge pie-bald cat rubbed against her hands, purring with pleasure.

"Luck to you, neighbour," she said to the tongue-lolling wolf stealing through the tall, flowering weeds. "You run to-night, I run to-morrow. The devil be with you!"

The cat purred louder, stretching and contracting its claws in pure delight.

An enormous golden-red moon was lifting above a shoulder

of the tilth, and a string of bats passed across the uppermost half. As it grew to its full circle, the under rim on the edge of the ploughed land, the twin uprights of a gallows drew two black lines of the blank face of it, and between them hung something that seemed no larger than a dangling beetle. About it was the circling flicker of crow's wings. At the gallows foot a pick-axe rose and fell, minute as the claw of an insect against the vastness of the ruddy, lightless moon. It stopped in the mid-height of its tiny swing, and a thin scream, like the voice of a child in agony, shrilled up, and snapped, as though a heel had been set upon the child's throat. Then a dog howled. To draw forth the man-shaped root is death. The she-wolf that was Hevar slid into the midnight within midnight of a close wood. Here it was all astir, and so crowded that the palpable air had thickened. Troops of will-o'-the-wisps hopped in and out of the contorted tree-roots, as like to white candle flames as pea is to pea, save that they were evil in their very essence, and knowingly. Slimy shapelessnesses, akin to the one-night growths of spotted fungi, coated with a yellow mucus, sprawled and crept, leaving the silver trail of slugs. Bubbles of wan fire, in which milky light churned, wandered close to the earth, and pigmies, some prickly as a burr, some legged like hunting spiders, swarmed. Suddenly a pure glowing grew out of the quickened dark, broadening and broadening, softer and more pervading than keen daylight. Down the wood-path moved a girl in her night smock, holding a lit candle, whose flame she shielded with her other hand, and her darkened eyes were expressionless as the glass stare of a doll. Only her baptismal mark showed as if a forehead diamond lay just below the parting of her plaited hair. But on her right, and behind, a shape that was like a spear of intense white light moved with her, and before them the path thickened with close grass, bright as a good folk's dancing-ring, and the fungi blackened away, and the nameless spawn lapsed back to the scum from which they bred. The light and the sleeping girl passed slowly; then the two walls of malignant darkness rushed in and met rejoicing, and the place seethed. But Hevar had fled swiftly, ears flat, and tail tucked between hind legs, and when the sharp voice within that screamed, "Run!—this is no place for us!" was silenced, she was on the grey high road, and the sow-thistles behind the grave-yard wall nodded their tops at her, though the night was airless. About the open belfry, spiked with an iron cross, where the church bell hung as if the bell-rope had been turned to rigid stone, a ring of linked impets circled swiftly as a top spins, and on the church roof they were thick as starlings. A figure moved on the road, but after the manner of no living thing, and Hevar checked to watch. It was a woman, or what had once been a woman, in the brown shroud of her burial. She was yellow-grey—the colour of the second day of death—and her eyelids were sealed down as though the coins still weighed upon them. But her mouth was redder than any girl's, and to the full underlip hung a tear of blood. Her naked feet moved wood-enly in the dust, and her arms were stiff at her sides as they had been put by the layers-out. She passed in by a wicket in the wall. Somewhere in the tangle of hideously-rank weeds there would be a narrow, open pit.

Hevar had trotted on the cross-ways. Here there were only vague suckings in the water meadows, and a splitting of the earth above a suicide's burial-place, that closed and drew apart again. She sat on her haunches, waiting. From beyond the turn of the road two sounds came to her—human, for they were coarser and had more body to them than the sounds of that night—a man's voice, and a man's heavy-footedness. Now he was round the turn, and a swinging lantern tossed light back and forth. The length of the stride was a trifle overdone, as was the working arm. As he came he bawled the Te Deum at the top of a voice throaty from fatigue and fear, and with his free hand dragged after him by its leash a most unwilling dog that whined anxiously, its tail completely out of sight.

"This," said the sharp voice that spoke in Hevar, "is a fool. A coward also. He has not even the courage to tell himself that he is afraid. See to him." The she-wolf flattened herself, trembling.

The man who bawled a triumphant hymn in his nervous terror was very close. The water-meadows had silenced, and the earth-crack shut like the halves of a touched oyster.

"Now!" said the voice.

But Hevar leapt one little moment late, and the man had seen the eyes of a she-wolf.

"Holy Saint Nicholas!" howled the singer of Te Deums, with blue panic clutching his entrails. Then, from pure brute instinct, and with the force of his almighty fear, he swung and crashed the lantern on the beast, dropped it, and bolted, bellowing to the countryside to save his life, while the dragged dog yelped. Far and far away the first cock crew faint as an elfin horn. A pause of breathlessness, and the next took up the challenge, nearer, and the next, and the next. The world turned in its sleep, muttering, and now every dung-hill, straw-stack, and rick-yard rail blew a defiant trumpet.

"The day is coming!"

In the cross-ways lay the unclad body of a woman with a bloody head, and having a strip of some dark hide about her waist. A heavy lantern was cast in the stained dust. It had the look of a most abominable murder.

ABOUT THE EDITOR

JAMES DOIG works at the National Archives of Australia in Canberra. He has edited several volumes of colonial Australian supernatural fiction, including *Australian Ghost Stories* (Wordsworth Editions, 2010). He has also edited single-author collections by H. B. Marriott Watson and J. S. Leatherbarrow, and has published articles on obscure authors of horror and the supernatural, including R. R. Ryan, Keith Fleming, and H. T. W. Bousfield. He has a Ph.D. in medieval history from Swansea University in Wales.

Lightning Source UK Ltd.
Milton Keynes UK
UKHW011324231020
372106UK00001B/96